ADVANCE PRAISE

"This essential resource is a must-read for all health care providers. Regardless of how frequently you encounter Black women or men with eating disorders in your practice, Small and Edwards-Gayfield offer a compassionate and practical guide to developing cultural humility and delivering culturally competent care. The book is enriched with insightful clinical vignettes, robust resources, and the authors' deep clinical expertise. Even seasoned professionals will gain fresh perspectives—about themselves and about working with Black people facing eating disorders—through this invaluable text."
—**Cynthia M. Bulik, PhD, FAED,** founding director, University of North Carolina Center of Excellence for Eating Disorders

"Of all the superlatives that might be used to describe *Black Women with Eating Disorders*, liberatory is the one that seems most relevant for our times. The book is an unapologetic foray into theoretical and practical issues that are often avoided, silenced, or unseen. Using a theoretical framework that includes both extant bio–psychosocial research as well as clinical experience, Small and Edwards-Gayfield expose the ecosystems of injustice that inhibit healing movement in the relationship between healers and clients. The guidance offered in this book is both theoretically grounded and eminently practical, thus opening pathways to the courage that enables both therapist and client to more authentically engage in the relationship: to show up and be seen each by the other. In their rejection of deficit-based diagnostic protocols, the authors guide healers and their clients toward treatment approaches that minimize the shame often associated with disordered eating behaviors. They do so by offering analyses of prominent evidence-based practices, highlighting their usefulness as well as their limitations. The authors' use of storytelling is illuminating; their language is relatable, accessible, and occasionally punctuated with good humor. This book belongs in the hands of anyone who is committed to doing healing work with Black women and who has the courage to embrace the possibility of mutual growth."
—**Maureen Walker, PhD,** licensed psychologist and author of *When Getting Along Is Not Enough: Reconstructing Race in Our Lives and Relationships*

"Both a challenge to and guidebook for the eating disorder community, which is too often blind to the impact of chronic racism that leaves Black clients further marginalized, misunderstood, and mistreated. Expertly weaving in the unique pressures Black clients face with concrete examples of Black-centered treatment, the writers offer specific strategies for creating spaces for clients that are emotionally and energetically supportive. Filled with the wisdom of lived experience, this book is *essential* reading for clinicians."

—**Amy Banks, MD,** founding scholar of the International Center for Growth in Connection and coauthor of *Wired to Connect: The Surprising Link Between Brain Science and Strong, Healthy Relationships* and *Fighting Time*

"I don't know how they have done it again—Dr. Small and Ms. Edwards-Gayfield have created another treatment tool that is essential for clinicians who have the honor of working with Black women with eating disorders. I felt so seen as a fellow Black woman clinician and researcher reading this text. With such limited resources in the marketplace, this book will undoubtedly offer clinicians guidance to expand their expertise to treat Black women navigating disordered eating."

—**Rachel W. Goode, PhD, MPH, LCSW,** associate professor of social work and psychiatry, University of North Carolina–Chapel Hill

BLACK WOMEN WITH EATING DISORDERS

BLACK WOMEN WITH EATING DISORDERS

CLINICAL TREATMENT CONSIDERATIONS

CHARLYNN SMALL

PAULA EDWARDS-GAYFIELD

Norton Professional Books
*An Imprint of W. W. Norton & Company
Independent Publishers Since 1923*

Note to Readers: This book is intended as a general information resource for professionals practicing in the field of psychotherapy and mental health. It is not a substitute for appropriate training or clinical supervision. Standards of clinical practice and protocol vary in different practice settings and change over time. No technique or recommendation is guaranteed to be safe or effective in all circumstances, and neither the publisher nor the authors can guarantee the complete accuracy, efficacy, or appropriateness of any particular recommendation in every respect or in all settings or circumstances.

The names and identifying details of clients described in this book have been changed and some clients and the descriptions of their treatment are composites. Any URLs displayed in this book link or refer to websites that existed as of press time. The publisher is not responsible for, and should not be deemed to endorse or recommend, any website other than its own or any content that it did not create. The authors, also, are not responsible for any third-party material.

Copyright © 2025 by Charlynn Small and Paula Edwards-Gayfield

All rights reserved
Printed in the United States of America
First Edition

For information about permission to reproduce selections from this book, write to Permissions,
W. W. Norton & Company, Inc., 500 Fifth Avenue, New York, NY 10110

For information about special discounts for bulk purchases, please contact
W. W. Norton Special Sales at specialsales@wwnorton.com or 800-233-4830

Manufacturing by Versa Press
Production manager: Ramona Wilkes and Gwen Cullen

ISBN: 978-1-324-05274-6

W. W. Norton & Company, Inc., 500 Fifth Avenue, New York, NY 10110
www.wwnorton.com

W. W. Norton & Company Ltd., 15 Carlisle Street, London W1D 3BS

1 2 3 4 5 6 7 8 9 0

To all the Black women who persevered
when their symptoms were misdiagnosed,
undiagnosed, or neglected—and to the masterful
practitioners who will help make them well.
—Charlynn Small

To my mother, Sandra—because of you, I am.
—Paula Edwards-Gayfield

Contents

Acknowledgments		*xi*
Introduction		*xiii*
Chapter 1:	So, You Have a Black Client—Now What?	3
Chapter 2:	What Do Eating Disorders Look Like in Black Women?	15
Chapter 3:	What Contributes to and Maintains Eating Disorders?	30
Chapter 4:	Black Women Embrace Their Bodies, Right?	47
Chapter 5:	How Do I Build a Culturally Informed Therapeutic Alliance?	68
Chapter 6:	How Do I Adopt Treatment Techniques and Recommendations for Black Women?	88
Chapter 7:	How Do I Help Black Women Reimagine a Healthier Relationship With Food and Their Bodies?	108
Chapter 8:	Which Medical Complications Should I Be Aware Of?	128
Chapter 9:	Wait . . . Black Men Get Eating Disorders Too?	156
	Conclusion	*175*
	References	*177*
	Index	*205*

Acknowledgments

First and foremost, I, Paula, want to express my deepest gratitude to my partner, Marlin. Your dedication to my professional growth and the encouragement you've given me has been a source of strength and motivation. Your unwavering support, willingness to assist, and belief in me have been the foundation of my journey. I couldn't have done this without you.

To my family—my mother, Sandra, my sisters, Pamela and Patrina, my nephew, Quinten, and my extended family—I am deeply thankful for your constant belief in me. Your support has always reminded me that I can achieve anything I set my mind to. Thank you for being my biggest cheerleaders and for always having my back. You've all been there through thick and thin, reminding me that I can conquer anything. Your encouragement, love, and occasional unsolicited advice have been my secret ingredients for success.

A special thank you goes to Dr. Laura McClain, whose consistent support throughout this process has been truly remarkable. Your willingness to assist with reviewing and editing, along with your constant belief in me, has meant the world to me.

Dr. Gayle Brooks, my mentor: your guidance, belief in my potential, and steadfast encouragement have been invaluable. You have inspired me to reach higher, and I am forever appreciative of your support. I am equally grateful to my Renfrew family, whose support and encouragement over the years have provided me with opportunities for professional growth and development.

To my friends, who have been a constant source of encouragement, joy, and perspective, I am deeply thankful. Your companionship and understanding have provided me with the balance I needed to see this project through. Your belief in my abilities has been a constant source of motivation.

A special note of gratitude is owed to my coauthor, Dr. Charlynn Small. I am honored that you considered and trusted me to embark on this project with you. Your collaboration has been a privilege, and I appreciate the opportunity to work alongside you.

Lastly, I want to thank our publishers for believing in our work and giving us the opportunity to bring this project to life. Your support has been crucial in making this book a reality.

* * *

I, Charlynn, am thankful for the support of all of the people who love me unconditionally, and whom I love unconditionally—the list of which is far too long for this page. But it certainly includes the two loves of my life, Taylor and Chuck; my siblings, Charles and Sheldon, and so many other loved ones including my brilliant and talented coauthor and Soror, Paula; as well as Dr. Mary Churchill, Tiffany, Lissa, GloryB, Marisa, and Blanche to name just a very few.

Thank you, Deborah M., for reaching out to me out of the blue, giving further validation to my work.

Introduction

Charlynn Small

It's been nearly a decade since my colleague Mazella Fuller, PhD, and I made it our mission to help bring Black women out of the shadows of eating disorders (EDs) by bringing widespread attention to their concerns. Hitherto, their needs have largely gone unnoticed and unmet. There was—and tragically still is—a misconceived assumption that Black women don't experience eating disorders. This assumption is based on a number of reasons including sociocultural theories, criteria for diagnostic classification of these disorders in Black women, the extant assessment measures, conflicting research results, and a lack of discussion around mediating factors in the development of EDs in Black women (Small, 2021b).

Our plan for bringing Black women out of the shadows was to create ways to center and amplify their voices such that their stories would be heard by a wider audience of persons positioned to help improve their landscape, beginning with a commitment to viewing their concerns with cultural sensitivity and humility, and through a culturally responsive lens overall. Our first book, *Treating Black Women with Eating Disorders* (Small & Fuller, 2021), was a part of our plan. And while I love it when a plan comes together, there is still so much further to go.

WHO THIS BOOK IS FOR

This book is a vital resource for any professional who is licensed to give some form of care to clients and counts Black women (and Black men) among their clientele. This diverse group includes mental health professionals (psychotherapists, counselors, clinical social workers, psychiatric nurse practitioners, etc.), medical specialists (pediatricians, OB-GYNS, gastroenterologists, ER doctors, bariatric surgeons, etc.), other health care professionals (primary care physicians, dentists, dieticians, etc.), and those in other helping professions (teachers, coaches, etc.). Professionals from these disciplines are often among the first to identify symptoms of an eating disorder or disordered eating.

WHY THIS BOOK IS IMPORTANT

As we encounter more diverse clients, the gap widens between the number of clients and the availability of resources that address the lived experiences of Black women. In order to provide the most effective quality of care, practitioners have a responsibility to embrace a cultural humility approach to care and to seek out resources tailored to these clients' unique needs.

Black Women with Eating Disorders is written expressly to address the concerns of Black women. This book serves as a guide for practitioners to ensure fidelity in the application of evidence-based treatments with these groups.

In addition, the book explores many relevant topics in the eating disorder field including social media, body image, weight stigma, historical trauma, and aging. This book is important because it details with specificity the ways these factors manifest in the Black community. Broadening the lens to examine the therapeutic relationship, the authors demonstrate how best to center Black womens voices so they feel heard and understood. In this way, practitioners are well-positioned to apply effective strategies in treatment and support, ultimately facilitating the reimagining of their relationships to food and body, and paving the way toward a full recovery.

CLIENT CARE THROUGH A CULTURALLY SENSITIVE LENS

Viewing Black women's concerns through a culturally sensitive lens means, among other things, not taking a colorblind approach to client care. This is very important because race and racism, and issues relating to these concerns (i.e., racial disparities, discrimination, inequities, violence, and trauma), are associated with both negative psychological and physical health outcomes (Raney et al., 2023), including the development of eating disorders in these groups. A colorblind approach is often marked by some clinicians behaving as if they do not notice or are unaware of a client's race (Apfelbaum et al., 2012), perhaps believing they are acting in accordance with trending and politically correct best practices. However, approaching interactions with Black individuals as if their racial identity doesn't matter can actually harm their well-being. Dismissing, neglecting, minimizing, or ignoring racial differences—the very obvious attribute that in large measure defines or describes these clients—can be quite hurtful. While providers may believe they are being considerate, or even think they are offering a compliment, a colorblind approach neglects the significant impact of race on their Black clients' mental health. Use of this approach also functions to negate any injustices and trauma experienced by their clients, or historically by members of their clients' race, even if it occurs without a provider's awareness or intent.

The recent focus on social justice, condemnation of racial bias in medicine, and calls for the decolonization of health care have encouraged many non-Black providers to become more aware of their own explicit racial biases (Penner & Dovidio, 2016). Explicit biases and prejudices are consciously held endorsements, and expressions of such are typically deliberate (Penner & Dovidio, 2016), unlike implicit biases, which occur at an unconscious level. Implicit biases are largely the result of negative cultural associations that have become internalized (Penner & Dovidio, 2016), less accessible to awareness, and are quite resistant to change as a result. Conversely, desires to reflect an acceptance of positive race-related values such as diversity and equity can be expressed with greater ease as non-Black providers develop greater self-awareness of their explicit biases. However, continued learning and guided introspection are required to avoid unknowingly (or knowingly) adopting use of colorblind approaches to client care in the hopes of appearing racially unbiased when working with Black clients. I've heard some colleagues boast proudly of treating everyone the same. While for some, employing such an approach may allow them to experience some modicum of relief, secure in the feeling that they are doing what's right by attempting to treat everyone the same, the salient issue is that *everyone is not the same*. Providers may adopt colorblind approaches to lessen the chance of being labeled racist or prejudiced by clients. But these providers will be less likely to engage Black clients on some of the very difficult issues of race that mediate the development and maintenance of their eating disorders. As Williams (2011) notes, these practices merely relieve providers of their obligation to address racial differences and the issues that arise from them. Conversely, some other providers have justified their dismissive behavior on the basis of an ideological premise grounded in the misperception of living in a post-racist society (Neville et al., 2013).

In either case, behaving in such a manner can allow for something that is very important to be considered unimportant (Brooks, 2014) or missed completely, effectively dismissing the client's lived experience. As a result, many of the issues that make these women sick do not get addressed—and they do not get well. It must also be noted that there is evidence that supports that many

Black practitioners and therapists have also found it challenging at times to address clients' difficult life experiences (Jonsson, 2021).

Another area of bias that can yield the same outcome for Black women with eating disorders, and should therefore be carefully considered when treating this group, is the practice of race-based medicine. The alleged intent of the centuries-old practice is to identify biological differences between the races in order to provide tailored health care to those groups (Dutchen, 2021). The outcome of this system which defines race as an essential, biological variable, translates into clinical practice that leads to inequitable care (Cerdeña et al., 2020).

While quite different from colorblind approaches to treatment, race-based medicine biases are very important to consider because they typically assume facts not in evidence. For example, many physicians believe that Black bodies have thicker skin and fewer nerve endings than White bodies and thus experience pain less acutely than White bodies (Hoffman et al., 2016). As a result, Black persons have been systematically undertreated for pain management (Hoffman et al., 2016). Race-based medical practices are very dangerous not only because they have been used without regard for what is true, but also because there is generally no regard for how the lives of individuals (i.e., Anarcha and J. Marion Sims) and groups of persons (i.e., U.S. Public Health Service [USPHS] Syphilis Study at Tuskegee; FDA approved use of BiDil for Black patients only [Vyas et al., 2020]) have been or will be impacted. And these efforts have often been made under the guise of being helpful, or with the best of intentions to aid traditionally under-served populations (Dutchen, 2021). These concerns will be addressed in greater detail later in the book.

WHY WE WROTE THIS BOOK

For me, the journey toward my mission of bringing awareness of Black women with disordered eating to the attention of the discipline began about 20 years ago. On this day, my University of Richmond colleague Mary Churchill, PhD (also a contributor on *Treating Black Women with Eating Disorders*), and I took two of our mentees to dinner at a popular, nationwide chain restaurant near campus. While waiting to be seated in the often-crowded establishment, we noticed that most of the Black women were in larger bodies. The fact that many of these women were young, college-age, Black women captured my attention in particular.

In that moment, I pondered some of the possible reasons or contributing factors for what we were witnessing. I speculated about what might have been happening in the personal lives of these women that could account for the weight. I wondered about whether it was because many colleges no longer have a physical education requirement. And then I considered a more obvious, tangible factor, that was related to the allure of this particular restaurant. Like some others, it is quite popular in part because it features a variety of economically priced, hard-to-refuse meal deals, effectively—albeit not intentionally—setting the stage (or table) to encourage binge eating.

As a Black woman knowing what I knew about the adverse physical impact of being overweight on Black bodies (hypertension, diabetes, heart disease, arthritis, stroke, asthma, etc.), I became quite curious about how and when this all of a sudden happened. At least it seemed that this was a new occurrence. And as I became more and more curious about this, I became quite introspective.

I thought about my own family. Heretofore, I could only identify 5 first or second-degree relatives (4 women and 1 man) who were in very large bodies. I thought about the impact of the additional weight on their bodies. Four of the 5 were treated for Type 2 diabetes, and every one of the 4 incurred life-threatening issues related to the disease during its course. I thought again about the young women we saw that evening at the restaurant and wondered whether or when their livelihood might be compromised or otherwise impacted by diabetes or other weight-related conditions. As my interest and concern about these matters continued to grow, I also became aware of the many other instances when I was in the midst of Black women and a great number of them were in large bodies. No, this was not a new occurrence. Somehow, I had just not noticed this dynamic. This awareness and my reflections about the associated health risks of being Black and overweight became my catalyst for our clarion call to action.

After publication of *Treating Black Women with Eating Disorders,* Dr. Fuller and I were even more energized to continue our campaign to spread our message of cultural humility and to bring awareness of Black women's issues with eating disorders to practitioners within the eating disorders discipline and other disciplines as well.

Because the book was released at the start of the pandemic, I thought our efforts would be hampered by the world-wide physical distancing imperative. However, with the innovations in virtual learning technology that seemed to happen overnight, I'm fairly certain we reached many more persons than we could have possibly reached in person during the same timeframe. For example, we made live presentations close in time at a number of different colleges who asked us to lecture about Black women with eating disorders (EDs), including Historically Black College/University (HBCU) Spelman College, as well several Predominantly White Institutions (PWIs) including Appalachian State University, Wake Forest University, and University of North Carolina–Chapel Hill.

We believe that our presentations at PWIs are particularly important because of the increase in the numbers of women of color enrolled in these schools, some of whom cope with EDs, but may not be identified as such. Although, due to the efforts of Dr. Fuller and I (along with our colleagues who share our concern), and with all of the recent talk of diversity, equity, and inclusion (by the way, I don't understand how the word *race* is left out of this equation, when it seems actually to be the impetus for the movement), cultural sensitivity, decolonization of health care and such, many practitioners in the discipline have a greater awareness that Black persons do experience disordered eating. However, many still may not recognize the importance of incorporating different treatment approaches when working with diverse groups. Thus, we continued to forge ahead, sharing our message wherever we found an audience whether across the U.S. or abroad.

For example, by chance, Karen Carberry, the director of Family and Systemic Therapy at Orri Eating Disorders Treatment Clinic in the United Kingdom, saw our book online and reached out to me. During our association with Carberry, who now lectures at Oxford University, we learned that the experience of Black women grappling with EDs in the UK, mirrored that of Black women in the U.S. Through our connection with Carberry, we presented our live message virtually to three London audiences, and one in Glasgow, Scotland. We were invited to present in person in Glasgow for the UK's BEAT sponsored 2022 Eating Disorders International Conference (EDIC). Unfortunately, a surge in the COVID virus put an end to that trip, but still we presented our live message virtually to that audience.

During a London conference on intersectional perspectives on eating disorders, Dr. Fuller and I shared the stage with British pioneering ED psychotherapist Susie Orbach, where we engaged in a moderated panel discussion on several issues including feminism and body image concerns. Later, I was invited to consult on the set of a Showtime television series about a Black woman with bulimia. Again, this invitation was made after the series showrunner found *Treating Black Women* while researching eating disorders. As the COVID-19 pandemic came under control, I was able to travel internationally again and presented my message of hope for Black women with EDs at the Canadian Nutrition Society's Thematic Conference, 2023, in Toronto. In between, Dr. Fuller and I continued our mission to bring awareness of these concerns via different platforms including podcasts, interviews, and conference keynotes and presentations. Most recently in December 2024, I presented a keynote address on these topics at the University of the West Indies, Mona Campus in Kingston, Jamaica at their annual Dying to Be Beautiful conference.

Dr. Fuller frequently emphasizes the community aspect of our mission. Renfrew Center's regional assistant vice president and cochair of The Renfrew Center's Diversity and Inclusion Taskforce, Paula Edwards-Gayfield, MA, LPC, is part of our community. Edwards-Gayfield is also a member of the Board of the National Eating Disorders Association (NEDA), NEDA's Clinical Advisory Council (CAC), and teaches part of the core certification curriculum of the International Association of Eating Disorders Professionals (iaedp™). We first met several years ago, when I attended a diversity workshop she cofacilitated with our mentor Gayle Brooks, PhD, at the Renfrew Center's conference. Noting similarities of backgrounds and interests, we quickly joined forces and continued our crusade to educate practitioners and clinicians about the eating disorder challenges faced by a large segment of underrepresented persons.

In addition to copresenting at multiple conferences, Edwards-Gayfield joined membership with Dr. Fuller and I in iaedp's African American Eating Disorders Professionals (AAEDP) committee, serving as one of our two first-time cochair successors. As such, she cocreated and cofacilitated the innovative Culturally Competent Conversations, which is a platform inviting members of the EDs discipline to exchange views on important topics and issues impacting the profession. Edwards-Gayfield joined with us again as a contributor to *Treating Black Women with Eating Disorders.*

Besides her extensive knowledge of EDs, Edwards-Gayfield has nearly 20 years of eating disorders treatment and treatment facility management experience. Maintaining an emphasis on the importance of educating consumers and noting the increase she's seen in the number of Black persons seeking treatment over the past two decades, Edwards-Gayfield continues to speak on diversity issues and the treatment of people of color (POC) with eating disorders. Her efforts to raise awareness can also be accessed across various platforms including podcasts, interviews, blogs, and conferences. She recalled one profoundly memorable instance when parents chose one of her facilities to treat their teenage daughter after they learned there was a person of color in leadership there. This presence gave them confidence that the predominantly young, White staff would be culturally considerate when designing a treatment plan for their teen.

Edwards-Gayfield described another meaningful moment that occurred during an outreach event she coordinated in one Haitian community. An adolescent boy's mom explained that her son had lost a tremendous amount of weight after he began cutting carbs from his diet. While being unfamiliar with the concept of EDs, the parent initially became concerned about her son's diet when she noticed he would no longer eat rice which was a staple with most of their meals. Following their exchange of information during the outreach event, Edwards-Gayfield left that encounter feeling that her interaction with the parent had been quite helpful.

Some years earlier, I had a similar, though somewhat converse encounter with a Nigerian college undergrad seeking care after gaining what she described as an unusual amount of weight for her, and having later learned she had developed slightly elevated blood sugar levels. She recounted feeling in a quandary after her physician told her to stop eating rice. The student understood that his cautionary instructions may have been indicated, but with no other plan or assessment, she didn't know what to do next given that rice was a staple in her diet. These are the types of experiences that lead us to believe that this book is so crucial.

WE ALL CAN MAKE A DIFFERENCE

In a field dominated by stereotypes and biases, Black women continue to be underdiagnosed, overlooked, unheard, misinformed, or left out of important conversations concerning their own best interests. This book adds much needed dialogue to our understanding of eating disorders, by exploring a range of eating disorder terminology, symptomology, and interventions that providers across all disciplines can integrate into their knowledge base. More research is essential to center the experiences of Black women with eating disorders, and to understand the interplay and the impact of the various factors that contribute to their eating disorders. By exploring these intersections, we can better understand how to effectively treat and adapt interventions to improve treatment outcomes and promote healing among Black women affected by eating disorders. These pursuits will not only enhance our knowledge but will also encourage empowerment and resilience within this population.

BLACK WOMEN WITH EATING DISORDERS

Chapter 1

SO, YOU HAVE A BLACK CLIENT—NOW WHAT?

Eating disorders (EDs) are serious and complex mental health issues affecting people from every demographic, every ethnic group (National Eating Disorders Association [NEDA], 2005) and every race (Acle et al., 2021). Yet these disorders are frequently undiagnosed or misdiagnosed in Black women. However, most of the current literature negates the long-standing misconception that EDs are disorders impacting only wealthy, young White women, and slightly more attention is now being given to the fact that Black women do experience EDs. First, let's define what we mean by "Black women."

BLACK WOMEN DEFINED

Black women are not monolithic. Because of the myriad Black and Brown persons comprising all of the various ethnic and cultural groups termed people of color, it's important to define the women who are the focus of this book. The Historical African Diaspora was created by the involuntary subjugation and dispersion of persons from Africa to many parts of the world through the transatlantic slave trade (Institute for Cultural Diplomacy, 2024). One result of this was the creation of very large communities of persons of African origins, particularly in the U.S. (Institute for Cultural Diplomacy, 2024). Women from these communities who self-identify as Black are the focus of this book. They are further defined here as women of African ancestry, though born in the U.S., and whose current social and political stations and treatment are largely and undeniably due to the history of slavery (Lewellen et al., 2021).

RESEARCH ON EATING DISORDERS AND BLACK PERSONS

Research has shown that Black teens are as much as 50% more likely than White teens to engage in bingeing and purging behaviors (Goeree et al., 2011). Similarly, Goode et al. (2018) reported a binge-eating prevalence rate of nearly 5% in Black women, compared with 2.5% in White women. These and other results provide evidence that Black women experience these disorders at similar or greater rates than White women, making the lack of visibility around this issue even more significant.

Still, Sonneville and Lipson (2018) found that people of color who present with EDs continue to be half as likely as White persons to be diagnosed or treated for such. The reasons for this vary and include different racial biases (i.e., implicit and explicit biases), cultural factors, practitioners' lack of cultural competence and humility, lack of diversity in the EDs workforce, stereotypes, and other misconceptions and misinformation.

For example, this disparity was demonstrated in a now classic study by Gordon et al. (2006) seeking to evaluate whether race-based stereotypes affect a clinician's ability to recognize ED symptoms in Black girls. Participant clinicians were presented with one of three versions of a case study describing the behaviors of a 16-year-old adolescent girl with ED symptoms. The three case studies were identical except for one variation—the teen was presented as either White, Latinx, or Black. Clinicians were tasked with determining whether the teen's symptoms were problematic. Results suggested that the teen's race or ethnicity influenced the clinician's recognition of whether she had eating problems. When the teen was believed to be White, 44.4% of clinicians recognized the symptoms as problematic and 40.5% of the clinician participants recognized symptoms when the teen was viewed as Latinx. Interestingly, when clinicians believed the teen was Black, only 16.7% of them recognized these identical behaviors as symptomatic of an eating disorder. (Indeed, this issue may also be true for men of all races and ethnicities with eating disorders as well, and warrants further examination. However, the topic is beyond the scope of this book.)

Furthermore, additional analysis showed that while some clinicians did acknowledge occurrence of those same ED symptoms in the Black teen, they considered them individually, rather than collectively as a syndrome, thus underestimating the severity of these symptoms in what they believed was the Black teen. As one might surmise given this underestimation, results showed clinicians were less likely to refer the Black teen for help with her symptoms, compared with the rate at which the White and Latinx teens were referred for help.

In a similar study, Pike et al. (2001) found that although Black and White women diagnosed with binge-eating disorder (BED) were almost equally as likely to have been treated for weight management problems (28.8% and 30.6%, respectively), Black women with BED were almost three times less likely than White women with BED to receive treatment for EDs (7.7% and 22.4%, respectively).

These results beg the question: *How is it possible to view identical clinical pictures, but make such vastly different assessments and referrals?*

FACTORS CONTRIBUTING TO VASTLY DIFFERENT ASSESSMENTS AND REFERRALS

The researchers suggested that the "low usage of treatment may reflect a cultural bias within the Black community regarding mental health care," or that there may be some other reason for not securing such care (Pike et al., 2001). While the cultural biases described are not untrue, the researchers' summary doesn't account for many clinicians' decisions not to refer these women for ED treatment, even though it may be indicated.

A few of the other reasons cited for these types of disparities include clinicians' lack of cultural competence and humility (Small, 2021a), practitioners' fears of engaging clients in difficult discussions about racial differences, biased clinician assessments (Small, 2021a; Gordon et al., 2006; Becker et al., 2003), attitudes and implicit biases (Tong & Artiga, 2021), race-based stereotypes (Gordon et al., 2006), clients' identity issues (Small, 2021a) and their bodies (Gay, 2017), and their differential access to health care (Becker et al., 2003). Results of these and similar studies suggest that many practitioners have likely seen a significant number of Black women clients with EDs without knowing it or thinking to assess for it.

It is also likely that Black women themselves don't know that their symptoms are associated with EDs. Therefore, it seems unlikely that they would think to suggest to their primary care physician—frequently the first point of entry for behavioral care (Huggard, 2020)—that they might be experiencing some type of disordered eating issue. If these women had some idea of what was happening to their bodies, in this respect, primary care facilities would be important settings for detecting various mental and behavioral health concerns (Jetty et al., 2021; Bland, 2007) including stress, depression, and anxiety. Huggard (2020) reported persons 18–24 accounted for 20% of primary care visits that were associated with behavioral health care. EDs often develop during this time, or even earlier, between adolescence and young adulthood.

RESOLVING THE EVALUATION PARADOX

More urgent than the question of how groups of persons presenting the same clinical picture can be evaluated so differently is the question: *How can we best resolve this paradox?*

In the first study presented above by Gordon et al. (2006), the behaviors depicted are examples of restricting. The fact that few clinicians considered the possibility that the teen presenting the restricting behaviors could be Black is an example of *clinician assessment bias*. One way to address the paradox in this case is for the clinician to increase their level of cultural competence and humility through continued education and training, thus expanding their lens and challenging stereotypes. This topic is addressed in Chapter 5.

Likewise, in the study presented by Pike et al. (2001), the results seemed to indicate that clinicians did not refer Black women with binge-eating disorder for eating disorder treatment perhaps either because the idea of Black women having an ED is simply beyond their frame of reference, or because of some stereotypical views of fat, lazy Black women, or yet because of some other related reason. These and other factors that maintain EDs are addressed in Chapter 3.

In my first book (Small, 2021a), I (Charlynn Small) discuss in some detail that some practitioners fail to recognize these disorders in Black women because we are not talking about them—as a society we aren't centering Black women in our conversations, and as practitioners we aren't asking our Black clients enough relevant questions to obtain a thorough clinical picture. Black women show up for appointments with their general practitioner or OB-GYN physicians in larger bodies, but there is not enough exploration about *why* they are in these bodies.

Often, Black women are told that to address weight concerns, they must diet and exercise—which is perhaps more often true than not—lest they become diabetic, or succumb to heart failure, or some cerebrovascular accident. However, adjusting diets and adding an exercise routine are only part of what needs to happen to effect significant changes. In this scenario, what is missing is any discussion regarding why Black women are in these larger bodies.

An exploration about why Black women are in these larger bodies must necessarily begin with a conversation between practitioner and client. This requires both active and reflective listening from the practitioner, which includes the fundamental skills of deep listening, attending to the client's verbal and nonverbal communication, and acknowledging that the client has been heard. However, these dialogues can sometimes be quite difficult to navigate. The difficulty stems from the fact that EDs (binge eating) manifest most often in Black women as a result of racism, acculturative stress, adverse childhood events (ACEs), various other traumas, and environmental circumstances (Small, 2021a). Unfortunately, practitioners often fear asking the hard questions about their clients' weight and appearance because they often lead to very uncomfortable conversations (Small, 2021a). A lack of training on how to have these difficult conversations leaves practitioners ill-equipped to manage these sorts of interactions.

Cultural humility is an interactive approach to understanding parts of one's identity (Hook et al., 2013; Office of Minority Health, HHS, 2013), that when practiced will aid in navigating these difficult dialogues. The practitioner's investment in learning about the client's lived experience through the client's own perspective is emphasized. And while there must be a comfort with not knowing some things with this approach (Office of Minority Health, HHS, 2013), in this case, the initial consultation is where the practitioner can begin the search for why clients are in larger bodies by seeking answers to some very difficult questions.

If the practitioner gleans important information during the initial consultation (or at any point over their course of treatment), their clinical judgment may lead them to offer the client various referrals depending on the clinical picture, beginning the multidisciplinary team (MDT) process. In the case of a Black woman client presenting ED symptoms and related concerns (low self-esteem, body dissatisfaction, depression and anxiety, etc.), an ED specialist with additional training in *cultural competence* would likely be a good place to begin. They may consider the possibility of an ED and assess the client, accordingly, including exploration of the impact of racism, other cultural concerns, trauma, etc., on her presenting symptoms. Interventions would be tailored to the specific needs and preferences of that client.

EIGHT TRUTHS EVERY HEALTH CARE PROFESSIONAL SHOULD KNOW WHEN WORKING WITH BLACK WOMEN

As stated previously, whether you are a primary care physician or psychotherapist, dietitian, dentist, or other specialist, you will likely have (or may have already had) at some point in time a Black female client who has an undiagnosed

ED or a significant pattern of disordered eating behaviors verging on a diagnosable illness. This book offers diverse perspectives and practical applications for working effectively with these persons.

There are a number of provider types who are in a unique position because of their individual disciplines to identify symptoms and potentially save lives. *An estimated 10,200 deaths each year are believed to be the direct result of an eating disorder—that's one death every 52 minutes* (Deloitte, 2020). We have the ability to change this frightening statistic for the better. In this book, we provide concrete tips on how begin making change.

The fact that few eating disorders studies have been conducted that include Black women is yet another reason why health care professionals have misconceptions regarding the disorders within this population. What follows is a list of what we believe are essential truths that any health care provider working with Black women with EDs should understand.

1. Racism is a primary factor in the development of EDs for Black women.
2. Colorism, or discrimination within the Black community, figures prominently in the development and maintenance of eating disorders.
3. Mistrust of the medical community means Black women may not seek help for ED symptoms.
4. There is a strong link between eating disorders and sexual assault.
5. There is a strong link between eating disorders and trauma (i.e., adverse childhood experiences [ACEs]).
6. ED symptoms manifest differently in Black women than in White women.
7. Socioeconomic status is often a major factor in the onset and maintenance of EDs.
8. The purpose of food (i.e., to self-soothe vs. for nutritional value) plays a major role in contributing to and maintaining EDs in Black women.

Black women face the challenges of acculturative stress, racism, class, and gender daily. These psychosocial stressors erode health through chronically elevated cardiovascular responses (Merritt et al., 2006). They make Black women sick. So, in addition to fighting for their mental health, they're fighting for their physical health, as well (Fuller, 2021). Effective clinicians will be respectful of Black women's lived experiences and join with them in treatment at every level of care for successful healing to occur (Fuller, 2021).

Practical Tips

Each of the eight truths is addressed in greater detail later in this book. Below are a few things you can do now to start to understand these truths in context:

- Read *Treating Black Women with Eating Disorders: A Clinician's Guide*, edited by Charlynn Small and Mazella Fuller (Routledge, Taylor & Francis); *Not All Black Girls Know How to Eat* by Stephanie Covington Armstrong (Lawrence Hill Books); and *Freeing Black Girls: A Black Feminist Bible on Racism and Revolutionary Mothering* by Tamura Lomax (Duke University Press).
- Ask your Black female client about any history of adverse childhood experiences (ACEs).
- When a Black woman shares her symptoms, don't dismiss them. Engage her in discussion about them.
- Many hospitals, mental health or other treatment facilities offer opportunities to join with other professionals to engage in intersectional or culturally competent conversations, virtually or in-person. Such discussions typically are designed to help practitioners facilitate difficult discussions with greater comfort when working with clients from diverse backgrounds.
- Read the entirety of this book and share it with your colleagues.

TREATMENT CENTER LEVELS OF CARE AND TREATMENT TEAM COMPOSITION

The level of care provided for someone with an eating disorder is determined by a number of different factors including, but not limited to, the following: manifestation of symptoms, frequency of presenting behaviors, existing coping skills, course of the disorder, protective factors, previous treatment, trauma history, co-occurring conditions, the institution or setting where service is provided (college campus, hospital, clinic, etc.), the client/patient's age, age of onset, available treatment modalities (i.e., CBT, DBT, IPT, FBT), acuity of symptoms, suicidality, and nonsuicidal self-injury.

Similar to the appropriate level of care, the composition of a multidisciplinary eating disorders treatment team depends on many factors—of which level of care is a primary determining factor. While comprehensive treatment should be provided at every level of care, the size of the team will vary depending on patient or client needs. Particular treatments are provided by different health care professionals from many different disciplines, across various levels of care, and typically ranging on a continuum from least to greatest intensity as necessary. Levels of care offered by larger, well-established centers (The Renfrew Centers, Eating Recovery and Pathlight Centers, etc.) usually provide a full spectrum of services that includes some variations of the following: intensive outpatient (IOP) therapy, virtual (mostly since the pandemic) IOP therapy, partial hospitalization program (PHP), residential (RES), and inpatient (IP). Some facilities distinguish between IP and acute medical stabilization, with the latter designated expressly for persons who are severely medically unstable. In general, fewer services are required at less intensive levels of care. However, the number of services required can increase significantly with the complexity of a person's symptomatology and as the level of care increases.

For instance, a client may present only a few symptoms and, perhaps infrequently. As such, she may appear to not require many services. This could be because she has an effective repertoire of coping strategies and skills to help manage their disordered eating behavior or symptoms, thus requiring only minimal services, such as from a mental health therapist, a nutritionist, and perhaps a general practice physician. If the client began to experience an increase in severity and occurrence of symptoms, she may require a higher treatment level to include the services of one or more practitioners to provide highly specialized treatment.

TYPES OF PROVIDERS AND TREATMENT CONCERNS RELATED TO EATING DISORDERS

General Practitioners, Family Physicians, and Urgent Care and Emergency Room Physicians

Someone experiencing disordered eating or other more acute symptoms may first bring them to the attention of a family doctor or other general care physician, including an urgent care or emergency room physician. A general practitioner may have several roles on the multidisciplinary care team, among them, providing the client with psychoeducational information about eating disorders. Learning about the possibility of having an eating disorder, despite its potentially serious implications, can often provide a certain measure of relief as the client learns there is an explanation for their particular symptomology and behavior, and also that treatments are available.

A general practice physician will continue gathering information following results of routine screenings (blood pressure, weight, etc.) and brief assessments (i.e., SCOFF [Morgan et al., 1999]) to confirm or rule out conditions with greater certainty. For example, an accelerated heart rate perhaps with other symptoms or behaviors commonly associated with eating disorders, may inspire a general care physician to either begin a more comprehensive assessment, including specialized labs not typically ordered if an ED is not suspected (this will be discussed in greater detail later), or to make referrals to other practitioners, especially those with specialized expertise in treating eating disorders.

In some cases, depending on the patient or client's age when disordered eating symptoms appear, a pediatrician (or gerontologist) may be the first practitioner to address these complaints. In this case, the pediatrician may make a diagnosis and also take the lead on developing a treatment plan and assembling the core team, which typically consists of at least a physician, a mental wellness provider, and a dietician or nutritionist. Family members also join with the patient or client to comprise the core team. Apart from recommendations to other medical specialists to treat various physical concerns related to EDs that may occur, a general practitioner (or pediatrician) will likely refer patients to a mental wellness care provider early in the team process.

Mental Wellness Professionals

Mental wellness professionals can include a number of different practitioners who provide psychological support, and a variety of different services and treatment via evidence-based therapies (National Eating Disorders Collaboration [NEDC], 2023). Practitioners in this group include psychologists, social workers, professional counselors, mental health nurses, and addiction specialists. Services pertaining to eating disorder symptoms and behaviors may include assessment, consultation, diagnosis, treatment planning and implementation.

Psychiatrists also provide psychological support. They are medical doctors who can prescribe medication to address patient concerns as necessary and may also take the lead on medication management. Psychiatric nurse practitioners have additional medical training and may also provide medication as needed. The mental health care and treatment a client receives depends on a number of factors, or a combination of factors, such as the diagnosis; symptoms; presence of any co-occurring disorder(s); client's age, acuity, chronicity, existing family and friends support; recommended level of care; the practitioner's theoretical orientation, training, and experience; availability of services, and barriers to care.

EDs can develop as the result of myriad reasons or events including dieting, depression, anxiety, stress, trauma, suicide gestures and ideation, nonsuicidal self-injury, adverse childhood experiences (Centers for Disease Control and Prevention [CDC], 1997), adjustment disorders, transitions, substance use/dependence, addictions, binge eating, purging, and restricting. Conditions or issues can also occur or become exacerbated during the course of treatment. In addition, it is not uncommon for persons diagnosed with one eating disorder to migrate to symptoms or behaviors of another disorder (Small, 2019). Mental wellness care providers are trained to address these issues at any point during the course of treatment.

Dieticians and Nutritionists

A dietician or nutritionist is one of the most essential elements of the ED team and is also likely to become involved early in the treatment process. Like other team members, the dietician/nutritionist educates the client from their specialty perspective on the ways their physical and mental well-being can be impacted by the effects of their ED. A primary role of the dietician is to determine the severity of any malnutrition and assess for any deficits in nutritional skills and knowledge that may inhibit a client's nutritional recovery (Jeffrey & Heruc, 2020).

In addition to completing a nutrition assessment and providing continued evaluation and monitoring of treatment goals (National Eating Disorders Collaboration [NEDC], 2023; Jeffrey & Heruc, 2020), the dietician will play a significant role in weight management; refeeding in acute cases; assisting the client with creating menus, food plans, and exchanges; working around challenge foods; and helping to determine practical, effective strategies around food and eating (i.e., encouraging the client to place snacks on a plate vs. eating from the container, which might lead to overeating). The dietician's expertise is also needed in particular circumstances (i.e., diabetes mellitus, pregnancy, food allergies, and gastrointestinal or other disorders or conditions; NEDC, 2023) to prevent and/or monitor acute and chronic complications associated with certain co-occurring diseases and conditions.

Additional Medical Specialists

Eating disorder behaviors impact the whole body. Therefore, there is an increased risk of developing a number of symptoms or disorders affecting virtually any bodily system that are best treated by practitioners with expertise in those systems, including endocrinologists, cardiologists, neurologists, occupational and rehabilitation therapists, dentists, nephrologists, bariatric surgeons, bariatricians and gastroenterologists, obstetrics and gynecologists, orthopedic surgeons, dermatologists, and gerontologists.

In addition to physical and mental health specialists, the ED multidisciplinary team may include teachers, tutors, and other school personnel. Children and adolescents with EDs are at risk of missing significant school instruction depending on certain factors, such as diagnosis, treatment level, or stage of recovery. In the case of a young person admitted to partial hospitalization or residential care, the student will likely be eligible to receive learning accommodations through a 504 Plan (U.S. Dept. of Education, 2008), or other recovery support plan designed to help the student meet academic standards while focusing on recovery. Such plans are created through a collaboration between the school and the treatment facility. It provides the details of the goals and objectives, and identifies the person or persons responsible for facilitating achievement of the goals.

MOVING FORWARD

Although systematic reviews of the empirical studies that have included Black women show this population remains underrepresented in ED clinical trials (Parker et al., 2023; Acle et al., 2021; Goode et al., 2020), increasing evidence suggests that ED prevalence is rising in this group (Acle et al., 2021; Goeree et al., 2011). For example, Goode et al. (2018) report that Black women in the U.S. have the highest rates of obesity and engage in frequent binge-eating behaviors. Similarly, the National Center for Health Statistics (NCHS, 2017) estimates that 82% of Black women are affected by overweight or obesity, compared to 63.5% of White women.

Depending on the severity and chronicity, EDs have the potential to impact every system of the body. As such, effective treatment may require the expertise of health practitioners from a number of disciplines. Because Black women with EDs have different problems, the disorders manifest in ways differently than might be expected, and they often require different and/or additional ways to address them. In Chapter 2, we will examine in greater detail the ways in which EDs present in Black women.

Chapter 2

WHAT DO EATING DISORDERS LOOK LIKE IN BLACK WOMEN?

The *Diagnostic and Statistical Manual of Mental Disorders* (*DSM-5-TR*; American Psychiatric Association, 2022) defines a number of eating disorders, some of which can be deadly. Each is characterized by a variety of different features and behaviors that occur with varying frequencies and severity. Different behaviors are associated primarily with particular disorders (although there is some overlap across disorders in some cases), each having the ability to impact the body in different ways. A brief overview and review of some of the major disorders and the ways they manifest in Black women is presented here.

Despite conclusive evidence showing that Black women experience eating disorders (i.e., Goode et al., 2020; Goode et al., 2021; Goode et al., 2022; Taylor et al., 2007), studies about Black women, and more often studies on clinical trials that include Black women continue to be underrepresented in the ED literature.

However, the literature has shown that of the most well-researched eating disorders (e.g., anorexia nervosa, bulimia nervosa, and binge-eating disorder), binge eating disorder is the most prevalent ED occurring among Black women (Goode et al., 2020; Goode et al., 2022; Taylor et al., 2007; & Hudson et al., 2007), with lifetime prevalence rates of 2.36% (Taylor et al., 2007). Taylor et al. (2007) also found a lifetime prevalence of 5.82% for any discrete episode of binge eating among Black women, compared with a lifetime prevalence of 2.5% among non-Latinx White women (Marques et al., 2011).

TYPES OF EATING DISORDERS

Binge-Eating Disorder

Binge-eating disorder (BED) is a pattern of eating most notably characterized by discrete episodes of eating a very large amount of food during the episode. The amount of food eaten is significantly greater than what most others would eat during the same amount of time (e.g., approximately a 2-hour period) in almost identical situations. To meet *DSM-5* (APA, 2022) criteria, the episode must occur at least 1 day a week for a period of 3 months. BED onset typically is between adolescence and young adulthood, though instances of later adult onset of BED is not unusual. Some studies have found BED to have the highest age of onset among Black women, between 22–25 years (Taylor et al., 2007; Hudson et al., 2007).

During binge-eating episodes, individuals eat rapidly and describe the experience as a loss of control over their eating. Typically, food is eaten until the person feels uncomfortably full. It is also quite common for persons with BED to eat large amounts of food even when they do not feel physically hungry. When aware of their behavior, persons with BED often experience a hodge-podge of emotions ranging from shame to guilt to embarrassment, among others (Hazzard et al., 2019). And because so much of EDs is about control, self-criticism, and perfectionism (Schafer & Rutledge, 2003), these feelings can lead to eating alone in order to avoid humiliation, and also to self-loathing and disgust. Grappling with so many mixed emotions simultaneously causes marked distress (APA, 2022), which can often lead to co-occurring conditions such as anxiety and depression (Mitchell & Mazzeo, 2004). In such cases, substance use can often become a factor as individuals seek ways to cope with mood issues. Treatment and recovery efforts can be quite difficult in these situations because treatment facilities haven't routinely integrated treatment to address both issues concurrently (Claudat et al., 2020).

Bulimia Nervosa

Bulimia nervosa (BN) bears some resemblance to BED in several important ways, but also differs from BED in one particularly important way. The feature that sets them apart primarily is BN's corollary, inappropriate compensatory behaviors designed to offset or prevent weight gain from calories taken in during the binge episode. Like BED, BN is characterized by discrete episodes of eating a very large amount of food during the episode. Also, as with BED, the amount of food eaten is definitely larger than what most others would eat during the same amount of time under similar circumstances. However, to meet *DSM-5* (APA, 2022) criteria for BN, both events—the binge-eating episode and the inappropriate compensatory behavior—each must occur at least 1 day a week for a period of 3 months. Similar to BED, the onset typically is between adolescence and young adulthood, though rarely occurring initially after 40 (APA, 2022). Regarding the prevalence of BN in Black women, Taylor et al. (2007) reported a lifelong prevalence rate of 1.90%, and a 1.04% 12-month prevalence.

Because of the fear of gaining weight and the concurrent desire to lose weight, the bulimia cycle generally begins with dieting or restricting behaviors, resembling those of individuals with anorexia nervosa (APA, 2022). However, despite stringent efforts at maintaining enough control to restrict or fast for days at a time, almost inevitably, persons need to eat. And for those with BN, the period of starvation typically leads to bingeing. And similar to the binge-eating episodes that occur with BED, persons with BN often eat ravenously and they experience a sense of being out of control, as if unable to stop. Some have described their binges as having a dissociative quality. Also because of the fear of gaining weight and the desire to lose weight, body shape and weight are inextricably tied to self-esteem and self-valuation (APA, 2022).

Recall that control, perfectionism, and self-criticism are the pillars of disordered eating. Thus, bingeing is interpreted as a loss of control. It's important to remember that an essential feature of the disorder is the amount of food eaten and the speed at which it's eaten, versus the type of food eaten. Although unlike BED, with BN, binge foods are typically avoided. However, the compensatory, or purging behaviors that usually follow the binge may allow the individual with BN to partake of the ordinarily forbidden foods, believing they are counterbalancing the binge by purging. While this may be partially true, it should be noted that during the binge, persons may also retain enough calories and nutrients to sustain themselves. This may account for the relatively average size of many persons with BN.

With the loss of control eating, persons with BN feel bloated and uncomfortably full. And quite commonly, guilt and shame are their companions. Purging serves to relieve these feelings. And the cycle begins again. There are several ways to purge. Some of the most frequently used methods include vomiting, diuretics, enemas and laxatives, fasting, and excessive exercising. It should also be noted that individuals with BN often purge even after eating small amounts of food. In addition, in recent years, we've seen the emergence of diabulimia. Although not yet named as such by the *DSM*, diabulimia has been called an eating disorder (Kinik et al., 2017), and is described as a form of purging because of the way individuals with diabetes mellitus either limit or skip taking their prescribed insulin doses, which reduces metabolism of the food eaten during bingeing.

Anorexia Nervosa

Three essential features characterize anorexia nervosa (AN), and each is required to meet *DSM-5* (APA, 2022) criteria for the diagnosis. The first is restriction of energy intake that leads to significantly low body weight in terms of what is minimally expected given one's age, gender, developmental trajectory, and physical health. There must also be either an intense fear of gaining weight or becoming fat, or alternatively, persistent behavior that obstructs or inhibits weight gain despite one's already significantly low weight. The third criteria for diagnosis is a distortion in the experience and significance of one's body and shape, which includes a persistent lack of recognition of the seriousness of their current low body weight status. It may also be necessary to specify whether the AN is of the restricting type (no episodes of bingeing or purging during the last 3 months) or whether the AN is of the binge-eating/purging type (the individual has episodes of bingeing or purging during the last 3 months).

Taylor et al. (2007) reported an AN lifetime prevalence rate of 0.14% in Black women, which is consistent with the scant, previous research findings of low occurrence of AN in these groups. (i.e., Hudson et al., 2007). Findings of Taylor et al.'s (2007) seminal research examining the prevalence of eating disorders among Blacks in the National Survey of American Life (NSAL) study showed that lifetime prevalence estimates for Black women were greatest for any discrete episodes of binge eating (5.82%), BED (2.36%), BN (1.90%), and AN (0.14%), which is the reason we, the authors, present the disorders in that order. However, despite that binge eating is the most prevalent ED among Blacks, please be cautious about the fact that while risks for Black women developing AN are low, they are not nonexistent.

Though prevalence was low for adults, Taylor et al. (2007) reported a younger age (14.89 years) of onset for AN in Black adolescents, which is younger than is typical for children in the U.S. These results suggest that Black children, who have a lower risk of developing a disorder but may do so at an early age, are at greater risk of the disorder going undiagnosed and untreated for a longer time. These findings provide support of the need for clinicians and practitioners to be well-trained in working with diverse groups (Taylor et al., 2007).

Other Eating Disorders

The *DSM-5* (APA, 2022) lists several other types of disordered eating concerns that may be less prevalent across different populations, but not necessarily less serious, including *avoidant resistant food intake disorder* (ARFID), *Pica*, and *rumination disorder.*

With ARFID the essential feature is avoidance of, or a lack of interest in eating some foods based on sensory aspects of foods, like texture. There may also be some concern for possible consequences of eating the foods (i.e., vomiting).

Pica is defined as persistent eating of nonnutritive, nonfood substances for a period of 1 month. The behavior is not developmentally age appropriate, nor is it connected to any culturally supported ritual or practice.

Rumination is repeated regurgitation of food over a period of at least 1 month. Regurgitated food may be re-chewed, re-swallowed, or spit out. The repeated regurgitation is not attributable to an associated gastrointestinal or other medical condition (e.g., gastroesophageal reflux, pyloric stenosis). However, while working with persons in special populations (intellectually deficient, severe autism, etc.) I often observed them, one more than others, to regurgitate whole, unchewed, boneless cuts of meats (i.e., pork cutlets or chicken thighs) several hours after first eating them, and then begin to chew them and re-eat them. While it seemed clearly that this behavior is rooted in some type of medical condition, by definition, it is not.

Orthorexia nervosa, while not a *DSM-5* (APA, 2022) diagnosis, also warrants attention because of its potentially severe outcomes. Its essential features are an exaggerated emotional distress regarding food choices, as there is a focus on eating only "clean" or healthy foods. Severe weight loss, malnutrition, and other serious medical conditions may result.

Other Specified Feeding and Eating Disorders

The *DSM-5* (APA, 2022) recognizes *other specified feeding and eating disorders* (OSFED) as a category of subclinical feeding and eating symptoms and associated behaviors or patterns causing clinically significant distress or impairment in social, occupational, or other important areas of functioning that may be problematic but that do not meet the full criteria for any one particular disorder in the feeding and eating disorders diagnostic class.

DISORDERED EATING BEHAVIORS VS. EATING DISORDERS

The terms disordered eating (DE) and EDs have frequently been used interchangeably. Although similar, there are some important differences between the two. For example, EDs are the clinically diagnosable eating conditions, having met all of the specified criteria for a particular disorder. However, while similar to the OSFED nomenclature, DE is a separate category of eating behavior patterns used often to refer to subclinical presentations of symptoms or behaviors that have the potential to cause tremendous emotional upset such as intense embarrassment, shame, self-loathing, or guilt following presentation of the symptoms or behaviors (Chaves et al., 2023). For example, a subclinical depiction of AN might be most accurate if an individual's behaviors meet every criterion for AN, except that there is absolutely no disturbance in one's body image pertaining to how one experiences weight or shape, which is required for the diagnosis. Another instance where the subclinical DE depiction would be more accurate would be in the case of an individual who presents all of the criteria for BED, except that the behaviors occur only once per month for 3 months, versus the required once per week for 3 months. In this way, as with many other *DSM-5* disorders, syndromes, illnesses, and conditions, an important differentiation between DE and EDs is one of extent, measure, or scope, specifically with regard to the frequency of occurrence and the severity of the various symptoms and behaviors (Chaves et al., 2023).

EATING DISORDER PRESENTATION IN BLACK WOMEN

Let's look at how EDs may uniquely present in Black women.

Binge-Eating Disorder: Toni

Toni is a recently divorced woman in her late 50s who worked as guardian ad litem in a small rural town, a job about which she feels quite passionate. Toni had grappled with binge eating for as far back as she could remember. Unhappy with her appearance and her size, which was now causing serious health issues (e.g., diabetes), Toni's health and well-being goals were weight loss and weight management, which she had hoped to achieve through Food Anonymous (FA).

While she had never experienced any substance dependence, gambling, or other hard to extinguish behavior, Toni explained that her understanding of FA was that they believed overeating can be managed, in part, by abstaining from addictive foods. Though achieving her target weight loss goal and having had some remissions in FA, Toni was frustrated about her inability to maintain long-term success in the FA program, like many others who had achieved moderate success. Toni thought this was partly because she was constantly thinking about food (i.e., "When can I eat?", "I can't eat out, because I can't weigh or measure my portions . . ."), creating meal plans, or touching food (e.g., shopping for it, chopping it up, storing it in freezer bags). Although there was never condemnation for relapses in FA, there was no real processing of what led to relapses in their peer-led meetings. And while support of the fellowship was comforting, she didn't feel that her disordered eating behaviors were being addressed adequately.

During many of our discussions, Toni began to realize that job-related issues were what usually led to her relapses. It wasn't her meager wages—she would have done the work for free. What was hardest for her was when, after finally gaining their trust, children were sometimes removed from her caseload and reassigned without notice. She didn't get to say goodbye to them or to wish them well. These things made her very uncomfortable, angry, and anxious.

To feel better, she'd give herself permission to eat out. She'd search the menu for food items with "clean" ingredients. This meant she could eat larger than usual portions. Dining out also gave her permission to overeat. She binged when feeling happy. Wonderful news at work gave her permission to binge. A positive performance evaluation or a well-received presentation gave her new justification. And, while she felt badly about relapsing, she was relieved about being able to recognize the circumstances during which she was most likely to binge.

And I was relieved for her, because she was better able to avoid relapses if she could anticipate when they might occur. During relapses and when negative events occurred, I encouraged Toni to practice self-compassion. Specifically, I helped her learn to use positive self-talk, and to not be judgmental or self-critical because of shortcomings or mistakes, or events over which she had no control. Ultimately, she began treating herself with more kindness, using softer tones, and reacting less harshly to negative events. I also encouraged her to maintain her practice of regular self-care, such as connecting with her supportive family and friends, working with her nutritionist, journaling, going to the gym, and taking short breaks while working. Toni continues her self-care regimen and manages her weight concerns with significantly less anxiety.

Bulimia Nervosa: Yolanda

Yolanda is a 24-year-old Black law student whose family moved from the Dominican Republic to New York soon after she was born. As a child, she was a competitive swimmer, sang in the church choir, and excelled at most activities. She was always an A student. She was offered full scholarships to several top institutions. As an undergraduate, most of her professors described her as brilliant. She was working toward earning her JD at a large, well-regarded university. Both of her parents and her paternal grandfather were attorneys.

Yolanda was raised primarily by her paternal grandmother, who died during her freshman year of college. Yolanda began bingeing and purging soon afterward. Most people described Yolanda as very attractive, though she never felt that way. Because of her average weight, she always felt overweight. She seemed always on the periphery of different friend groups, not feeling confident enough to assert herself. During her sophomore year, she had a bariatric procedure during a break from school. She continued bingeing and purging. Without these behaviors, she felt unproductive and believed she could not earn A's. As her bulimia grew in intensity, she frequently complained of heartburn, had visible signs of edema in her cheeks, and calloused knuckles (Russell's signs) from biting down on them while purging.

Most of the men in Yolanda's family were heavy drinkers. During law school, she began drinking heavily also. She believed this gave her the courage to engage more easily with friends. Over the course of counseling at the campus wellness center, Yolanda came to the realization that these behaviors were quite unhealthy. She also discovered that as the frequency of her eating disorder behaviors decreased, her drinking increased, and vice versa. Unfortunately, while there were several treatment facilities near where she attended school that were equipped to treat either her bulimic behavior or her problems with substance use (the costs of which were quite prohibitive), there were no facilities that could treat her co-occurring issues. And, because she had not told her parents about her health issues, she did not want to ask them for help. More than anything, she did not want to disappoint them.

Anorexia Nervosa: Emme

Emme is a 16-year-old Black high school student who presented for treatment following her pediatrician's concern over a significant weight loss of 20 pounds within three months. Over the past three months, Emme restricted her daily caloric intake to approximately 500–800 calories, engaged in excessive exercise, and eliminated pasta from her diet. While she enjoyed cooking and baking with her sisters and mother, she often avoided eating, claiming she had already eaten or lacked an appetite. She noticed physical symptoms like lightheadedness, increased cold sensitivity, and lethargy but dismissed them as normal, resorting to drinking Gatorade when needed. Attending a predominantly White high school, Emme reported feeling increasingly out of place and struggling with body image issues, particularly in comparison to her less curvaceous peers. She expressed a desire to "disappear" and fit in better, often comparing herself unfavorably to her naturally thin mother and grappling with why she didn't resemble her. Emme frequently compared herself to her sisters too, who were also naturally thin. She reported having a good relationship with her parents and siblings and did not want them to be impacted by her behaviors.

Emme described herself as a perfectionist, driven to maintain her status as an A student, which exacerbated her restrictive eating behaviors. She believed these behaviors were just part of being "healthy" and dismissed concerns about developing an eating disorder, viewing them as uncommon among Black girls. Her decision to join the cheerleading squad was influenced by the belief that weight loss would help her feel more comfortable and attractive in the uniform. She expressed concerns about her attractiveness, particularly the lack of attention from Black boys at her school, noting that there were few boys of color and questioning why they didn't seem interested in her compared to her non-Black friends. Although she denied experiencing overt racism, she acknowledged feeling pressure about her desirability and attractiveness, particularly in the context of school stress and anxiety.

Initially reluctant to engage in therapy, Emme began to disclose more frequently as she continued to feel more supported and "free" to discuss her experiences. The therapist encouraged her to track her food intake while working with her family to connect them with a dietitian. As therapy progressed, Emme began to recognize her body image concerns, particularly how they were influenced by comparisons to her family, peers, and societal beauty standards.

Despite her weight loss, she expressed dissatisfaction with her body, particularly her stomach, thighs, and hips. Family therapy sessions emphasized the importance of shared family meals to normalize eating and strengthen connections. These sessions provided Emme with a platform to discuss the pressures she felt at school and home, as well as an opportunity to explore the impact of societal expectations and microaggressions on her self-esteem and body image. Emme acknowledged that these experiences and the lack of representation she missed at school, affected her self-perception.

Through therapy, Emme began to understand the broader implications of her actions and their impact on her health. She initially believed that Black girls didn't have eating disorders and saw her behaviors as common dieting practices. However, therapy helped her explore these misconceptions and recognize the significance of her emotional and physical well-being. As treatment progressed, Emme developed a more balanced relationship with food, adopting the "all foods fit" approach with the support of her dietitian and family. She also started reconnecting with extended family members, seeking a stronger sense of identity and community. Despite presenting a confident exterior, Emme revealed deep insecurities about her abilities and appearance, which impacted her relationships and self-worth. Emme's therapy journey unveiled the underlying insecurities masked by her confident façade, leading to significant personal growth and a better understanding of her emotional and physical needs. She began to challenge societal standards that contributed to her restrictive behaviors and worked on embracing her natural body shape.

RECOVERY

During all of the years we, the authors, have worked with persons who have EDs, we have discovered that recovery, like many other constructs (i.e., grief) is highly individual and personalized. It is defined differently by different people. The interaction of any number of variables and personal values (readiness to change, self-love, determination, fortitude, community, hope, etc.) is involved in the complex, multidimensional process. As such, a person's treatment and recovery journey are facilitated by more factors than just diagnosis, and the chronicity, severity, and remission of symptoms. Gordon (2013) underscores this belief, cautioning that a preoccupation with symptom reduction and elimination effectively negates the mental anguish and life impairment resulting from the mental illness. These consequences (i.e., lost relationships, work, security, time, and resources) can often be greater in impact and intensity than the symptoms. Because the distress experienced as a result of the illness does not resolve magically with symptom remission, there must be a continued focus on relearning how to engage with self and others, and on reestablishing relationships (Gordon, 2013).

Similar to what we have learned about the highly individualized nature of one's perspective of recovery, Kenny et al. (2022) have found that recognizing just one singular definition of recovery is too narrow to capture each person's very own unique experience. They argue against the widely accepted "full or partial" definition of ED recovery (Bardone-Cone et al., 2010) in which persons are considered recovered or not depending on whether they have met certain criteria, explaining that a definition, which in this case aligns with the medical model emphasizing symptom reduction as a primary indicator of recovery, is inadequate. Kenny et al. (2022) also question the generalizability of the Bardone-Cone et al. (2010) recovery model, citing their limited sample data. They instead espouse a recovery model grounded in the phenomenology of a person's unique, firsthand, personal experience of a mental illness. They also conceded that important information can be overlooked when measures of recovery are applied too narrowly and do not account for the views of underrepresented groups, which would include Black women. Given their acknowledgment of this potential problem, it is interesting that the 2022 study did not include more Black participants, and was called "Lived experience perspectives on a definition of eating disorder recovery in a sample of White women: A mixed method study." Perhaps they were unable to attract more Black participants, which in turn might have been because BED is infrequently diagnosed to start with.

Part of why narrative perspective is such an important consideration in the recovery of Black women is because of the course of the illness as they experience it. The course begins with their EDs being overlooked and undiagnosed or underdiagnosed in many cases, which contributes to their relatively low treatment participation. EDs in Black women are mediated by very unique factors such as racism and systemic oppression, which are not generally considered by ED clinicians. Also, this group often faces barriers to treatment because of social equity issues and disparities in health care coverage. For these and other reasons, we believe that clients are more invested in the work of recovery when they have access to culturally responsive treatment techniques (Blount et al., 2024) that allow them to feel seen and heard. The ultimate goal of which is to encourage clients' reimagining their relationships to food and body, facilitating their recovery.

RELAPSE

As reflected in some of the cases above, relapse can be considered the rule and not the exception. It's very simply a part of just about any type of recovery process. Prochaska and DiClemente's (1982) original Stages of Change component of their Transtheoretical Model of Behavior Change did not include a relapse step. However, nearly every subsequent discussion of change includes it as an "unofficial sixth step." And as such, there is much to be learned about relapse during the change process. For example, one can learn how to identify triggers, persons, and events that might lead down the path to relapse. Even if there is a slip, relapse does not need to signify failure. Still, there can be very serious consequences associated with relapse. For instance, the current trend of glucagon-like peptide-1 receptor agonists (GLP-1A) use could have the potential to be quite deadly in eating disorders populations. Semaglutide (brand name Ozempic) and other drugs in this class are being hailed as transformative and game changing in the fight against weight loss. These medications were developed originally to treat Type 2 diabetes and to reduce the associated risks of cardiovascular illnesses. Ozempic was approved by the Food and Drug Administration (FDA) for those purposes in 2017. Subsequently, a number of other medications in this category have recently become FDA approved for chronic weight management. They have become enormously popular world-wide for cosmetic weight loss. However, despite the intended long-term use of these medications in clinical populations, there is insufficient evidence to support the widespread, long-term use of these medications in eating disorder populations. While there are clear benefits associated with these medications for some populations, the same benefits may yield a paradoxical effect for others. For example, GLP-1 agonists have been shown to reduce brain chatter and obsessive thoughts about food by slowing down stomach-emptying, causing early satiety, and reducing one's appetite. Persons with EDs may return to previous compensatory behaviors. This cycle can carry with it the emotional impact associated with the disorders as well.

EATING DISORDERS IN PERSONS 65 YEARS AND BEYOND

Eating disorders do also occur in older Black women. However, as noted, given that no one is checking for them routinely, they often go unrecognized, undiagnosed, and untreated. As such, with few clinical studies that include Black women participants, reports on their prevalence is generally inaccurate. In general, these illnesses include the same features in older, Black women, as the usual suspects (bingeing, restricting, purging, etc.), except that they may be experienced differently. They may also occur at varying stages over the lifespan due to any number of factors, including the impact of the natural aging process on one's physical and mental functioning. When I consider further that these disorders can occur at any point during one's life, and when I think of the influence of Western world notions of beauty (which measure that beauty in inches from Whiteness, along with a preoccupation with perky breasts and firm thighs, etc.), I can't help but wonder what a stage theorist like Erikson might say these days about the development of body image issues in older women. Older Black women in particular. While he talked about identity vs. role confusion, he didn't address physical appearance directly. I wonder if he would have incorporated body image issues as a developmental task or conflict at some stage(s). The quality or virtue to be gained would be a healthy body image issue.

I believe it's human nature to want to improve. Overall improvement includes attempts toward extending the lifespan and improving health and quality of life, simultaneously. Evidence from one of the most well-controlled and best-known human studies on nutritional intervention (Flanagan et al., 2020; Broskey et al., 2019) suggests the aging process can be attenuated through calorie restriction (CR). CR is defined as the sustained restriction of energy (e.g., nutrients), intake below that which is necessary for optimal weight maintenance (Flanagan et al., 2020; Broskey et al., 2019). The Comprehensive Assessment of Long-Term Effects of Reducing Intake of Energy (CALERIE 1) study had three different conditions: CR, alone; CR plus exercise; and a very low-calorie diet to induce weight loss as fast as possible. The very low-calorie diet aimed at inducing weight loss as quickly as possible was found to be the most effective intervention for attenuating the aging process and improving health (Racette, et al., 2022; Flanagan et al., 2020; Broskey et al., 2019).

While progression of the aging process is certain and inescapable, it varies greatly among individuals, groups, cultures, countries, and other demographics, as it is impacted by innumerable factors. The factors are categized into two broad groups: primary factors and secondary factors. Primary factors are the age-related declines in physiological functioning and physical ability (Flanagan et al., 2020). These innate factors account for the human body's natural wear and tear. Secondary factors are those that can impact primary factors. The impacts can be noxious (substance abuse, poor diet, disease factors, etc.) and deleterious (Flanagan et al., 2020) with the potential to hasten life expectancy. The impacts can also be beneficial or benign. CR plus exercise were found to be most beneficial for maintaining optimum primary health.

Despite proponents' beliefs in the potential health benefits to be gained from CR, there are at least as many potential health risks for elders. One of the most important concerns that arise when elders reduce energy intake is an increased risk for reduction in skeletal muscle mass and strength, which could affect mobility and lead to falls. If it is believed that the benefits of CR outweigh any associated risks, then a multidisciplinary team (MDT) approach should be considered. An occupational and/or physical therapist can assist with muscle strengthening, flexibility, and balance. A dietician to monitor nutritional concerns would be quite helpful given that meal planning can be challenging in terms of making substitutions to be certain that clients are receiving essential nutrients. Planning a balanced diet can be challenging under more ordinary circumstances. A balanced, reduced caloric intake diet could become quite prohibitive, particularly for persons on a low income. Although many older Black persons fit this demographic, it seems noteworthy that no effect of CR on primary aging was reported by race in the CALERIE 1 study because that study included very few Black persons (Flanagan et al., 2020). In addition, although few instances of eating disorders were reported as a result of CR, Flanagan et al. (2020) note that dietary weight loss interventions have been known to alter eating behavior patterns—increasing food consumption even in the absence of hunger. A dietician could be helpful working with a psychologist to address binge-eating that might develop. Other MDT members that would be helpful could include a nurse practitioner or other professional to manage medications, and a gerontologist or general practitioner to aid in the integration of all of the components.

These CR interventions, when boosted with optimal nutrients (added protein, dietary supplements, etc.) are called the CRON diet, or CRONIES. Despite some of the potential challenges, proponents believe it is a superior method for extending longevity and improving overall health. Given some of the challenges, certain intermittent fasting schedules have been suggested as alternatives to CR. For me, these approaches yield just as many red flags, because in my experience these scenarios have often resulted in poor outcomes.

MOVING FORWARD

It is difficult to accurately estimate the number of Black women in the United States who are impacted by EDs. Possible reasons for this include provider characteristics that may impact assessment and recognition of the disorders in these women, such as a limited knowledge about factors that mediate EDs in Black women, a lack cultural competence, and a lack of awareness of one's own implicit racial biases. In addition, the dearth of clinical studies that include Black women might suggest that EDs are not issues they experience. Of the three major types of EDs—binge-eating disorder, bulimia nervosa, and anorexia nervosa—binge-eating disorder, which is characterized by an individual consuming a large amount of food rapidly, while experiencing a sense of feeling a loss of control is most common in Black women. Treatment of these disorders is quite challenging. The road to recovery looks different for each person. And while it's not unusual for clients to relapse at some point during the course of treatment, full recovery is possible.

Chapter 3

WHAT CONTRIBUTES TO AND MAINTAINS EATING DISORDERS?

Momma, Black guys do want big lips and big booties. . . . They just don't want them on us.

—Taylor Small, 14 years old

Many different researchers have reported myriad reasons for the causes and maintenance of eating disorders, which are usually associated with either an overvaluation of weight or weight management, or both. In general, contributing factors range from biological and psychosocial factors to the experiences of traumatic events. Small (2021a) outlined a number of specific factors and conditions that can mediate disordered eating patterns and the development of eating disorders in Black women, such as racism and related concerns. In addition to racism, the impact of a singular or co-occurring issue pertaining to skin color, length and texture of hair, and differences in body shape and size can be the impetus for developing such maladaptive behaviors, as well as maintaining the behaviors. I guess that knowing the harm and hurt that can result from such issues is the reason I felt such a profound sadness when I heard my then 14-year-old, dark-chocolate-skinned daughter speak those words to me. Those words that seem to suggest that guys who look like she does prefer girls who don't. At first, I wondered how this happened. When did this happen? But then, in an instant, I became aware that it had been happening her whole life. This message is brought to her daily through all forms of televised media

From television shows, commercial advertisements, and music videos, to the internet (i.e., Instagram), and printed media. And I began to think more about the media presentation of prominent, celebrated Black men, a great many of which seem to have chosen White or very light-skinned women as mates. Their selections seem to make clear their preference. Similarly, media images of wonderful, ordinary Black men are presented with White or light mates with growing frequency. Sadly, there is nothing new about this. Remember the Kenneth Clark experiments? Recall that the little Black children chose the White dolls over the Black ones, believing somehow, something was wrong with the Black dolls? Again, this is how early these daily messages of "There's something wrong with me" begin. These messages really do impact developing self concepts and identity, which I firmly believe is at the heart of eating disorders. And, this study has been replicated many times before. Sometimes longer than 65 years later, with similar results being obtained. It doesn't stop with little children. Stephens and Thomas (2012) found that Black women college students' attitudes toward and feelings about skin color was that "compared to lighter skin color, dark complexions were a liability in dating contexts." Taylor attended a certain Historically Black College/University (HBCU), in the U.S. south. There were some absolutely extraordinarily brilliant and gorgeous women on campus. Still, somehow, many of the young men found their way to White women. Wherever dark-skinned Black men are found, so too are light-skinned or White women. Again, none of this is new. Black men with leading ladies, for instance, have been presented as far back as Hollywood's golden age, when producer, director, and screenwriter Oscar Micheaux distributed nearly 50 films aimed at Negro audiences. Micheaux's regular leading ladies were typically very fair and starred opposite dark-complexioned men. These trends continue today.

INTERNALIZED RACISM AND OPPRESSION

Since the time I wrote about mediating factors and conditions associated with eating disorders in Black women, several studies have been conducted further substantiating these correlations. For example, results of an analyses by Oh et al. (2021) support those of previous studies (i.e., Monk, 2021) suggesting that internalized racism or colorism could account in part for the continued social stratification as well as some of the mental health care disparities that Black persons continue to experience.

Among other findings of the study were significant correlations between colorism and an increased risk of eating disorders, substance and alcohol use disorders, and anxiety (Oh et al., 2021). Similarly, Raney et al. (2023) reported finding significant relationships between racial or ethnic background or skin-color discrimination and an increased risk of binge-eating behaviors and binge-eating disorder (BED) when examining data from a large U.S. study of racially diverse early adolescents (e.g., the Adolescent Brain Cognitive Development Study [ABCD], National Institutes of Health, 2015). Specifically, of the 5% of participants who reported having experienced racial or ethnic discrimination (e.g., participants, perceptions of being unaccepted in society, or being unwanted in groups based on their race, ethnicity, or skin color) by teachers, other students, or by adults outside of their school during the previous year, 1.1% of them met the clinical criteria for BED. This is a rate similar to the lifetime prevalence rate (1.7%) of BED among Black adults in the U.S. (Jackson et al., 2004).

In addition, in some conditions discrimination was associated with BED at a rate of risk that was more than three times greater than the 1.1% of those children who met the criteria for BED and reported discrimination. And not surprisingly, adolescents who reported racial or ethnic discrimination committed by peers were at significantly greater risks of engaging in binge-eating episodes and for developing BED (Raney et al., 2023). While the researchers did not give specifics about the participants' skin tones, I would hazard a guess that if the peers committing the discrimination were same-race peers with lighter skin tones, the risks for disordered eating and the propensity to develop eating disorders would be even greater.

Nagata et al. (2021) analyzed the same ABCD data set and reported similar results. When examining the prevalence of perceived discrimination due to race or ethnicity, they found that Black children's experience of racism was highest of all groups of children, across conditions. Specifically, 10% of Black children who experienced discrimination ascribed the cause to race or ethnicity; 12% of Black children reported that most discrimination was done by peers; and 8.4% of discrimination as reported by Black children was perpetrated by teachers and adults outside of school. In addition, Black children reported higher rates (6.4%) of not feeling accepted in society compared with other groups of adolescents (e.g., Latinx, Native American, and White).

In a recent review of the literature, focusing on the neuroscience of discrimination and racism, and the impact of digital media on the mental health of Black and Brown children, Njoroge et al. (2021) found support for the theory that multiple forms of racism can have deleterious consequences on these children, negatively affecting their developmental trajectory. Some of the various forms of racism investigated by the researchers are conditions well-studied and proven to adversely impact the physical and mental development of Black adolescents, including everything from inadequate access to equitable health care, to poor quality—if not substandard—public schools, access to few (if any) green spaces, to the toxicity of their living environments, which far too often includes water that may not be potable.

Results of this study reminded me of findings of toxic water in several major U.S. cities over the past decade. Many of the cities have large populations of Black and Brown persons—cities like Newark, Philadelphia, and Houston. In 2016, National Public Radio (NPR) detailed the account of the toxic water situation where people were allowed to, encouraged even, to continue to use the water there for at least two years after residents first began raising concerns about the contaminated water. Residents were assured their water met all safety requirements. The Flint situation ultimately resulted in a number of legal charges against nearly a dozen state and former state employees, as well as two corporation consultants. Charges included felonious neglect of duty and conspiracy to tamper with evidence. Several employees of the Michigan Department of Health and Human Services were charged with failing to release a report that evidenced unsafe levels of lead in the blood of children from Flint (NPR, 2016).

Of this crisis, which was declared a state of emergency by then-President Obama, Michigan's attorney general stated, "Many things went tragically wrong in Flint. Some people failed to act, others minimized harm done and arrogantly chose to ignore data, some intentionally altered figures and covered up significant health risks." Misconduct and willful neglect of duty (NPR, 2016) as in this case are examples of the kinds of actions that disincline Black persons from trusting and seeking assistance from U.S. medical providers. Failure to seek medical help is one of the factors associated with the maintenance of EDs in Black women.

Distressed by what was happening in Flint and other U.S. cities with poor water quality, I remained thoughtful about persons experiencing the fallout from those circumstances. Being mindful not to take my own situation for granted, I continued to give thanks for what I believed was the relative safety of the water supply where I live. However, on a recent trip home to Washington, DC (another city with a large number of Black persons), I thought I was seeing things when my children and I each received a public safety alert on our phones concerning the water quality of the nation's capital. In Northwest Washington, DC, customers were advised to boil their water for at least one minute before drinking it or cooking with it. The alert also provided a projected time for the advisory to end, as well as links to view maps outlining the affected regions. While I don't recollect anything like this while growing up in DC, I have learned that these kinds of alerts have been provided several times in recent years.

As stated, it has been well-documented that one of the many ways that Black adolescents' mental health has been compromised by racism is by the emergence of disordered eating behaviors and eating disorders. And while disordered eating can show up in different ways in Black women, binge eating is the behavior most often seen in Black women to address emotions experienced as the result of colorism and racism (Small, 2021b; Thompson, 1994).

Thompson (1994) was one of the first theorists to encourage a paradigmatic shift from thinking about eating disorders solely as expressions of vanity in young, skinny, wealthy White women, toward thinking also about the occurrence and function of disordered eating—binge eating in particular—in Black and non-Black women of color in the United States. Binge eating was described as a way that Black women coped with a number of interpersonal and societal traumas, including oppression and racism.

Still, while some theorists and practitioners have taken notice, advancing our concerns in these matters has been slow for several reasons, including perhaps because of a lack of interest. U.S. Black women's issues and health concerns have never really been anyone's top priority, except perhaps in the cases of American physician J. Marion Sims during slavery from 1845–1849, or Henrietta Lacks—*and* her children. In addition to a healthy cultural paranoia and mistrust of the U.S. health care system, it is likely that another primary reason that Black women's eating disturbances and other health concerns remain unaddressed in large measure is because we're still not talking about them. For as long as they continue to be overlooked, neglected, and minimized, Black women will remain untreated, and they won't be well.

SYSTEMIC ISSUES AND SYSTEMS OF OPPRESSION

In a study investigating the amount of agreement among study participants concerning environmental factors that influence adult BED, Bray et al. (2022) identified a number of fluid themes with great potential to impact assessment, diagnosis, and treatment of BED, and also the direction of the discipline. They assert that BED is a social justice issue, fomented by systemic oppression and a number of other conditions that maintain the disorder and its impact upon persons who experience it. Among the most pertinent such conditions are predatory food industry practices and the way messaging occurs via social media.

In a recent study by Bray et al. (2022) systemic issues and systems of oppression were disaggregated into subthemes addressing individual and overlapping systems of oppression. Bray et al. (2022) found that there was 100% agreement among study participants that these systems either precipitate BED or are co-occurring factors that impact or otherwise hamper BED research, treatment efforts, or remission of symptoms. One of three overlapping groups of systemic oppression identifies large scale forms of racism such as overinflated health care costs, lack of insurance coverage, and provider scarcity, which act effectively as barriers to BED treatment for Black women. For instance, there continues to be a dearth of practitioners and physicians with specialized training in the treatment of eating disorders (Bray et al., 2022), as well as an absence of many culturally sensitive practitioners (Small, 2021a; Edwards-Gayfield, 2021; Woodson, 2021). As such, it follows that many practitioners have had no instruction in, and/or very little experience in treating Black women with eating disorders.

DISTRUST OF THE MEDICAL COMMUNITY

Medical mistrust among Black clients can impede their access to both mental and physical health care services. This mistrust is influenced by historical injustices and ongoing systemic inequities that disproportionately affect Black communities (Hoadley et al., 2022). Negative past health care experiences often contribute to heightened medical mistrust and reluctance to seek health care services (Hammond, 2010). Concerns about privacy, stigma, and discrimination are commonly reported in health care interactions with people of color.

I would hazard a guess that vast numbers of Black persons (*and* White persons) may not be familiar with the nineteenth-century gynecologist J. Marion Sims and the nefarious cruelties perpetrated on multiple and nameless (except for Anarcha Westcott, Lucy, and Betsey) Black enslaved women in the name of advancing medical science. In addition to the Sims position for gynecological exams and the Sims vaginal speculum (precursor to today's two-bladed Sims speculum [Wall, 2021]), Sims developed a procedure for repairing vesicovaginal fistulas, which was accomplished through repeated experimental surgeries on this "vulnerable population" (Wall, 2006) of women between 1845 and 1849, without the use of anesthesia. Though health care providers had experimented with various forms of anesthesia since 1842, the first successful surgical use of it in the U.S. was in 1846 (Abhyankar & Jessop, 2022). However, it was believed that Black women did not experience pain as acutely as White women did (Women and the American Story [WAMS], 2020). Sims performed Anarcha's thirtieth procedure without anesthesia in the summer of 1849 (WAMS, 2020).

These beliefs still are widely held among many persons in the medical community (Trawalter, 2012). Hoffman et al. (2016) found that medical students and residents who held erroneous beliefs about racial differences (i.e., Blacks have fewer nerve endings than Whites), rated Black persons' pain lower, which affected their treatment recommendations. The study also found that even when study participants rated Black persons' pain as higher, they neglected to recommend a more aggressive treatment regimen (Hoffman et al., 2016). Responding in this way may contribute toward continued racial disparities in the assessment and treatment of pain (Hoffman et al., 2016).

The story of Henrietta Lacks is another case of an unethical and unlawful chain of events that contributes to many Black persons' unfavorable perspective of the U.S. health care system. In 1951 Lacks was treated at Johns Hopkins Hospital for a very aggressive form of cervical cancer. While there, a tissue sample of her cervical cancer cells was harvested without her consent. Scientists would soon discover that Lacks's cancer cells were unlike any others previously studied. Lacks's cells had the immortal ability to double every 20–24 hours, becoming the first-ever cells to be successfully cloned in a lab (Johns Hopkins University, 2024), forming the bedrock of modern medicine (NBC News, 2023b) and biomedical research. Hers is the first human living cell line (NIH, 2022) and has played a role in every major medical advancement of the twentieth century, including the development of vaccines for polio and

COVID-19 (Johns Hopkins University, 2024; NBC News, 2023b; & NIH, 2022). For decades, behemoth biotechnology corporations made unfathomable profits from Lacks's cell line, which was extracted without her consent (NBC News, 2023b). In August 2023, her family settled a lawsuit against one company for an undisclosed amount. Also around that time, Henrietta Lacks was posthumously awarded the Congressional Medal of Honor for her contribution to the world (NBC News, 2023b).

The conversation on medical mistrust has shifted focus recently, emphasizing the importance of transforming health care systems to be more trustworthy rather than solely addressing individual-level mistrust (Hoadley et al., 2022). Establishing trust between health care providers and Black clients helps to nurture secure therapeutic alliances, which hopefully will encourage Black women to keep returning, thus prioritizing their healthcare.

PREDATORY FOOD AND TOBACCO INDUSTRY PRACTICES

In the U.S., overweight children grow up to be overweight adults in over 70% of cases (Byrd et al., 2018). It should come as no surprise that similar to many other chronic, acute, and deadly health conditions, Black children are disproportionately affected by overweight and obesity (Byrd et al., 2018; Skinner et al., 2018). While almost one third of America's children are overweight or obese (Harvard, n.d.), the numbers in Black and Brown communities appear worse, with nearly 40% of those children being overweight or obese (U.S. DHHS, 2021).

Obesity and being overweight in childhood is associated with a number of serious health conditions, as nearly every organ can be impacted by these conditions (Harvard, n.d). Some of the more immediate concerns for children include breathing difficulties, increased risk of fractures, hypertension, early markers of cardiovascular disease and insulin resistance, as well as mental health and emotional problems (WHO, 2020) such as BED. Risks for serious illnesses over time including diabetes, cardiovascular diseases (e.g., heart disease and stroke), and musculoskeletal disorders, osteoarthritis in particular, and certain types of cancer (endometrial, breast, and colon) increase with age, and are impacted in part by age of onset and duration of childhood overweight and obesity (WHO, 2020). The WHO (2020) states these diseases are associated with an increased risk for premature death and multiple disabilities in adulthood. Many factors contribute to a near epidemic of overweight and obese children, including questionable food marketing strategies presented through every viable medium.

Numerous studies have been done detailing the food industry's marketing practices. Consumer purchasing is largely influenced by advertising strategies such as product branding, celebrity endorsements, and persuasiveness (Ahmed & Ashfaq, 2013), as well as more tangible product variables such as packaging aesthetics and product availability (Mialon et al., 2021). Employing strategies in ways that influence and encourage consumer purchases is also associated with binge eating (Just & Payne, 2009).

In addition, Brownell and Warner (2009) outlined a number of ethically questionable marketing tactics used by food industries, such as blaming the consumer for adverse health outcomes from product use and minimizing or denying the destructive and addictive qualities of the product being marketed, which they noted were similar in practice to those used by the tobacco industry. A particularly deceptive and insidious practice used by tobacco and food industry strategists is that of marketing expressly to adolescents, which often results in loyal, long-term customers (Brownell & Warner, 2009), yielding enormous benefits for the industries and, far too often, seriously adverse health consequences for the consumer—which seems not to be a great concern for some of these industries. One case in point is an infamous statement made by an executive at a certain big tobacco company, in which small children were referred to as "replacement smokers" (American Lung Association, 2023) to supersede those persons who would no longer use their products, having perished (ostensibly from prolonged use of their products).

For more than 60 years, the tobacco industry has practiced salesmanship that can at best be described as unscrupulous. Free cigarettes were doled out lavishly to small children, Black children in particular, living in low-income housing (Tobacco Control Legal Consortium, 2016). Food stamps secured by these families often came with the added bonus of coupons for discounted tobacco products (Brown-Johnson et al., 2014). But the point must be clearly made that it wasn't only Black children and families from low-income urban communities whose senses were designed to be excited by the lure of these goodies: it was Black *women* with limited finances who were targeted especially (Brown-Johnson et al., 2014). Their business was so highly coveted, so essential to their strategic success, that frequently for their patronage these women received automobile gasoline and other product rewards debit cards in hopes of maintaining their business.

What was at stake for the replacement smokers—most of whom were poor, urban dwellers that included vulnerable groups such as Black adolescents and younger children—was their health and well-being. Arguably, what is most morally reprehensible about all of this is that these marketing strategies were created by design, seemingly without any regard for the health and well-being of these young persons, for the express purpose of increasing tobacco industry profits.

Unfortunately, somehow tobacco companies continue marketing their products in the same manner, targeting the most vulnerable populations (CDC, 2021), with dispensaries disproportionately (American Cancer Society, 2023) and strategically placed in lower socioeconomic communities near schools and other places where children are easily accessible (Truth Initiative, 2018). Perhaps the most appalling aspect of all is that these companies are able to reap greater profits employing the same techniques to sell various e-cigarette products (i.e., marketing different flavors that are highly appealing to children) (CDC, 2021). E-cigarettes potentially have even more devastating health impacts because these products have been shown to contain a number of dangerous chemicals, including nicotine and formaldehyde (American Lung Association, 2023) and have greater addictive qualities than traditional fire-burning cigarettes (Addiction Center, 2023).

The level of deception of some of these industry marketing practices (Bray et al., 2022) seems even more insidious and convoluted when one considers the close, intertwining relationships of some tobacco industry giants partnering with some of the biggest food brands in the world. These mergers have the potential to influence children in a number of ways, largely because many of these companies acquired food and beverage products that they now market to children using the same techniques used to market cigarettes. For instance, Hawaiian Punch had primarily been marketed to adults as a cocktail mixer, but when R. J. Reynolds bought the brand, they started to market the beverage as a drink for children, using the drink's "Punchy" mascot in the same way that the Joe Cool character was used to market cigarettes. When Philip Morris bought the Kool-Aid brand, they created their own "Kool-Aid Man" and offered toys and other merchandise branded with the character, going on to create special child-tested flavors to market to children (Nguyen et al., 2019; Washington Post, 2023; see also Glantz, 2019).

As noted, attractive packaging is a highly successful marketing maneuver when targeting any audience. However, children are a particularly vulnerable market, as conservative estimates suggest that advertisers spend more than $12 billion per year to reach them (APA, 2024). The Obesity Evidence Hub (2022) has found that children's developmental immaturities make them particularly susceptible to certain marketing strategies. For example, children ages 4 to 6 years old believe food products taste much more scrumptious when cartoon characters are featured on the packaging, compared with the same food in packages without cartoon characters (Roberto et al., 2010). Similarly, Robinson et al. (2007) found that even younger children (3 to 5) who tasted twin food and drink samples reported that the samples dressed in the packaging of a very well-known, very well-branded, kid-friendly fast-food restaurant tasted better.

Correlations have been found between exposure to ads for high-calorie, low/non-nutritive, high fat content foods and an increase in childhood obesity (Boyland et al., 2016). Successful marketing campaigns have included use of collectible toys and sports sponsorship, delivered via a variety of mediums (i.e., television, internet advergames, viral marketing) reaching millions of loyal patrons and millions more potential consumers at once. In this way, societal norms confirming and authenticating the appropriateness and desirability of food become established (WHO, 2022), and consumers govern themselves accordingly.

BIOLOGICAL AND PSYCHOSOCIAL FACTORS

Regarding bio/psychosocial factors, controlling behavior, perfectionism (Egan et al., 2023), and low self-esteem or self-criticism have been recognized as types of temperament frequently associated with eating disorders (EDs). These latter two, in particular often work in tandem in the case of EDs. A large number of studies provide evidence showing perfectionism to be a *transdiagnostic process*. Transdiagnostic processes involve systems of behavior or mechanisms that may be present across several different disorders. Such mechanisms can increase the risk of one developing an ED, or serve to maintain an ED (Stackpole et al., 2023).

Smith et al. (2017) explain this dynamic in terms of the interplay between perfectionistic striving, that is, setting very high personal goals and standards, and perfectionistic concerns, which involve fear of negative evaluation (from self or others) and of making mistakes (slight or monumental). Because fear of failure often manifests as fear of gaining weight, or of bingeing (Fairburn et al., 2003), when the high standards of perfectionistic strivings are not met, the result is poor self-valuation and self-deprecation. Shafran et al. (2002) goes further in their definition of clinical perfectionism, describing it as a dysfunctional self-assessment system in which personal value and worth are judged by the successful accomplishment of stringent goals (i.e., restricting and weight loss) (Fairburn et al., 2003), but without regard for any adverse events that might follow.

Two remaining mechanisms shown to mediate or maintain EDs as well as hamper or impede recovery efforts are mood intolerance and interpersonal difficulties (Fairburn et al., 2003). Fairburn et al. (2003) define mood intolerance as an inability to identify, express, or cope well with emotions.

POLITICS, INJUSTICE, AND VIOLENCE

In addition to issues of colorism, social and political events have also been shown to influence patterns of disordered eating and development of EDs (Small, 2021a). A number of studies documenting the neuroscience of discrimination and racism have detailed their impact on the mental health of Black children (Njoroge et al., 2021) and women. Environmental stressors such as acculturative stress and real-life gratuitous violence and injustice firmly rooted in racism have long been associated with EDs, as Black women sought ways to cope with the daily subtleties of the indignities of microaggressions.

Many significant and traumatizing events have occurred within recent years, garnering attention worldwide, such as some very bold murders (i.e., Dante Wright, George Floyd, Breonna Taylor, Tony McDade, Manuel Ellis, Andre Hill, Rayshard Brooks), which have been described as modern-day lynchings at the hands of persons sworn to protect and serve the public. Experiencing and/or viewing these real-life events even one time, and certainly with frequency, can be traumatizing and makes people feel unsafe. These events together with the recent repeals of important legislation, specifically landmark decisions such as Affirmative Action (NBC News, 2023a) and *Roe v. Wade* (ABC News, 2022), have left people frightened for the safety of themselves and their loved ones. These feelings have been shown to be mediating factors in the development of EDs.

A disturbing and related phenomenon resurging within the past few years, most unfortunately, is the reincarnation of "Karen." Karen is a euphemism for that meddlesome, self-proclaimed neighborhood, community, or building monitor whom you would like to slap two or three times. She's that person with at least two powerful unearned advantages, who begs the question, "Who died and left you queen?" If only she would use her power for good.

Although we, the authors, have introduced her in a humorous light, Karen is anything but funny. A symbol of institutional racism (NPR, 2021), she's quite dangerous. Karen's self-entitlement has allowed her for centuries (under various pseudonyms, i.e., "Miss Anne," during Antebellum times, or "Becky" throughout the 1990s; NPR, 2021) to wield or attempt to wield her power over more vulnerable persons, or groups of people. Her favorite targets have been Black persons.

A favorite pastime of hers (or who knows, perhaps she believes she is doing someone a favor) is to make frivolous 911 calls on Black persons who are minding their very own business, completely within the confines of the law. For example, recently Karen's self-entitlement has led her to call 911 "to voice suspicions about an 8-year-old Black girl selling bottles of water on the sidewalk in San Francisco, a 9-year-old Black boy in a deli in Brooklyn whose backpack bumped against a White woman ('I was just sexually assaulted,' she told the police), and a Black man entering his own apartment building in St. Louis, all in 2018; a Black uniformed UPS worker delivering packages in Atlanta in 2019; and, in 2020, a Black man bird-watching in Central Park and Black children swimming in a pool at the hotel where their family was staying in Williamston, N.C." (*New York Times*, 2021).

Slowly, some cities are enacting legislation to address these travesties. One of the first to sign such a bill beginning in 2020 was San Francisco. Caution Against Racial and Exploitative Non-Emergencies Act, also known as the CAREN legislation, makes placing racist 911 calls a hate crime.

Karen's behavior and probable intentions have the potential to be deadly, as they could have been in a recent incident concerning my then 18-year-old son. While knocking on a friend's door in an apartment building one day, he was approached by Karen. She wanted to know who he was and why he was there. He had been there countless times before. I had even been there once with him. Under no obligation to respond to her, he chose not to. Karen was holding a door jammer security bar. She tapped him on the shoulder with it and repeated her request. His friend was not in the apartment and my son walked toward the other end of the hallway and began texting his friend to say he had arrived. He still had not responded to Karen. Apparently, she didn't like that so much, because at that point she stepped inside of her apartment and called the police. Within about three minutes, my son turned around to see six policeman—including a camera crew—all with their hands on their weapons. My son is taller than 6 feet, and he is a body builder and athlete. Having been raised by his mother, who was raised by her career police officer father, my son kept his hands in plain sight and knew better than to make any sudden moves. Brilliantly though—and very sad too, because of the necessity to do so—my son took a seat on the floor when allowed. He is a large individual who wanted to look as nonthreatening as possible. He was interrogated for a few moments before being allowed to leave. In a short video my son was able to take during the incident, Karen can be heard in the background pleading her case, explaining why she tapped him with her security bar. Of the incident, my son said, "Momma, I could have been on a T-shirt."

TRAUMA

We Black women have so much extra "stuff" impinging upon us daily. In addition to coping with the same general stressors as many other groups—such as food deserts, single-motherhood, and many co-occurring factors including substance misuse, OCD, cutting, and different types of trauma (accidents, loss of loved ones, natural disasters, etc.)—we also bear the burden of the impact of disproportionate levels of adverse childhood experiences (ACEs) such as physical or emotional abuse, parental divorce, a family member's illness or incarceration, etc., much more than most other groups (Whiteside-Mansell et al., 2019; Sacks & Murphey, 2018).

Whether acute, chronic, or complex, the experience of traumatic events can manifest in any number of insidious or nondeceptive, long-lasting mental health and/or physiological problems, EDs among them. Because EDs have long been associated with a history of trauma exposure (Briere & Scott, 2007), culturally sensitive practitioners should be cautious to assess for any experience of trauma, being alert to certain ACEs in particular. This is because in addition to being faced with a rate of ACEs that exceeds that of most other groups, Black persons often experience particular types of ACEs more often than most other groups—childhood sexual abuse being among the most common. Black children have nearly twice the risk of sexual trauma as White children (Sedlak et al., 2010). Without a sophisticated repertoire of strategies for managing the jumbled assortment of hurt feelings, frustration, confusion, and guilt, children will often binge in an effort to feel good, or to escape the pain.

CONTRIBUTING AND MAINTAINING FACTORS IN BLACK WOMEN 65 YEARS AND BEYOND

A multiplicity of conditions and factors can work together or singularly to encourage development of ED symptoms and to sustain the potentially deadly condition in Black women aged 65 years and older. A sense of uselessness and being seen as undesirable, for instance, can stir such feelings in any group of women, particularly with the onset of menopause, as this developmental phase is commonly accompanied by physical, emotional, or psychological changes that are the tell-tale signs that women are entering into a new phase of life. Normative physical changes, due in large measure to hormones, may occur in the months or years preceding menopause (perimenopause). These changes include a slowed metabolism and weight gain, loss of breast fullness, graying and/or thinning hair on all parts of the body, changes in skin (dry, oily, sagging, discolored, wrinkled, etc.), brittle nails, and vaginal dryness. Other health issues and concerns common to the aging process (i.e., arthritic conditions) may lead to mobility problems.

These conditions together or separately have the ability to make some women, however mentally sharp and vibrant, feel unattractive, if not hideous. As such, body image concerns are not the exclusive domain of younger adults and adolescents. The impact of these kinds of physical changes very often plays a role in the development of eating disorders in women in their 60s and beyond. For example, Khalil et al. (2022) found that menopausal stages were associated with binge eating and restricting among a sample of middle-aged Lebanese women. In particular, they found that binge-eating was significantly higher than restricting behaviors in perimenopausal women.

Additional physiological changes during menopause, including vasomotor symptoms such as hot flashes, night sweats, and chills, can cause sleep disturbances, anxiety, depression, and mood changes, all of which can impact quality of life and increase women's vulnerability to psychological distress, which contributes to, or exacerbates feelings of loss of control. These kinds of feelings can increase the risk of eating disorders in women in this age group.

Khalil et al. (2022) reported further that a review of the literature shows perimenopausal women experienced not only a higher prevalence of disordered eating behavior, but also significantly higher self-rating scores of "feeling fat" than premenopausal women. They further discussed the complex physical, hormonal, psychological, and social changes commonly experienced by many women during the transition from perimenopause to menopause. Similar depictions become even more intense, however, when you consider the lived experiences of many Black women, which includes a lifetime of structural racism.

Harlow et al. (2022) presented an analysis of the differences in the experience of menopause and associated health outcomes between cohorts of Black and White women in a 25-year study (Study of Women's Health Across the Nation; SWAN). They believed that to obtain the truest, most accurate measure of the differences in experience between these groups of women, they needed to have some modicum of understanding of the social context for their experiences. In addition to an examination of the differences in the experience of menopause between these groups, the researchers were interested in the impact of racism with its concomitant social disadvantages, discrimination, etc., on Black women's reproductive aging and midlife health.

Researchers emphasized that the Black participants lived the entirety of their lives in a United States society firmly embedded in the institutional, systemic racism that defined the Jim Crow era. And while the researchers of the SWAN study were cautious to present the essence of the Jim Crow era with authenticity, what they did not underscore is that the cornerstone ideas of that era have made a resurgence. In fact, considering the latest string of murders at the hands of law enforcement officials, recent backward changes in legislation, as stated above (e.g., repeal of affirmative action, *Roe v. Wade*), and thus perhaps experiencing a sense of déjà vu, one could argue that Jim Crow never really ended. It seems that the more things change, the more they stay the same. As such, it might prove interesting to compare results of the SWAN study with those of a replication study examining the impact of racism on the experience of menopause and indices of midlife health of Black women Boomers (1946–1964), or Gen Xer's (1965–1980) born at the beginning of that range.

MOVING FORWARD

The myths that eating disorders only affect thin, young, White women, and are only about body image, are not only dismissive and dangerous, they are deadly. From young to old, Black women are sicker than their peers, and eating disorders play a role in surprising ways—surprising, perhaps, to those outside of the lived Black experience. But within it, the pileup of trauma, environmental racism, injustice, overt and covert racism, inequity, deceptive marketing practices, food deserts, mistrust of the health care system, poor living conditions, stress, and more is an obvious mountain of factors that contribute to and maintain EDs. Therefore, we in the healing professions must be vigilant about inquiring about our clients' histories, experiences, and environments. We must consider that continually reaching for food after a storied history of presumed guilt until proven innocent is not merely a case of stress eating.

Chapter 4

BLACK WOMEN EMBRACE THEIR BODIES, RIGHT?

Body image is typically defined as the way you see yourself in your mind's eye, the way you believe others see you, and what you believe about how others see you. However, for Black women, body image is not just about size, shape, and weight. Body image incorporates overall appearance such as hair, shapes and sizes of physical features, and skin color. Providers who maintain a narrow view of body image may affirm feelings of invisibility and inferiority.

It is important for clinicians to think about why body image is important and why it is important to Black women. What messages are being communicated by family, members of one's own community, and society? Are the messages based on White supremacy? These very significant questions have gone unanswered largely because they aren't being asked nearly as much as they should be.

We frequently hear Black clients' report that what they think and feel does not matter to their providers. They often attribute this sensibility to provider bias and the assumptions that are frequently made about Black people. However, when providers engage with clients, asking questions and listening attentively, it makes a difference.

Keith et al. (2010) acknowledged that issues of racial identity, skin color, and attractiveness are profoundly important for women of color, shaping their lived experiences and societal perceptions in significant ways. The intersectionality of race and gender can exacerbate challenges related to beauty standards, discrimination, and cultural representation. Providers who are willing to address these issues help to foster a therapeutic relationship that demonstrates understanding, inclusivity, and equity.

While physical appearance holds significance for women overall, women of color often emphasize *facial features* (such as lips and eye color), skin tone, and hair texture to a greater extent. Similar to the absence of cultural considerations in many existing eating disorder assessments, features significant to Black women are rarely included in body image assessments. Providers should recognize that body image attitudes may be influenced by conflicting societal expectations for Black women, racial/ethnic identity, health considerations, and economic constraints (Talleyrand et al., 2017), as these issues can and should be addressed in treatment.

Body image extends to the treatment of Black bodies, emphasizing the importance of acknowledging historical context. Throughout history, there has been a prevailing belief that Black women's bodies are seen as excessive or too much. The images of fat Black women became synonymous with "greed, laziness, and savagery" (Strings, 2019). These women were viewed as ugly and undesirable (Jackson-Lowman, 2014), moral failures, and stupid (Ciciurkaite & Perry, 2018).

During an interview, Roxane Gay said,

> *Our cultural perception is weird, why do we believe that if you're fat you're dumb, you're lazy, or a loser? Why (and when) did these become the preconditions for fatness? You're a failure, because only a lazy person, only a dumb person, would allow themselves to get into this situation. It's appalling that this is the mindset. People generally treat fat people like they don't know anything about anything. It's incredibly demeaning. And incredibly frustrating. (Machado, 2017, para. 24)*

White women and Black women were pitted against each other as fatness became stigmatized; White women sought to differentiate themselves from the image of "big, Black women" by embracing characteristics such as "slender" and "petite" as their ideal (Strings, 2019). The thin ideal gained considerable popularity during the 1960s, as society increasingly valued slimness as the epitome of beauty for women. Following this period, Black women and White women started to perceive themselves as fat at different thresholds of body weight (McMillan, 2021). Specifically, White women saw themselves as fat at much lower weights and smaller body sizes than Black women (Fernandes et al., 2010). Author Anissa Gray (2019) provides an illustration of this point in her book, *The Care and Feeding of Ravenously Hungry Girls*, when she shared that "compared to White girls I'd grown up with, body image standards for Black girls were different. A 'thicker figure' was not only acceptable, it was also normal."

Body image impacts Black women in significant ways. The societal ideal of a specific body type has established a hierarchy, leading to questions about the value of the Black female body (Taylor, 2018). I frequently hear from non-Black persons the echoes of the misconceptions that Black women are "lucky" because they are okay with being in a larger body and thus do not experience body dissatisfaction or eating disorders. Are these statements true? Are Black women protected from the influence of the thin-ideal? Is this belief finally fading, uncovering the harsh reality that Black women and girls experience hurt and anguish over these issues too?

Black girls and women may grapple with body image and not have eating issues, and the converse can also be true. We have had several clients believe they see their reflection accurately and just do not like what they see, and we have had some that report body image distortions. Black girls and women who desire to improve their physical appearance or obtain a desired look may resort to behaviors like dieting, exercise, or using diet pills. For some, these behaviors can contribute to the development of an eating disorder. We encourage you to engage in discussions about these factors with your Black clients, even if there are no signs of an eating disorder.

Research has supported the belief that Black women experience greater body satisfaction and engage in less restrictive eating practices when compared with White women (Talleyrand et al., 2017; Chao et al., 2008). Black women tend to engage in fewer restrictive behaviors, indicating potential differences in how various racial and ethnic groups approach certain behaviors (Talleyrand et al., 2017). Black adolescent girls exhibit a higher prevalence of binge eating and unhealthy weight control behaviors compared to non-Latina White and Asian American girls (Simone et al., 2022). Unhealthy weight control behaviors, such as laxative use, diet pill consumption, or excessive exercise are not synonymous with restriction and can occur independently of binge-eating episodes. Black individuals present with all forms of eating disorders (Cassidy et al., 2015).

Also, it's been said that a sense of pride and connection with one's ethnic community may serve as protective factors against body dissatisfaction and eating disorders for women of color (Pearce-Dunbar & James Bateman, 2021; Capodilupo & Kim, 2014; Shaw et al., 2004). However, more research, including clinical trials involving Black women, is needed before these statements can be made with absolute certainty.

BODY DYSMORPHIA

In addition to the factors discussed, body dysmorphia and lack of embodiment are highly correlated with eating disorders. There are several terms used to express the body image concerns that individuals experience—body image distortions, body dissatisfaction, and body dysmorphia, to name a few. Individuals with body image distortion are disconnected from their bodies and live in a world of images to protect themselves from feeling their emotions or experiences. Opara and Santos (2019) add that "body dissatisfaction refers to negative subjective evaluations of one's physical body, such as figure, weight, stomach, and hips." Higher rates of body dissatisfaction may be a correlation for eating disorder development as these individuals may engage in disordered behaviors and other extreme means to alter one's body.

It's important to remember that body image for Black women includes physical features, skin tone, and hair. Therefore, body dissatisfaction, body distortions, and body dysmorphia should be extended to include these components. Body dissatisfaction should not be confused with body distortion, which occurs when the individual perceives their body as significantly larger than it is (Moradi, 2010).

Body dysmorphia is increasingly discussed in our society but refers to a clinical diagnosis: body dysmorphic disorder (BDD). The *Diagnostic and Statistical Manual of Mental Disorders* (*DSM-5-TR*) (APA, 2022) characterizes BDD by a preoccupation with perceived bodily defects and flaws. It can be any aspect of the body, not only size, shape, or weight. It's important to recognize that not everyone who notices flaws in the mirror has body image concerns or body dysmorphic disorder. Understanding a Black client's experiences can indeed be a complex process. It requires careful listening, empathy, and effective communication, asking open-ended questions, and providing a safe space for them to share their thoughts and feelings. We concede that as providers you are aware of what's needed, but our Black clients' experience of health care is fraught with distrust.

For Black clients, the distorted view or beliefs about their body may result from a myriad of sources. Understanding the stressors Black women face requires seeing things from their perspective.

> *Imagine being a passenger in a car driven by a Black woman. While each passenger sees the journey from a different angle, only the driver has the full view and experience. As passengers, our position in the car limits our perception, we cannot fully comprehend her experience, as we are not in her seat. (Lashley et al., 2017, pp. 215–216)*

Acculturative stress has been found to affect body dissatisfaction and bulimic symptoms in ethnic minority women, including Black women (Gordon et al., 2010; Perez et al., 2002). If a Black client adopts the beliefs, attitudes, and behaviors of the dominant culture, they may have a higher degree of acculturation, leading to increased stress, shame, mental health issues, feelings of marginalization, and greater body dissatisfaction and eating disorder symptoms.

A former client recounted that during her early childhood, she didn't have concerns about her body or appearance and could not recall significant comments related to her size, shape, or weight. However, upon entering elementary school, she noticed differences, feeling the pressure to conform as she interacted with peers who didn't resemble her. This intensified over time, particularly as she progressed academically, leading her to believe she needed to conform to fit in.

Black women have contended with feelings of shame stemming from the belief that they are perceived negatively by others as "defective, inferior, inadequate and unattractive because of shaming personal characteristics (e.g., physical appearance or behaviors)" (Duarte et al., 2017, p. 200). Dr. Small (2021b) reminds us that ". . . acculturative stress events are correlated with an increase in bulimic symptoms in Black women" (p. 6), and if providers are not aware of these stressors, they will overlook these contributing factors.

LACK OF EMBODIMENT

Lack of embodiment refers to a disconnect between a person's mind and body, often resulting in a lack of awareness or connection to bodily sensations and emotions. This can lead to disordered eating behaviors as individuals may not be attuned to their body's hunger and fullness cues or may use food to numb or suppress emotions. The Theory of Embodiment (Piran, 2016, 2017) suggests that physical, social, and mental experiences that promote positive embodied experiences may cultivate a positive body image, and in turn protect girls and women from disordered eating behaviors. Experiences of embodiment involve fostering awareness of bodily sensations, feeling connected to one's body, a sense of competence, and feelings of inclusion (Piran, 2016, 2017).

Disruptions in embodiment raise the risk of disordered eating and decrease body image acceptance among girls and women. Access to embodiment-promoting experiences varies based on social position. For example, ethnically and racially minoritized individuals face racial discrimination and negative stereotypes, known as *minority stressors*, which undermine personal agency and disrupt embodiment (Vitus, 2015). Piran's Developmental Theory of Embodiment (2016, 2017) supports these notions and suggests that the risk of disordered eating behaviors may increase due to disempowerment, threats to agency, and when positioned in social contexts that lack a sense of belongingness. Marginalization and discrimination are strongly associated with body image concerns and disordered eating behaviors among Black girls and women.

PRESENTATION IN BLACK WOMEN

Ethnicity is a complex, multifaceted variable that is comprised of ethnic identification and acculturation, each considered quasiorthogonal from each other.

> *Quasiorthogonal implies that ethnic identification and acculturation are relatively independent. A person's level of ethnic identification does not predict their level of acculturation, and vice versa. Ethnicity should be understood as comprising two distinct, yet related, components: ethnic identification and acculturation. These components can vary independently, meaning strong ethnic identification does not imply low acculturation, and high acculturation does not imply weak ethnic identification. (Carter & Sbrocco, 2018, p. 183)*

Providers are encouraged to consider the following questions:

- To what extent does your Black client identify with their ethnic group?
- To what extent has your Black client adapted to another culture?

Ethnic identity can shape how symptoms are expressed, the interpretations of their significance, and the choices for treatment approaches. For example, individuals strongly identifying with their ethnicity may attribute symptoms to coexisting medical conditions. This could lead them to perceive symptoms through a physiological perspective, thinking, "High blood pressure runs in my family, so it was bound to happen." Such beliefs may affect how symptoms are communicated and managed, potentially leading to a preference for medical rather than psychological interventions (Carter & Sbrocco, 2018). Acculturation serves as a variable that can either mitigate or amplify the impact of ethnic identity.

Concerns such as body dissatisfaction, body dysmorphia, and appearance preoccupation manifest in various recognizable ways. However, it is critical to understand that body image concerns show up differently in Black women than in White women. Without this awareness, clinicians may miss important signs. Therefore, it's essential to consider a range of nuanced issues that are common in the Black community, including:

- ethnic identity
- a strong desire to "look good"
- size, shape, and weight
- skin and hair
- feeling compelled to compare to other women
- grappling with Black features that are not appreciated on their bodies
- a "go get it done" attitude

Ethnic Identity

In the African American community, there's a pervasive belief that Black people, particularly Black women, are often judged based on stereotypes portrayed in media. This notion is not new; scholars have demonstrated that encountering African Americans, especially Black women, often evokes negative associations shaped by media portrayals (Burton, 2017), a pattern observed across all persons throughout the United States. People of color with strong attachments to their ethnic origin, who feel pride and a sense of connection, are less vulnerable than Black girls and women who may be more assimilated into mainstream society (The Association of Black Psychologists, 2013).

Individuals with an *ethnic identity* are likely to have internalized different cultural messages, values, beliefs, and traditions that are contrary to the European thinness ideal for women. Ethnic identity refers to self-identification with a specific ethnic group; the sense of belonging and attachment to such a group; the perceptions, behaviors, and feelings one has, due to such membership; and involvement in the cultural and social practices of the group (Opara & Santos, 2019). Stronger ethnic identity may be a protective factor to promote healthy and positive behaviors, but Black girls and women are not immune to wanting to fit in or be accepted.

Black women often face challenges when interacting with individuals whose perceptions of their cultural identity are shaped by popular media, potentially leading to challenging or dangerous real-life encounters (Burton, 2017). This desire may be a result of acculturation pressure and an attempt to counteract negative stereotypes. For Black women, adhering to this phenomenon is tied to self-issues that damage their overall self-image, leading to feelings of invisibility, inadequacy, and poor health (Lashley et al., 2017). Many Black women have turned to unhealthy coping mechanisms in response to negative assaults on their self-esteem.

Desire to "Look Good"

Overall appearance is important to Black women! It's essential to look "presentable," a message that has often been reinforced since childhood. *Looking good* is often about more than just appearance; it's about feeling put together and confident. Edwards-Gayfield (2021) recalls several Black individuals, at various stages of life, who had certain essentials they wouldn't leave the house without—whether it was heels, earrings, or eyeliner. These adornments weren't just about looking their best; they played a pivotal role in fostering confidence and a sense of completeness, contributing to their self-assurance and presentation. Asking individuals to change or forgo these items can pose challenges, as they often view them as extensions of themselves and integral to their identity or self-presentation.

Black girls may worry about the clothes they wear, the quality and color of their skin, what their hair looks like, and what their actions might suggest. Black girls grow into Black women who face similar struggles. Images of perceived flaws perpetuate feelings of inadequacy and insecurity about racial characteristics and lead to the acculturated belief that something must be done to be beautiful, acceptable. Providers should be aware of beauty practices when assessing body image among Black girls and women. These practices may be used to correct perceived flaws or improve appearance, but the underlying motivations may often be concealed.

An important takeaway is that the desire to look good does not always align with the European thin ideal; therefore, a provider biased toward a White ideal when assessing (or not) for disordered eating or body image concerns may miss or misunderstand important cues. Body image, like the experiences of Black women, is not a monolith and can present conflicting beliefs and ironies. We encourage you to view your client as the expert in their own experience while remaining mindful of these complexities, as they can significantly impact the Black client you are working with.

Size, Shape, and Weight

In 2016, I (Paula Edwards-Gayfield) facilitated a body image presentation to a group of (primarily) Black adolescent girls. I explored what body image meant (to them) or what they thought of when they heard the term, the majority shared that they wanted to be "slim-thick." They wanted to maintain their curves but have a flat stomach and a small waist. This may not be the ideal body type for all Black women, but it has been present for years, with different labels.

"To understand the risk of disordered eating behaviors among Black women it is pertinent to acknowledge the interconnectedness of sizeism—discrimination or prejudice directed against people because of their size and especially because of their weight (Merriam-Webster, n.d.)—and racism in the United States, such that sizeism is the direct product of anti-Blackness" (Simone et al., 2022, Discussion section, para. 5). Historically, non-Black individuals have assumed that race is a protective factor against body dissatisfaction due to the perceived larger body ideal for women of color (Capodilupo & Kim, 2014). While some individuals may exhibit greater resilience or have healthier attitudes toward their bodies, it's rare for anyone to be completely immune to feelings of dissatisfaction with their appearance. Is there anyone who is completely unaffected by body image dissatisfaction? However, Black women of all ages engage in some sort of self-monitoring of their bodies and use exercise, controlling food intake, and plastic surgery to alter the shape of their bodies.

The degree of *acculturation*, the process by which an individual adopts the beliefs, attitudes, and behaviors of the dominant culture (Kroon Van Diest et al., 2014), may account for body dissatisfaction and eating disorder symptoms. Higher levels of acculturation are associated with increased reports of eating disorder symptoms, and for some, internalizing the new standard of beauty becomes the gauge by which the individual compares their perceived self.

In the eating disorder field, there is a growing emphasis on avoiding labels like *obese* or *overweight* for individuals in larger bodies. Correcting clients who use these terms can strain rapport-building efforts. When working with Black clients, it's crucial for providers to listen attentively and understand the origins of these labels—are they hurtful or accepted? Educating clients about the mental health impact of labels is encouraged. Language is important when discussing weight with Black women. Labels like "fat," "voluptuous," or other euphemisms used by individuals to discuss the larger body can reinforce weight stigma, especially when used by those who are hostile or critical. These labels are often intended to inflict pain and are not well-received.

The ways in which we speak about fatness is pathologized, and weight is weaponized in our culture; it has been since slavery. Sabrina Strings (2019) informs us that "the fear of the fat Black woman was created by racial and religious ideologies that have been used to both degrade Black women and discipline white women" (p. 14).

Roxane Gay (2017) states:

> *It's hard for thin people to know how to talk to fat people about their bodies, whether their opinions are solicited or not. I get that, but it's insulting to pretend I am not fat or to deny my body and its reality. It's insulting to think I am somehow unaware of my physical appearance. And it's insulting to assume that I am ashamed of myself for being fat, no matter how close to the truth that might be. (p. 201)*

Regrettably, fat Black women are (still) not accepted in society. Fat people are often targets of recurrent stigmatization. Targets of fat stigma describe it as "everywhere" and "unavoidable," often believing they deserve this prejudicial treatment and rarely challenging it (Lindloff et al., 2024, p. 335). Many women, including Black girls and women internalize these messages resulting in a lot of self-loathing. Although Black women may be more accepting of curvier or larger body types, there is an increase in body image disturbance.

Body image dissatisfaction can also stem from the experience of being objectified. Objectification theory suggests that women are frequently objectified and regarded as objects for visual enjoyment, rather than as individuals with their own thoughts, emotions, and agency. These experiences lead girls and women to internalize cultural standards of attractiveness and to *self-objectify*, using an observer's perspective to judge their own bodies (Moradi, 2010; Buchanan et al., 2008). Objectification contributes to gender and racial inequality for Black women and girls and reinforces harmful stereotypes about women, often resulting in low self-esteem, internalized sexism, and oppression. Self-objectification often manifests as constant body surveillance or monitoring (e.g., body checking), which can lead to body shame (Moradi, 2010) and may contribute to less frequent help-seeking for body image issues (Hewitt & Murray, 2024).

Skin and Hair

Skin color or tone has a significant role in a Black woman's body image and a role in shaping the opportunities and life experiences of Black people. Although experienced in other minority groups, Black people have experienced *colorism* since slavery. The Association of Black Psychologists (2013) define colorism as "skin color stratification that privileges light skinned people of color over dark"; it is discrimination based on skin tone (Uzogara, 2019). It has a stronger impact on the lives of Black women.

There are advantages to being a light-skinned Black person in the United States. Our society heavily judges and values women based on their outward appearance and beauty. Light-skinned Black women are often perceived as more attractive than dark-skinned Black women by both Black and White individuals. Some believe that the closer an individual is to being White, the "better" they are, while darker individuals may experience rejection and mistreatment more frequently.

Darker-skinned women are often stereotyped with derogatory attributes such as being unattractive, dirty, or unintelligent, while lighter skin tone is associated with more positive traits like intelligence, attractiveness, and politeness (Uzogara, 2019). Internalized racism impacts self-esteem, perceptions of beauty, and ethnic identity for all Black women, causing psychological distress.

However, dark-skinned Black women may face additional disadvantages in various aspects of their lives due to this type of discrimination.

Skin tone discrimination within the Black community, known as in-group colorism, has a significant impact on the occurrence of psychiatric disorders among Black Americans (Oh et al., 2021). This is linked to conditions such as anxiety disorders and eating disorders, among others. Health professionals should consider colorism when developing interventions and improving health care services to address health disparities among Black Americans. It is crucial to challenge and dismantle these harmful beliefs and celebrate the beauty and diversity of all skin tones. Beauty comes in all shades, and every individual is uniquely beautiful.

Hair is another important aspect of body image (Capodilupo & Kim, 2014), and a contributor to emotional issues for Black girls and women. Hair can reflect one's level of *Blackness* (or being Black enough)—sense of self or identity, self-expression, and how they present themselves to others. Deciding whether to keep their hair natural, relax it, or wear a weave carries social implications for Black girls and women. Yet, Black women often face scrutiny over their hair's style, texture, length, and color, as these aspects are often judged by others (Capodilupo & Kim, 2014). Several clients have recalled comments from parents like "You're going out with your hair like that?" This implies that they might embarrass their families simply because of their hairstyle choices.

Resembling colorism, society tends to view straight, long hair as more beautiful and desirable, aligning with Eurocentric beauty standards. References to Black hair frequently draw comparisons to White standards, reflecting deeply ingrained racial histories in the United States. Despite not seeking alignment with White norms, Black women experience the impact of societal expectations associated with Whiteness on their lives and sense of identity (West, 2018). Media influence has historically overlooked Black women's natural hair, though this is improving with initiatives like the CROWN Act.

The CROWN Act, which stands for "Creating a Respectful and Open World for Natural Hair," is a law that prohibits race-based hair discrimination, which is the denial of employment and educational opportunities because of hair texture or protective hairstyles including braids, locs, twists or bantu knots. (The Crown Act, 2023)

Black hair acculturation pressures have left many Black girls and women feeling compelled to silence aspects of their cultural self-expression to fit in and function effectively within the White culture. They choose their hairstyles based on others' reactions, shaped by stereotypes and assumptions, as well as internalized messages about what is considered acceptable or not. As echoed throughout this book, creating spaces for Black clients to be seen and heard is an essential requirement for providers working with Black women. Recognizing the connection between a Black woman's hair, her self-acceptance, and her mental well-being is crucial.

Feeling Compelled to Compare to Other Women

Comparing oneself to others is seemingly a natural phenomenon. How often do you walk past someone or notice something in media and then appraise yourself based on the image that is observed? Most of us are surrounded by characters, images, or stories that perpetuate the message that certain bodies are acceptable or attractive. Standards of beauty are constantly changing and influenced by social media, celebrities, and what is deemed desirable or acceptable by prospective partners. These sociocultural standards increase comparisons, body shame, disordered eating, and other unhelpful behaviors. Black women may evaluate or make changes to their appearance to conform to the standards of beauty that they adopt. For example, facial features that are attributed to Black people (i.e., wide nose, big lips) are made smaller by using makeup—contouring, liners, etc. In fact, an Instagram search for these makeup tutorials yields 42 million results.

Providers are encouraged to approach discussions without preconceived notions of what body image entails for their Black clients. Body image satisfaction may be influenced by factors beyond size, shape, and weight as appearance satisfaction for Black girls and women may differ from Eurocentric standards, impacting their ability to discuss appearance concerns without an open conversation. Perceptions of body image may be influenced by the increased presence of Black female celebrity images, but what bodies/body types are accentuated? Black girls and women also experience pressure from Black males to possess Eurocentric features (e.g., straight hair, light skin) and pressures from their family to fit in. Imagine the process of adolescent development—trying to identify who you are as an individual and navigating identity development, the process of acculturation, while being consumed with thoughts of "am I attractive enough for a desired partner," "do I fit in (any place)," "am I Black enough—connected to my community" (Blazek & Carter, 2019; Howard et al., 2019; Capodilupo & Kim, 2014). Conflicting messages often result in individuals feeling undervalued and underappreciated. Black women are not immune to the societal standards of beauty. Those external standards integrated with their own beliefs about what is attractive can result in discontent and disconnections.

Grappling With Black Features That Are Not Appreciated on Their Bodies

Black women's bodies and their beauty ideals have generally been devalued and rejected by mainstream culture (Awad et al., 2015). However, White women and some non-Black women of color adopt some of these features: increased curves, ample butts, hair styles, and more. Imagine receiving messages that your lips are too big, and other non-Black women are increasingly obtaining lip injections or purchasing products to enhance their lips. What does this say to a Black woman? Is it their Blackness that's unacceptable? What conclusions do Black girls make when they are deemed unattractive because of these features? It's easy to question the thinking traps that may occur, but if this is the repeated experience of your client, is it a thinking trap? Or is there validity in the client's experience, the internalized message of not good enough or not pretty enough?

A "Go Get it Done" Attitude

The culture of weight loss seems to be embedded among some Black women and girls, often driven by the pressure to conform to shifting beauty trends, which complicates self-acceptance and celebrating individuality. Many Black women turn to waist trainers, detox teas, or rigorous social media workouts, especially when preparing for significant events, and push themselves to extremes. Weight loss efforts—whether through dieting, exercise, or even weight loss drugs and surgeries—are often seen as necessary steps to enjoy life fully. Motivations for these efforts vary, encompassing personal satisfaction, health, appearance, the need to fit into previously worn clothing, and the influence of family and societal expectations. A former client expressed frustration, saying it feels like the world is constantly telling her that she is wrong for simply existing as she is, only to find that efforts to change don't bring the desired results. Privileges related to race, gender, and other factors play a significant role in how fatness is perceived and contribute to fat-phobic narratives (Oswald, 2024).

Durham (2024) noted that in the United States, fitting into a smaller clothing size is often celebrated as a significant achievement. The societal obsession with weight loss has intensified with the introduction of GLP-1 drugs like Ozempic. GLP-1, *glucagon-like peptide-1*, is a hormone that helps regulate blood sugar levels (Richards et al., 2023). These drugs work by stimulating the release of insulin, slowing down digestion, and reducing appetite (Bartel et al., 2024). Originally designed to treat Type 2 diabetes, these drugs are now used for obesity and heart disease—conditions that disproportionately affect Black Americans (Durham, 2024). However, many studies on these drugs lack diversity, raising concerns about accessibility, affordability, and the historical discrimination Black communities face regarding weight and health.

Many Black women and girls carry the weight of past experiences with fat phobia into adulthood, where physician-recommended weight loss often triggers shame, disordered eating, and even eating disorders. The misuse of drugs like Ozempic to manage anxiety about eating, body shape, or weight can worsen these issues and hinder recovery (Bartel et al., 2024). These experiences underscore the impact of societal biases and historical stereotypes on how Black individuals view their bodies and health. The cultural allure of a "magic" solution to fatness, as Durham (2024) notes, reflects a broader societal yearning for quick fixes, despite the complex realities of weight and health.

Weight loss surgery is widely regarded as the most effective treatment for moderate to severe obesity and its associated comorbidities (Welsh et al., 2020). In the U.S., Roux-en-Y gastric bypass and vertical sleeve gastrectomy are the most commonly performed bariatric procedures. However, African American patients are significantly less likely to undergo these surgeries compared to non-Hispanic White patients, indicating a lower overall prevalence among Black Americans (Hui et al., 2020). The rate of bariatric surgery among African Americans is approximately 17.35% to 17.36% (Welsh et al., 2020). Additionally, Black patients tend to experience poorer outcomes, including less weight loss, higher complication rates, increased readmissions, reoperations, major complications, mortality, and the need for further interventions compared to non-Black patients (Wisniowski & Samakar, 2023; Welsh et al., 2020; Hui et al., 2020).

Plastic surgery used to be taboo, but not anymore. Plastic surgery and nonsurgical treatments are on the rise! Cosmetic procedures among Black women are typically referred to as an enhancement. It has been suggested that Black women are more conscious visually than ever before. Cosmetic surgery has sort of become just part of the beauty regimen. Surgery is more accessible and affordable. Stigma has lessened because more women (i.e., actors, models, musicians) are getting work done, which grants "permission" to "go get it done." Some procedures often requested are rhinoplasty (a thinner nose), liposuction and tummy tucks, breast lifts or reductions (Jeffries, 2020).

Roxane Gay shared in an interview:

> *If I was Lane Bryant fat, I would be joyful about fatness. I'm fat positive, in that I don't see fat as a bad thing. But what I do see as a bad thing is how I'm treated. I can have the most positive outlook in the world, but that is not going to change how hecklers and people walking down the street are yelling at me. Can you understand how this individual may want to be invisible? It can be challenging for some to feel positive about their size, shape, and weight, especially when they are not able to find clothing that fits, or feel accepted within their peer groups, or are bombarded with messages to lose weight, get fit, be better. (Machado, 2017, para. 35)*

A FILTERED WORLD

Black women are portrayed in the media in different ways than White women. The widespread misrepresentation of Black women and girls in the media can have harmful consequences. Historically in film, Black women and girls are oversexualized and Black girls in particular are often dressed as little women rather than being portrayed as children. Black girls are often faced with the task of rejecting negative portrayals while also aspiring to unrealistic and sometimes unachievable body standards. Exposure to sexually objectifying media aligns with poorer body image.

Unfortunately, the social norms regarding Black women have not improved, often resulting in Black girls being victimized, distrusted, and treated as adults. Black women's bodies are not viewed in the same manner as others and it's important to assess media's influence on these viewpoints. As a result of the misconceptions about Black girls, stereotypes form and negatively affect children and adolescents. If a young Black girl is curvy and has larger breasts than her peers, she is considered overly sexual. Conversely, "the thin ideal White body frame is often viewed as innocent and modelesque" (Romo et al., 2015). With easy access to the internet, young women are continually inundated with images depicting mainstream beauty standards (Williams & Ricciardelli, 2014). Due to the accessibility of these images, young women may become desensitized, leading to the normalization of the desire to achieve unrealistic beauty standards.

A study conducted by the Georgetown Law Center for Poverty and Inequality revealed that adults tend to perceive Black girls as more mature, less innocent, and more accountable for their behavior than White girls of the same age (Epstein et al., 2017). This is an example of *adultification,* when Black youth's childhood behaviors are diminished or disregarded. Two forms of adultification may affect Black clients seeking treatment: (1) *socialization*, where children mature early due to environmental factors, particularly in low-resource communities, and (2) *cultural stereotypes*, where adults perceive children as more mature, often influenced by race (Epstein et al., 2017). Black girls who experience adultification often encounter heightened mental health concerns and may feel a pressing need to protect themselves. The stress and disconnection associated with assuming caretaking roles or being perceived and treated as more mature can be particularly difficult to navigate.

Epstein et al.'s (2017) study reports that compared to White girls of the same age, adults believed:

- Black girls need less nurturing
- Black girls need less protection
- Black girls need to be supported less
- Black girls need to be comforted less
- Black girls are more independent
- Black girls know more about adult topics
- Black girls know more about sex

Adultification strips Black children of their innocence, dehumanizing them and undermining the unique essence of childhood. This false narrative suggests that certain behaviors of Black youth are deliberate and malevolent rather than the result of immature decision-making. They are not allowed to make mistakes, which continues to manifest in expectations to be a "Strong Black Woman" or exhibit "Black Girl Magic." Black girls and women experience these stereotypes directly. When viewed as coping mechanisms for emotional distress, eating disorders can be significantly influenced by the experience of adultification.

Adultification can severely impact mental health in several ways:

- Increased anxiety and stress: Elevated expectations and responsibilities lead to heightened stress and anxiety.
- Lost childhood: Deprivation of typical childhood experiences results in feelings of isolation, loss of innocence, and lack of peer support.
- Emotional regulation issues: Expected to handle adult emotions without necessary skills, leading to difficulties in coping with stress.
- Internalized pressure: The need to meet unrealistic standards can cause chronic stress and perfectionism.
- Identity and self-esteem problems: Struggling with self-worth, feeling valued only for adult-like responsibilities.
- Risk of depression: Cumulative stress and lack of support increases the risk of depression.
- Maladaptive coping mechanisms: Development of eating disorders, substance abuse, or self-harm as temporary relief.
- Relationship challenges: Difficulty relating to peers and strained family dynamics due to altered roles and expectations.

Adultification places undue psychological and emotional burdens on children, leading to significant mental health challenges that can persist into adulthood (Bounds & Posey, 2022). Recognizing and addressing these impacts is crucial for providing appropriate support and interventions.

Practical Tips: Interview Protocol for More Accurate Depictions of Client Experiences

For treatment efficacy, Talleyrand et al. (2017) recommend an interview protocol to provide a more accurate depiction of your clients' experiences. Here are a few questions you can ask your client:

1. Can you describe what body image means to you as a Black woman?
2. Can you talk about your concerns with your body image?
3. What influences have you had in your life when it comes to your body image?

4. How would you describe a healthy body image?
5. Talk to me about what you view as important in defining your appearance.
6. Can you describe what influences how you view your appearance?
7. Can you describe what you view as important to your overall well-being?
8. Is there anything else you can tell me about your experiences with eating and body image that would help to understand your struggles or concerns?

BODY IMAGE IN OLDER ADULTS

Body image concerns are not reserved for adolescents and young adults. Women across age and race are vulnerable to experience body dissatisfaction and engage in disordered eating behaviors. The fear of aging is prevalent in our society, particularly as women experience natural changes in their bodies. Perimenopause is a critical period for the development of eating disorders (Finch et al., 2023). Symptoms such as depression, fatigue, low mood, fear of weight gain, feeling overweight, and body dissatisfaction are common during this time. This combination of factors can create a challenging situation for some women, as they may feel compelled to start dieting during this natural period of bodily changes (The North American Menopause Society, 2023).

Menopause can also significantly impact metabolism, weight, physical fitness, and body dissatisfaction, potentially increasing the risk of developing an eating disorder (Manzato & Roncarati, 2022). Older adults may have differing nutritional needs compared to younger people, which can exacerbate complications associated with eating disorders. Despite these changes being a normal part of aging, societal pressures often lead women to believe that their bodies should remain static. Midlife is a period of significant role shifts, juggling careers, and caring for both children and aging parents. These dual pressures—internal role transitions and external body expectations—can amplify body image issues. In response, individuals may resort to restrictive eating or increased exercise to feel in control during this transitional phase. Mature women admit that they internalize societal expectations of beauty and feminism, often engaging in diet behaviors to manage weight or alter their appearance.

It is common for adults as they age to begin questioning their social location. Loss of identity and purpose can result in disordered eating patterns or a greater focus on physical appearance and the quality or lack of quality relationships, both platonic and romantic, in their lives (Reela et al., 2008). Older Black women want to feel desired, attractive, and as though they made a difference. They want to feel "worth it." As with anyone who may question their worthiness or value, there could be an increased focus on body image—making the necessary changes to acquire the status of being good enough; desirable. There may be increased emotions of envy of a younger woman's ability to do more with her body or the attention that they receive, or regret for not taking advantage of similar opportunities when they were younger.

Satisfaction with one aspect of the body does not equate satisfaction with the entire body. McLaren and Kuh (2004) found that women aged 54 who felt positive about their body weight reported greater distress about other aspects of their appearance (e.g., skin). The need for a multifaceted approach to assess body image is prudent as this demographic is understudied. It is important to note that Runfola et al. (2013) reports in their race-inclusive study that "body size satisfied women appear to exert considerable effort to achieve and maintain this satisfaction, and they are not impervious to experiencing dissatisfaction with other aspects of their appearance, particularly those aspects affected by aging."

MOVING FORWARD

Black women may have distinct and diverse standards of beauty that are shaped by their unique cultural experiences and perspectives (Talleyrand, 2006). Understanding and respecting these differences is important in promoting inclusive and affirming conversations about body image and self-esteem. There are many social justice movements or attempts to improve body image: body positivity, body neutrality, body liberation, and many more. However, many body positivity activists, particularly those with privileged bodies, have failed to recognize the presence of the fat Black women that paved the path to liberation to exist in their bodies.

I have stated this so frequently that I cannot recall the original source, but it is adapted from relational-cultural theory: "Culture shapes our perceptions of health, healing, and relationships." Cultural factors can have a significant impact on one's attitudes, beliefs, and behaviors related to food and body image. This understanding is crucial in the assessment and treatment of eating disorders, as it helps address the broader contextual factors that contribute to an individual's experiences. Understanding your Black client's experience can be a complex process and requires the provider to be culturally informed (Fuller, 2021; Cassidy et al., 2015; Talleyrand, 2006). Culturally informed providers create a more supportive and empathetic therapeutic environment, allowing for a more effective and relevant approach to treatment and support.

Chapter 5

HOW DO I BUILD A CULTURALLY INFORMED THERAPEUTIC ALLIANCE?

Building a culturally informed therapeutic alliance involves active efforts to understand and address the unique experiences of our clients. As professionals it's important that we begin to recognize the stigma around having an eating disorder, especially with Black women and girls. Systemic barriers (e.g., lack of health insurance and clinician bias), and personal barriers (e.g., lack of motivation, family privacy, fears of not being understood, readiness to change, or lack of knowledge of available resources) are examples of treatment barriers identified by women of color with a history of an eating disorder (Reyes-Rodriguez et al., 2013).

I, Paula, am frequently reminded of the importance of a culturally informed therapeutic alliance when I encounter clients of color requesting to work with a provider of color. A former client expressed a desire to work with a Black therapist, and when she learned that one was not available, she expressed her discontent. Acknowledging the client's disappointment and recognizing the significance she places on working with a Black therapist for a more *relatable* therapeutic experience is crucial in fostering understanding and establishing a supportive therapeutic relationship.

The challenge of limited diversity in certain fields, including the eating disorder field, is recognized. It highlights the ongoing need for increased diversity and cultural competence in both medical and mental health services to better meet the unique needs of Black clients. Efforts to increase representation and cultural competence must be ongoing. Recognizing the importance of a culturally informed alliance, we the authors recommend that you consider reaching out to providers who may be better equipped to meet those specific needs while you continue deepening your cultural humility.

UNDERSTANDING BLACK FEMALE STEREOTYPES

Providers must self-assess for unconscious bias, or implicit bias, because holding on to stereotypes can negatively impact the assessment and treatment of clients. In addition, clients can internalize their own stereotypes that make an authentic client–provider relationship impossible. Preconceived beliefs can hinder authentic relationship building by overshadowing the important process of discovery in the early stages of a client–provider relationship (Crawford Mann, 2021). Open-mindedness and understanding are crucial for effective communication and collaboration.

In "Girlhood Interrupted," Epstein, Blake, and Thalia (2017) shared "caricatures of Black femininity are often deposited into distinct chambers of our public consciousness, narrowly defining Black female identity and movement according to the stereotypes described by Pauli Murray (1963), as 'female dominance' on the one hand and loose morals on the other hand, both growing out of the roles forced upon them during the slavery experience and its aftermath" (p. 5). Labels of Black females as hypersexual, conniving, loud, and sassy prevail. Black girls are often assigned adult-like characteristics (see Chapter 4), which can expose them to the same harmful stereotypes and defamatory representations, making them equally vulnerable to negative assumptions and biases. Stereotyping is offensive, and for some, it may be ingrained due to societal influences. Disliking any form of stereotyping is rooted in the understanding that individuals might conform to these patterns based on learned norms rather than personal choice. Promoting understanding and challenging stereotypes can help foster a more inclusive society.

Three dominant paradigms of Black femininity originating in the South during slavery that have persisted into present-day culture are often associated with stereotypes (Mammy, Jezebel, and Sapphire) that "paint Black females as hypersexual, boisterous, aggressive, and unscrupulous" (Blake et al., 2015; Crawford Mann, 2021). In our current culture, these stereotypes may be referred to as freaks, gold diggers, divas, and baby mamas. These archetypes have historical roots but oversimplify and perpetuate biased views of Black women. These stereotypes are described below.

Matriarch

The "overbearing and harsh Black mother is the remnant of the mammy" (Crawford Mann, 2021, p. 70); she appears to lack kindness for her partner and children after being in a subordinate role and serving others. Her expression is candid, unrestrained, and unpolished evoking both fear and longing in those around her. "She is laden with the responsibility of creating the appearance of success by ensuring that her family purports the best behavior at all times" (Crawford Mann, 2021, p. 70). Her physical appearance aligns with the female gender, yet she is perceived to lack femininity and sexuality, possibly due to societal expectations that tie her worth to providing direction and correction as a Black woman. "Her relationships are controlling and transactional. Her essence is strength, but in her unyielding strength she lacks the capacity to tolerate true social and emotional vulnerability with herself and others" (Crawford Mann, 2021, p. 70).

Mammy

In Crawford Mann's (2021) portrayal, the Mammy is described as a domestic servant, often depicted as larger-bodied, dark-skinned, focused on duty without much time for self-care, and tends to shield herself from the harsh realities of her role. Her demeanor is described as neither happy nor sad, but rather dutiful, with her life centered around serving others. She neglects her own well-being, thoughts, talents, and desires—her "self" (Crawford Mann, 2021). The Mammy is often depicted as "self-sacrificing, nurturing, loving, and asexual" (Epstein et al., 2017). She often serves in caregiver roles perceived as asexual, such as a nanny or housekeeper (Dunn, 2018). She is the idealized caregiver who is amiable, loyal, nonthreatening, and obedient.

Jezebel

Crawford Mann (2021) describes Jezebel as "hypersexualized, seductive, and an exploiter of men's weaknesses. She is an object to be desired" (p. 70–71). This stereotype portrays Black women as hypersexual in media (Dunn, 2018; Lewis et al., 2013). She embodies uncontrolled sexual lust and promiscuous behavior. She does not have time for mundane roles or tasks, her body is her worth, and she is preoccupied with her appearance. She may be a loner who neither gives nor receives from other women (Epstein et al., 2017).

Sapphire

Sapphire is described as a Black woman who is loud, argumentative, and devalues men (Dunn, 2018). She is beautiful, but emasculating, aggressive, angry, and stubborn (Epstein et al., 2017). Her tendency to lash out at those who disrespect her may lead to her being perceived as bitter. She exudes a mysterious and sexually tantalizing aura but remains unattainable to men (Crawford Mann, 2021; Dunn, 2018).

According to Crawford Mann (2021), Jezebel and Sapphire are the oversexualized Black stereotypes, "their physicality is made of the fantasies of those who would desire them—flawless skin, voluptuous curves, and a cinched waist" (p. 70). These images and historical stereotypes continue to have real-life consequences for Black women and girls today. According to Blake and colleagues, "these stereotypes underlie the implicit bias that shapes many [adults'] view of Black females [as] . . . sexually promiscuous, hedonistic, and in need of socialization" (Epstein et al., 2017, p. 5). It is disheartening that stereotypes perpetuate such narrow portrayals, limiting the recognition of individuality and diverse experiences among Black individuals. For some Black women, this serves as a challenge, motivating them to surpass stereotypes and strive for their best self.

Strong Black Woman

When an archetype is considered positive, it may still be a stigma, like the Strong Black Woman. Lashley et al. (2017) admonishes that assuming a stigma is not a badge of courage; it leads to the invisibility of one's true identity due to the continuous suppression of self-interests within the social persona (Taylor et al., 2014). Black women and girls presenting for eating disorder treatment are often exhausted from having to maintain the role of the Strong Black Woman, which may result in negative health outcomes. Rather than recognizing the impact of stress associated with maintaining societal roles and stereotypes, providers may potentially overlook both the physical and mental health outcomes.

Many Black clients I have worked with express self-imposed expectations higher than those of other women, which are shaped by societal pressures. They believe it's their responsibility not just to open doors but to keep them open, resulting in considerable internalized stress. The myth of Black women being stronger than other women can hinder the expression of emotional distress and lead to harmful emotion-driven behaviors, impacting both physical and mental health. Seeking professional help is sometimes avoided due to the fear of being perceived as weak and incapable of upholding the Strong Black Woman image.

BOOSTING CULTURAL COMPETENCY

Cultural competence is the ability to recognize the importance of race, ethnicity, and culture. Specifically, it is awareness and acknowledgment that people from other cultural groups do not necessarily share the same beliefs and practices or perceive, interpret, or encounter similar experiences in the same way (Substance Abuse and Mental Health Services Administration [SAMHSA], 2014). Cultural competence "refers to the ability to honor and respect the beliefs, languages, interpersonal styles, and behaviors, understand, communicate with, and effectively interact with people across different cultures" (SAMHSA, 2014, p. 296). It involves being aware of and respecting cultural differences, as well as adapting one's behavior and communication style to be inclusive and respectful of diverse backgrounds.

Cultural misunderstandings, clinician bias, and a breakdown in linguistic competency can create barriers that deter Black individuals from accessing and utilizing care, preventing them from receiving appropriate mental health and medical support. One way to create culturally sensitive spaces for Black individuals to seek mental health and medical treatment is to build provider cultural competence. It's important to define a few terms:

> *Ethnicity*: Encompasses the social identity and shared sense of belonging among a group of people, characterized by common historical or familial origins, beliefs, and cultural standards of behavior (SAMHSA, 2014; Yang, 2000).
> *Race*: Commonly perceived as a biological classification based on inherent traits like skin color or facial features. It's important to note that there are no biological criteria supporting the division of races into distinct categories. Race is a socially constructed concept rather than a strictly biological one (SAMHSA, 2001).
> *Culture*: Defined by a community or society, influences how individuals

perceive the world. It encompasses a specific set of beliefs, norms, and values governing relationships, lifestyles, and environmental organization. Culture is a complex and enriching concept that significantly shapes human experiences and interactions (SAMHSA, 2014).

PRACTICAL TIPS: HOW TO PRACTICE CULTURAL COMPETENCY

Culturally competent care is about the creation of an environment in which the best health care practices can be safely and conscientiously implemented; it affirms all persons and shows contempt to no one for any reason; it supports and assists each person by incorporating behaviors and interactions from the medical personnel that serves to help restore the individual's well-being (Downer, 2021). The U.S. Department of Health and Human Services Office of Minority Health (2021) identified the following strategies for practicing cultural competency:

- Learn about your own and others' cultural identities
- Combat bias and stereotypes
- Respect others' beliefs, values, and communication preferences
- Adapt your services to each client's unique needs
- Gain new cultural experiences

Racial Identity Development

Justice Sonya Sotomayor, of the United States Supreme Court, reminds us that "Race matters. Race matters . . . because of persistent racial inequality in society—inequality that cannot be ignored" (National Museum of African American History & Culture, n.d.). Race is used to establish and justify systems of power, privilege, disenfranchisement, and oppression (National Museum of African American History & Culture, n.d.). Black women are impacted by these systems daily—they are subjected to classifications based on skin color, physical features, family systems, and their low status is reflected in pay inequality, health care disparity, and employment opportunities (Kirwan Institute for the Study of Race and Ethnicity, 2015; SAMHSA, 2014; Sue, 2001; Sue & Sue, 1999). Race is a social construct, but racial identity is real! Believe it or not, everyone has a racial identity.

What Is Racial Identity?

Racial identity is externally imposed: "How do others perceive me?" Racial identity is also internally constructed: "How do I identify myself?" (National Museum of African American History & Culture, n.d.).

Understanding not only your own identity, but how your client's identities and experiences shape who they are is imperative when building a relationship with Black clients. Clients may explore their racial or cultural identity development with their providers while experiencing a multitude of emotions. This exploration often requires introspection from both the provider and the client. Like stages of change, racial identity is a fluid and nonlinear process, meaning it can change over time and does not follow a fixed or predictable path. Racial identity development is composed of several stages: conformity; dissonance and appreciating; resistance; and immersion, introspection, and integrative awareness (National Museum of African American History & Culture, n.d.; Sue, 2001; Sue & Sue, 1999). Racial identity development theory describes the process of moving from internalized racism to a position of empowerment (Sue, 2001; Sue & Sue, 1999). Navigating this process—the desire to "fit in" to the

TABLE 5.1

RACIAL IDENTITY DEVELOPMENT: MINORITY ETHNIC GROUP	
Conformity	• Expresses a favorable attitude toward and a preference for dominant cultural values. • Assigns significant importance to traits that are representative of dominant cultural groups. • May hold negative views or devalue their own race and/or other racial/ethnic groups.
Dissonance and appreciating	• Begins to explore and question their personal identity. • Aware of conflicting messages and observations that challenge existing beliefs and stereotypes about their own cultural groups and the value of mainstream cultural groups. • Develops a deeper understanding of their own cultural heritage and the reality of racism. • Shifts away from viewing dominant cultural groups as entirely positive.

Resistance and immersion	• Embraces and maintains a positive attitude toward their own race and cultural heritage. • Rejects the dominant societal and cultural values. • Concentrates on addressing and eliminating oppression within their own racial or cultural group. • Likely harbors significant feelings of distrust and anger toward dominant cultural groups and their representations.
Introspection	• Begins to contemplate the psychological impact of directing intense emotions toward dominant cultural groups. • Seeks to redirect focus toward personal identity while maintaining respect for their own cultural groups. Adjusts their perspective to recognize that not everything about dominant cultural groups, their own racial/cultural group, or other diverse groups are entirely good or bad. • May experience internal conflict and feel torn between loyalties as their understanding evolves.
Integrative awareness	• Possesses a strong and assured sense of racial and cultural identity. • Adopts a multicultural perspective. • Sustains pride in their racial and cultural heritage. • Dedicates oneself to advocating for and valuing all marginalized and diverse groups.

Credit: National Museum of African American History & Culture, n.d; Sue, 2001; Sue & Sue, 1999

dominate culture's social norms and questioning their own identity—may be a stressor for Black girls and women and contribute to engagement in disordered eating behaviors. The following examples illustrate how these stages may manifest with Black clients.

> *Conformity*: A young Black woman is reluctant to participate in cultural celebrations with her family. She believes these gatherings reinforce stereotypes about Black people being "ghetto" or too "loud," and wants to distance herself, fearing that her peers would judge her as being like other Black people.
>
> *Dissonance and appreciating*: A biracial (having parents from two different racial or ethnic backgrounds) adolescent who identifies as Black, *passed* (as White) until she was in high school, when she experienced a

traumatic encounter of being called a racial slur. Despite her previous social acceptance among her mostly White friends, she felt unsupported by her peers as they did not understand her emotional response. She began exploring her racial identity more deeply.

Resistance and immersion: A Black student transferred to a predominantly Black university after spending a couple of years at a predominantly White educational institution. This change was motivated by a desire to reconnect with her cultural roots and address the feelings of alienation she had experienced. Since transferring, she has become intensely involved in Black student organizations and social justice movements, often expressing strong negative feelings toward White people and dominant cultural institutions.

Introspection: A biracial woman (person who has parents from two different racial or ethnic backgrounds) has navigated multiple cultural identities throughout her life. She has predominantly identified with her White mother's side of the family, has a White partner, and often downplays her Black heritage unless she visits her father. A recent incident at a family gathering where a relative made a racially insensitive comment about Black people prompted her to reevaluate her racial identity and her place within both cultural groups.

Integrative awareness: An older Black woman has undergone a long journey of navigating complex racial and cultural identities throughout her life. In her earlier years, she experienced internalized racism and conformity, followed by stages of intense cultural immersion and resistance, where she distanced herself from dominant cultural groups and focused intensely on her Black identity, ultimately reaching a point where she feels a deep sense of harmony and balance in her identity. She reports increased confidence and authenticity.

The racial identity development model applies to individuals from both ethnic minority and majority backgrounds. Our focus is on its relevance to ethnic minorities (see Table 5.1), while also encouraging practitioners to consider its application to majority ethnic groups as well.

Values

Values play a significant role in a Black client's experience of their culture, influencing perceptions, expectations, and norms. Conflicts or congruence between personal values and cultural norms can influence mental health, potentially contributing to stress, identity struggles, and eating disorders. Reyes-Rodriguez (2022) reminds us that "working with diverse populations . . . requires providers to be mindful of cultural values, culturally related stress and the context" (p. 23). Black populations navigate through multiple cultural aspects (e.g., acculturation, minority status, acculturative stress, discrimination, and food insecurity), which adds another level of stress to the treatment process.

The process of acculturation is familiar to Black individuals, who strive to preserve and express their cultural heritage. Despite these efforts, there are persistent societal messages pushing them to conform to mainstream cultural values, such as the ideals of being thin or having long, straight hair (Conley, 2021). This tension can impact self-perception and identity.

Practitioners, should reflect on the following:

- What impact might overlooking the values of our Black clients have within clinical spaces?
- In your experience, have you noticed any clashes between provider and client values, particularly concerning cultural aspects?
- Is there a tendency to assume shared values between the provider and the client, and how does this assumption influence the therapeutic relationship?
- If ruptures arise due to differences in values, what strategies or approaches do you think could effectively address and navigate these challenges in the therapeutic relationship?

Intersectionality

Kimberlé Williams Crenshaw's theory of intersectionality began with an exploration of the oppression of women of color and has expanded to include race, gender, orientation, class, colonialism, ableism, and sexism (Crenshaw, 1991, 2000). We are all a mosaic of intersections of many identities that either give us access to privilege or oppression in the world. In this way, the focus on group differences can promote a pattern of scrutinizing minority identities and cultures but not applying a parallel critical lens to dominant identities and cultures. The intersectionality theory is rooted in Black feminism and Critical Race Theory (Carbado et al., 2013; Lashley et al., 2017).

Intersectionality identifies advantages and disadvantages that are felt by people due to a combination of factors. Being stigmatized is a traumatic experience that can have a lasting impact. When you layer in multiple ways that someone from a marginalized group may experience stigma daily, it is not surprising that eating disorders are one of the maladaptive coping mechanisms that may emerge.

Providers will find value in attending to the ways in which Black clients may draw upon intersectionality as a source of strength and resilience. It is crucial to acknowledge that Black women face continued marginalization, often as a means of social control influenced by factors such as race, social class, and gender (Lashley et al., 2017). There is increased attention on the topic of intersectionality, and with this growing interest, intersectionality has become a "handy catchall phrase" (Love et al., 2018; Phoenix, 2006). Moradi (2017) suggests that there is a need for caution as intersectionality has become a buzzword, leading to confusion about its meaning and practical application.

PRACTICING CULTURAL HUMILITY

So, what's the difference between cultural competence and cultural humility? *Cultural competence* is a developmental process that involves gaining awareness, knowledge, and skills over time (Hook et al., 2017). This progression enhances the ability to work and communicate effectively in diverse and cross-cultural situations (Office of Minority Health, HHS, 2021).

Cultural humility is a reflective process of understanding one's biases and privileges, managing power imbalances, and maintaining a stance that is open to others in relation to aspects of their cultural identity that are most important to them (Kirwan Institute for the Study of Race and Ethnicity, 2015).

This is a lifelong process! Cultural humility requires consistent self-reflection and self-critique, allowing us to not only learn about Black women's culture (and others), but starts with the provider examining their own belief and cultural identities. Hook et al. (2017) reports that "cultural humility involves the ability to maintain an interpersonal stance that is other-oriented (or open to the other) in relation to aspects of cultural identity that are most important to the client" (p. 9). Continuous growth and improvement are crucial for providers, enabling them to adapt to evolving needs, enhance their skills, and provide better care for their Black clients. Nevertheless, all providers may encounter pitfalls when working with Black individuals because we can make mistakes and we have blind spots, which emphasizes the importance of ongoing self-awareness and learning.

Practical Tips: How to Practice Cultural Humility

The Office of Minority Health, HHS (2021) identifies the following strategies for practicing cultural humility:

- Practice self-reflection, including awareness of your beliefs, values, and implicit biases.
- Recognize what you don't know and be open to learning as much as you can.
- Be open to other people's identities and empathize with their life experiences.
- Acknowledge that the client is their own best authority, not you.
- Learn and grow from people whose beliefs, values, and worldviews differ from yours.

CHECKING YOUR BIAS

Bias: Preconceived notions and stereotypes that influence our understanding, behaviors, and decisions (Office of Minority Health, HHS, 2012). It encompasses both positive and negative evaluations and often forms early in life, potentially serving as a survival mechanism for some individuals.

Bias can lead to inadequate assessment and understanding of the client's unique experiences and challenges. It can result in the failure to provide appropriate support and interventions tailored to the individual's needs. Additionally, bias perpetuates harmful stereotypes, erroneously reinforcing misconceptions that affect Black individuals (Georgetown University National Center for Cultural Competence, n.d.). This limited perspective risks marginalizing anyone whose experiences diverge from these stereotypes.

Clients have shared experiences of feeling overlooked when providers inquire about difficulties with completing meals or if meals are challenging. They perceive that these questions are often directed at those with anorexia nervosa, neglecting individuals with bulimia nervosa or binge-eating disorder. Is this an example of bias? By only focusing on difficulties with completing meals or challenges with eating, providers may be unintentionally reinforcing stereotypes and assumptions about eating disorders being solely related to restriction. For Black clients, providers may want to consider how experiences of anti-Blackness and systemic bias result in increased levels of distress, morbidity, and mortality.

Recognizing and actively countering bias in therapeutic settings is crucial for providing inclusive and effective care.

UNDERSTANDING WEIGHT STIGMA

Weight stigma: Refers to the negative attitudes, beliefs, stereotypes, and discriminatory behaviors directed toward individuals based on their body weight or size. Weight stigma is a social stigma predominantly directed at individuals with higher weight, affecting almost every aspect of daily life and manifesting in diverse settings such as health care, education, media, employment, and social interactions (Osa et al., 2022).

Weight stigma influences how people understand, perceive, and behave towards others based on their body size, shape, and perceived weight. Weight stigma occurs across social groups. Members of multiple marginalized groups experience the burden of being othered and higher instances of stigma in a fat biased society. Weight stigma is discrimination, and it hurts everyone. Weight stigma is prevalent, existing throughout our daily life including employment education, health care, housing, the legal system, media, and interpersonal relationships. And unfortunately, weight stigma often goes unrecognized. (National Eating Disorders Association, 2023)

Experienced and internalized weight stigma has been associated with severe health repercussions for individuals with higher weight, including disordered eating, substance use and dependence, self-harm, health care avoidance, and an elevated risk of chronic morbidity and mortality. Stigma associated with weight is rooted in stereotypes that unfairly portray individuals with higher weight as lazy, impulsive, unhealthy, unattractive, unintelligent, and lacking in willpower and self-discipline. These weight-based stereotypes exist alongside beliefs that weight is controllable, and that weight loss is desirable and achievable for those who try hard enough (Osa et al., 2022). Weight stigma affects people of all body sizes.

Fat phobia refers to the fear, dislike, or prejudice against individuals who are perceived as overweight or obese (Kinavey & Cool, 2019; Matacin & Simone, 2019; Davis-Coelho et al., 2000). It involves negative attitudes, biases, and discriminatory behaviors directed toward people based on their body size. Fat phobia is closely related to weight stigma and can manifest in various aspects of society, including health care, media, education, and interpersonal relationships (Moller & Tischner, 2019).

In many professions, fat bodies are viewed as contrary to notions of professionalism, personal responsibility, and health. Fat individuals are frequently judged as less active, assertive, athletic, attractive, happy, hard-working, masculine, popular, and successful compared to their thinner counterparts (Hutson, 2013). They are often relegated to jobs with less social contact, perceived as more suitable for roles that are out of sight. Fatness is conspicuous, noticeable in every setting.

Health care professionals often lack training in discussing and considering the body in a nuanced manner, tending to concentrate on nonverbal cues and preconceived notions about physical appearance instead of engaging with the deeper facets of physical experience and embodiment (Mchugh & Chrisler, 2019). Black clients may internalize anti-fat bias, sometimes echoing harmful comments about body weight heard from their parents, and may use their body to manage other anxieties to avoid replicating these harmful patterns. Imagine being a marginalized Black woman in a larger body, facing weight bias and anti-fat beliefs that impact employment, psychological well-being, health care experiences, and media portrayals, alongside significant social stigma. When Black clients seek treatment or care, the next steps involve exploring their unique experiences.

Fat-affirming therapy is critical for successful psychotherapy with clients in larger bodies, particularly Black clients who have experienced shaming and mistreatment by medical providers due to their size and racial background (Davis-Coelho et al., 2000). Providers play a vital role in helping Black clients navigate their racial identity while also addressing internalized racism and fat phobia. This is crucial for fostering a supportive and validating therapeutic environment.

DOES YOUR CLIENT FEEL SEEN AND HEARD?

Stiles-Shields et al. (2016) recognize the therapeutic alliance as a relational bond formed through collaborative efforts and trust between a patient and provider, as both strive to establish and accomplish treatment goals. Understanding the unique challenges faced by Black women with eating disorders is essential for improving treatment outcomes. Establishing a strong therapeutic alliance and fostering an emotional connection with all providers can enhance engagement and support the recovery process. Collaboration and cultural competence play vital roles in addressing the ambivalence toward change.

Ensuring that clients are *seen and heard* is an essential approach to facilitate connection and demonstrate an understanding of their concerns and experiences. The concept of being seen and heard can vary for everyone. Examples that highlight the nuanced ways Black women and girls perceive and value the experience of being acknowledged include:

> *It's important for my thoughts and opinions to be validated, especially when they involve the need for change and you expect tangible actions, especially when they pertain to necessary changes. Providers that demonstrate a clear understanding of my concerns, backed by evidence and experience in treating similar situations, helps build my trust and belief that the provider wants to support me and will tailor effective treatment to my circumstances. (Anonymous, personal communication, January 1, 2024)*

> *I understand the need for a complete and accurate assessment for a provider to do their job, however, there are ways that this could be accomplished in a more relational way. I am a person; it would be nice if they (clinicians) tried to understand my experiences rather than make assumptions. (Anonymous, personal communication, January 1, 2024)*

> *Being seen and heard entails receiving acknowledgment for my hard work and genuine recognition, going beyond superficial rewards. It involves not being burdened with others' responsibilities just because of my competence. It also means that when I voice a concern, it is thoroughly investigated and addressed, without fear of retaliation for speaking up. (Anonymous, personal communication, January 1, 2024)*

> *Being seen and heard is significant, especially in interactions with professionals. Having a doctor who is open to discussing anything and genuinely listens is truly gratifying. (Anonymous, personal communication, January 1, 2024)*

The way information is delivered is crucial in establishing a connection. Building a genuine connection involves conveying general interest and avoiding rigid or overly structured approaches. For Black clients, a genuine connection involves interactions with attunement, and without judgmental or invalidating attitudes (Oyer et al., 2016). During personal communications, I am often reminded that being seen and heard means having a connection where others can relate, empathize, and understand the client's perspective without judgment.

Assess and Observe Your Client's Ability to "Take Up Space"

Exploring whether your Black client feels they can *take up space* involves understanding their cultural context, societal expectations, and family dynamics. To *take up space* metaphorically refers to asserting oneself, being visible, and having one's presence acknowledged or felt in conversations, relationships, or societal contexts without feeling the need to shrink or conform to expectations. It often relates to individuals expressing their opinions, needs, or identity without hesitation or self-restriction. It is a sense of belonging, identity, and autonomy. Some Black women express the importance of providers creating spaces where she can simply be herself during a session as significant for feeling truly seen and heard, allowing her to take up space.

> *When a provider shows awareness of even small details about me, or demonstrates genuine interest by bringing up specific information, it fosters a sense of being recognized and valued, contributing to a positive therapeutic relationship. (Anonymous, personal communication, January 1, 2024)*

The intersectionality of race, culture, class, and gender can contribute to individuals feeling undeserving, affecting their sense of existence, voice, and value. In therapeutic spaces, these feelings can be exacerbated if one doesn't feel heard or valued. The internalization of these experiences may lead to self-doubt, strengthening beliefs of misconceptions or insignificance. The struggle to feel deserving of taking up space or having a voice becomes a complex and challenging aspect of one's mental health and self-perception. Addressing these concerns within therapeutic relationships is crucial for fostering a sense of value and empowerment.

GETTING TO KNOW YOUR CLIENT

As providers, we learn that it is important to build rapport with our clients, this includes Black women. Black women do not have the privilege to "hide" their Blackness or their gender: it's apparent. It's also not uncommon for human beings to make assumptions about others based on stereotypes and their lived experiences—this is *implicit bias*, the process of associating stereotypes or attitudes toward categories of people without conscious awareness.

Have you ever skipped screening a Black client for an eating disorder because you presumed they didn't have one? Have you assumed someone in a larger body has binge-eating disorder? Has your tone ever changed when meeting with Black clients? Have you ever thought that an "educated," professional Black woman does not experience microaggressions or oppressive behavior because of the privileges they possess? Each of these are examples of implicit bias.

Practical Tips: How to Explore Important Issues With Black Women

Assuming we all have implicit biases, how do you get to know your Black female client? You must ask the hard questions, demonstrating your desire to know your client. Small (2021a) recommends asking questions such as:

- What is most important to you about your culture/ethnicity?
- What has it been like for you growing up in a culture of racism?
- What role has the region where you grew up and/or where you currently live played in shaping your body image and beauty standards?
- If you are spiritual or religious, what role has your spirituality or religion played in shaping your body image and beauty standards?
- What role has your socioeconomic class played in shaping your body image and beauty standards?
- What role has your gender and/or sexual orientation played in shaping your body image and beauty standards?
- What role has your hair (your own, that of others around you, or that of others you have observed) played in shaping your body image and beauty standards?
- What role has body shape and weight (your own, that of others around you, or that of others you have observed) played in shaping your body image and beauty standards?

TRANSFERENCE AND COUNTERTRANSFERENCE

Transference refers to the unconscious redirection of feelings and desires from one person to another, often occurring in a therapeutic relationship where clients' emotions toward significant figures in their life are transferred onto the therapist. *Countertransference* refers to the provider's emotional reactions and responses to the client influenced by the provider's past experiences, feelings, and unresolved issues. It involves the therapist projecting their own emotions onto the client.

Both transference and countertransference are crucial aspects of the therapeutic process that require awareness and exploration to maintain objectivity and provide effective treatment. Transference and countertransference, if not addressed, can complicate the therapeutic relationship significantly. Clients may project their own self-critical thoughts onto their therapist, assuming the therapist shares similar struggles with body image and self-esteem issues related to weight. This dynamic can create hesitation in clients to openly discuss their feelings of shame about weight, fearing they might offend or upset a fat therapist (Kinavey & Cool, 2019). As a result, clients may withhold honest communication about their self-loathing to protect the therapist from negative discussions about weight. Additionally, the differing body sizes between therapist and client can also influence the therapeutic process, potentially impacting the effectiveness of the therapy.

Fat bodies are frequently stigmatized, with the belief that clinicians and physicians should embody personal responsibility by addressing their own weight (Hutson, 2013). This connection between body size and professionalism implies that fat therapists may confront a challenging set of assumptions about their professional competence (Moller & Tischner, 2019). Patients often perceive fat therapists as psychologically unhealthy and unfit for their professional roles. Therapists sometimes view fat patients as lacking self-discipline or inherently self-loathing, leading to generalized assumptions compared to their thin patients (Fahs, 2023). Fat patients who feel their therapists overly emphasize weight can feel less valued or understood due to their body size.

Have You Ever Avoided Asking a Question Because It Was Uncomfortable or Embarrassing?

Yes! Many of us possess the privilege to not answer questions that are uncomfortable or embarrassing. Several providers that I have worked with shared that earlier in their careers they avoided asking clients how it felt to meet with them, a White clinician, and if they had any concerns. One provider shared that it was in part because she was uncomfortable with conflict and feared that her "super awesome therapist ego" would be bruised or she would be seen as a "lesser" or incompetent therapist.

Providers may harbor a fear of making inadvertent cultural missteps, both on a personal and human level. This concern revolves around the worry of unintentionally causing offense related to a patient's culture, potentially creating a barrier in therapy. While they may feel they have the right to broach cultural and racial topics with patients, there is also an apprehension about potential judgment from others for suggesting or desiring cultural adaptations in the therapeutic process (Kanakam, 2022). This fear operates on a personal and human level, impacting the provider's approach to cultural discussions in therapy.

WORKING WITH OLDER ADULTS

The experiences and perspectives within the Black population, even within a particular generation, can vary significantly based on social location, cultural norms, beliefs, and generational differences. Being attuned to these nuances allows for a more accurate and respectful understanding of background and identity. When working with older Black women, considering these multifaceted influences is essential for tailoring interventions and support that align with their specific context and needs.

While age itself is not inherently problematic, the dynamics of the relationship may be influenced by factors such as generational gaps, cultural differences, and power dynamics. In some cases, a significant age difference may be acceptable and even beneficial, particularly if the clinician has expertise in a specific age-related area. While age differences can bring diverse perspectives, it's essential for the clinician to maintain a professional and empathetic stance, ensuring the Black client feels understood and respected regardless of age disparities. However, in therapy, it's crucial for clinicians to be aware of potential biases, assumptions, or differences in cultural references that can arise due to age disparities.

Older Black women, like anyone else, have diverse experiences, perspectives, and reasons for seeking treatment. Various forms of loss, including the loss of friends, family, or significant life roles for Black women, may contribute to disordered eating behaviors. Engaging in discussions about the life roles and transitions that Black women experience is crucial, as these factors can contribute to the development and perpetuation of disordered behaviors. Assuming that certain concerns are irrelevant or that individuals shouldn't care about specific issues due to their age overlooks the individuality of each person. It's essential for providers to approach each client with an open mind, acknowledging the complexity of their unique circumstances and beliefs.

MOVING FORWARD

Expertise develops from a combination of clinical and scientific training, theoretical understanding, experience, ongoing self-reflection, staying informed about current research, and engaging in continuous education and training (American Psychological Association, Presidential Task Force on Evidence-Based Practice, 2006). This multifaceted approach contributes to a clinician's ability to provide informed, effective, and ethical care to their clients. Providers who approach their work with Black clients from a place of humility and empathy are actively nurturing a commitment to cultural awareness and prioritizing the therapeutic alliance. By continually examining their biases and understanding how they manifest in their interactions, these providers ensure that their Black clients feel acknowledged and understood. While this approach may pose challenges, it encourages providers to adopt new perspectives in their client interactions, seek guidance, ask pertinent questions, and engage in ongoing learning. Clients benefit from providers that are dedicated to their personal growth and development, enhancing their effectiveness as treating professionals.

Chapter 6

HOW DO I ADOPT TREATMENT TECHNIQUES AND RECOMMENDATIONS FOR BLACK WOMEN?

We have encountered numerous clients, family members, friends, and parents who express a strong desire to connect with health care providers who truly understand their needs. This often means professionals who share their racial or ethnic background, and possibly gender expression. However, finding such representation is often difficult.

This prompts important questions: How likely are patients to pursue treatment if they cannot find a provider who shares their background? Do they seek support—whether for physical or mental health—from providers who do not look like them? And if they do, how consistently do they return for ongoing care versus occasional visits?

Additionally, the availability of culturally responsive care can significantly impact the quality and effectiveness of health care interactions for minority patients. When Black women seek mental health services, they encounter disparities: less access to care compared to White women, heightened crisis points, frequent misdiagnoses, and premature treatment withdrawal due to unmet ethnic, cultural, and gender-specific needs (see also Chapter 3; Jones & Guy-Sheftall, 2017). This highlights systemic biases in current mental health systems and treatment models, rooted in racist and patriarchal frameworks (see also Chapter 5; Moussa-Tooks et al., 2024; Jones & Guy-Sheftall, 2017). Urgent development of new models is necessary to effectively meet the diverse needs of women across all racial backgrounds.

Evidence-based treatment (EBT) refers to therapeutic practices and interventions that have been rigorously tested and validated through scientific research and clinical trials. Considered the benchmark in health care, EBT integrates the latest research findings, clinical expertise, and patient values, offering a structured approach to enhance the quality, safety, reliability, and effectiveness of patient care (Rittenhouse, 2021a). While EBT aims to provide scientifically grounded treatment, it acknowledges individual variability, promoting adaptability to meet diverse patient needs (Rittenhouse, 2021a). Ultimately, EBT ensures optimal treatment standards by combining empirical evidence, clinical insight, and patient-centered care.

That said, the underrepresentation of Black and other minoritized populations, such as Latinx people, in clinical trials for eating disorders raises significant concerns about the applicability and effectiveness of current evidence-based treatments, which were primarily developed and tested on European White individuals (Reyes-Rodriguez & Franko, 2020). This gap highlights the pressing need for culturally responsive interventions tailored to diverse cultural contexts. Culture significantly influences therapeutic processes, and adapting interventions accordingly can enhance their effectiveness. Recognizing this need, the field has increasingly emphasized the importance of cultural adaptations of EBTs. These adaptations involve systematically modifying EBTs to align with clients' cultural backgrounds and contexts (Haft et al., 2022).

Research indicates that culturally adapted interventions yield promising outcomes for diverse groups (Haft et al., 2022). Studies, including randomized controlled trials, reveal that Black and ethnically diverse populations experience significant symptom improvement with culturally adapted interventions compared to non-adapted treatments (Haft et al., 2022). This reinforces the importance of cultural responsiveness in enhancing the effectiveness and relevance of treatments for diverse populations with eating disorders.

Unfortunately, not all providers adapt EBT to individual needs, including those of Black clients. It's crucial to explore clients' cultural experiences, acknowledging that best practices may differ from standardized EBTs. Providers should listen to clients and integrate treatments that align with their unique needs and experiences, especially in conditions like eating disorders.

When choosing a treatment approach, it's crucial to incorporate your Black clients' cultural, ethnic, and racial backgrounds. These clients may experience unique intersectional needs due to the overlapping challenges of their marginalized identities. Many theoretical orientations are not standardized on people of color, and the presentations of Black women cannot be neatly categorized within Eurocentric descriptions.

Integrating humanism and *relational-cultural theory* (RCT) can effectively support your client, given their complementary nature. This combined approach aims to recognize and address the distinct sociocultural and psychological experiences of Black individuals, enhancing therapeutic outcomes (Mason et al., 2024). It's essential to recognize that avoiding discussions about race with clients can perpetuate feelings of being overlooked and disregarded. While providers may fear being insensitive by constantly addressing race, clients often feel the opposite—they appreciate when their racial identity is acknowledged and respected. For them, racial identity is not something they can ignore; it shapes their daily experiences and interactions. They long to be seen and valued as individuals beyond their racial identity as Black women.

Consider adopting a feminist therapy as it seeks to empower women by addressing societal gender inequalities, such as prescribed sex roles and female socialization (Jones & Guy-Sheftall, 2017). This approach attributes mental health issues to disparities within patriarchal structures (Jones & Guy-Sheftall, 2017). Understanding the historical context of feminism helps contextualize its integration into mental health practices. In therapeutic work with Black women, it's essential to empower them to confront negative cultural messages and manage societal expectations that influence their experiences. By acquiring and applying new skills, Black women may experience reduced psychiatric symptoms.

FOR HEALING TO OCCUR

As mentioned in Chapter 1, treating eating disorders requires a multidisciplinary team consisting of a primary care physician (PCP), dietitian, psychiatrist, and therapist (see also Chapter 7). This chapter provides a theoretical overview of various evidence-based treatments that have been shown to effectively address eating disorders therapeutically. Eating disorders are emotional disorders characterized by disordered eating behaviors that stem from emotional distress. They often arise as a way for individuals to cope with intense feelings, manage internal conflicts, and regain a sense of control amid life's chaos. As providers approach eating disorders as emotional disorders, theoretical approaches prioritize addressing the underlying emotional distress that perpetuates disordered eating behaviors and associated comorbidities. These approaches are designed to empower clients by equipping them with essential skills to recognize, tolerate, and effectively manage their emotions. By fostering psychological flexibility, clients learn to respond adaptively to emotional challenges and reduce reliance on maladaptive coping mechanisms such as disordered eating.

Understanding the function of an eating disorder is pivotal in tailoring treatment approaches and choosing suitable theoretical frameworks or treatment models (Jones & Guy-Sheftall, 2017). This insight provides essential information without implying perfect alignment. For instance, a Black client's avoidance of discussing their eating disorder may reveal its significance to them. Therapies delve into the intricate emotional triggers that precipitate unhelpful behaviors, aiming to cultivate strategies that promote constructive management of these triggers.

Concurrently, theoretical frameworks integrate interventions tailored to manage co-occurring mental health conditions, recognizing the interconnectedness of emotional well-being with overall recovery. Ultimately, these approaches seek to not only alleviate symptoms but also to empower clients with the tools and resilience needed for sustained emotional health and lasting recovery from eating disorders. How do these theoretical orientations specifically address these issues when working with Black clients? Are they effective?

COGNITIVE BEHAVIORAL THERAPY (CBT) AND COGNITIVE BEHAVIORAL THERAPY FOR EATING DISORDERS (CBT-E)

Cognitive behavioral therapy (CBT) is the most widely used and evidence-based treatment for a variety of mental health disorders, including eating disorders. CBT is a versatile treatment used across various mental health conditions, aiming to modify negative thought patterns and behaviors through interventions like cognitive restructuring and exposure therapy (Fleming, 2024; Rittenhouse, 2021a).

CBT is built on two key principles crucial for its effectiveness. First, therapists conceptualize clients using a cognitive framework, positing that the meanings clients ascribe to their experiences influence their emotional, behavioral, and physiological responses (The Beck Institute for Cognitive Behavior

Therapy, 2024). These automatic thoughts about situations are connected to deeper beliefs about themselves, their world, others, and the future.

Second, building a strong therapeutic alliance with clients is essential (The Beck Institute for Cognitive Behavior Therapy, 2024). This alliance fosters collaboration and encourages clients to engage fully in the therapeutic process, both during sessions and in applying learned techniques in their daily lives. Together, these principles underscore the adaptability of CBT across various mental health issues, ensuring tailored and effective treatment strategies.

Cognitive behavioral therapy for eating disorders (CBT-E), which is closely related to CBT, is specifically tailored for individuals with eating disorders, such as anorexia nervosa, bulimia nervosa, and binge-eating disorder. CBT-E progresses through stages including establishing a therapeutic alliance, addressing specific eating behaviors, targeting broader psychological aspects like body image concerns, and focusing on relapse prevention (Fairburn, 2008). It employs techniques like regular eating patterns, self-monitoring, and challenging cognitive distortions related to food and body image, highlighting the need to address the unique psychopathology of eating disorders for effective treatment outcomes (Fairburn, 2008).

Limitations of CBT and CBT-E

While the significance of cognitive processes is widely acknowledged, this understanding has not consistently included Black people. There is a prevailing assumption that cognitive behavioral frameworks, deemed central to various disorders, apply universally across cultures (Carter & Sbrocco, 2018). However, recent evidence suggests otherwise. Over the past decade, studies have increasingly shown that the study and treatment of anxiety among Black individuals may require modifications in measurement and approach (Carter & Sbrocco, 2018; Reyes-Rodriguez & Franko, 2020). Specifically, several recent studies indicate that standard anxiety measures developed from a cognitive perspective and validated primarily among non-Hispanic Caucasians may not be psychometrically equivalent for measuring anxiety among Black people (Carter & Sbrocco, 2018).

When working with Black clients, it's crucial to be mindful of the language used in therapy. For instance, a limitation of CBT is the term *distorted thinking* or suggesting that a Black client needs to reframe their thoughts. This can imply that something is inherently wrong with the client, a perception many eating disorder clients already struggle with. CBT implies that the client needs to learn how to recognize one's distortions in thinking that contribute to difficulties, and then reassess them based on reality.

For Black clients, this issue can be further compounded by their experiences with racial and gender discrimination. Clinicians should explore how past experiences, including racial and historical trauma, influence their current thought patterns. Providers are encouraged to be sensitive in addressing thoughts that may be considered faulty within cognitive behavioral therapy, ensuring sensitivity for the broader context of the client's experiences.

Treatment effectiveness may vary between Black individuals and non-Hispanic Caucasians, partly due to historical oversight of cultural factors in understanding behavioral and medical conditions. Research has often neglected the impact of ethnic identity and culture on mental health assessments and the importance of culturally sensitive treatment approaches for Black individuals (Carter & Sbrocco, 2018). While this study did not pertain to eating disorders, researchers contend that most studies on anxiety among Black people have relied on a static definition of ethnicity (Carter & Sbrocco, 2018).

Treatment Efficacy

CBT has proven effective in treating a range of eating disorder diagnoses, including specific methods like CBT-BN for bulimia nervosa, CBT-E (enhanced CBT), and CBT for binge-eating disorder (CBT-BED). Given the underrepresentation of Black individuals and other people of color in the development of evidence-based treatments, providers using a CBT approach must consider potential biases and the impact of diversity gaps on the applicability of CBT to Black clients.

Often, clients may not discuss their experiences with racism in therapy unless prompted. Therefore, CBT therapists must proactively ask Black clients about their encounters with racism and discrimination and explore how these may impact their difficulties or challenges. Adapted CBT has been shown to effectively empower Black clients to address inadequate care, even when providers have internalized anti-Black attitudes (Fleming, 2024).

Failing to address these issues can reduce treatment effectiveness, while insensitivity in these discussions can lead to ruptures in the therapeutic relationship and result in premature termination. Incorporating a lens of racism when conceptualizing clients who have experienced it helps us understand why

Black clients may have strong negative reactions to certain situations, why they develop specific coping strategies, why they remain vigilant for potential harm, and why they often feel disempowered (see also Chapter 3). This approach underscores the importance of adapted psychoeducation, problem-solving, cognitive restructuring, and skills training for those who have encountered both blatant and indirect racism. Equally crucial is creating opportunities for racial empowerment, which includes consciousness raising and fostering racial pride.

An adapted cognitive-behavioral intervention for Black and minoritized individuals addresses the impact of systemic racism and marginalization on anxiety and vigilance, which contribute to mental health issues (Moussa-Tooks et al., 2024). By focusing on culturally specific stressors, this approach optimizes treatment outcomes. It allows providers to gain deeper insights into client experiences and effectively address relevant behavioral elements. This supportive method acknowledges and normalizes experiences with systemic racism, fostering awareness and creating a secure environment for reflection and therapeutic action (Moussa-Tooks et al., 2024). While the adapted intervention addresses systemic racism and minoritization, it may not fully account for other external factors affecting therapy effectiveness.

DIALECTICAL BEHAVIOR THERAPY (DBT)

Dialectical behavior therapy (DBT) is a type of cognitive therapy developed by Marsha Linehan. DBT emphasizes the integration of opposites, referred to as the dialectical (Haft et al., 2022). This is intended to combat an individual's black-and-white thinking and subsequent choices by emphasizing that one can be happy and stressed, love someone and be angry with them, or miss their eating disorder and acknowledge it is not good for them. DBT advocates for the acceptance of clients while also encouraging them to make positive changes, representing the therapy's core philosophy of dialectics (balancing opposites) (Linehan, 2015). This balance is integral to the therapy's approach to managing emotional dysregulation and its related issues.

DBT emphasizes teaching core skills such as *mindfulness* (existing in the present moment without judgment), *distress tolerance* (tolerating distress when the situation cannot be changed), *emotion regulation* (regulating uncomfortable emotion-states), and *interpersonal effectiveness* (communicating needs and boundaries while maintaining relationships) (Linehan, 2015). These skills are essential for improving mood stability, reducing maladaptive behaviors, and fostering recovery, especially in individuals with eating disorders. By focusing on both acceptance and change, DBT helps clients manage complex emotions and relationships, recognizing that conflicting feelings can coexist (Rittenhouse, 2021a).

Treatment Efficacy

Some scholars believe that individualized, behavior-focused therapies like DBT may inherently accommodate cultural differences because they are tailored to each person's unique characteristics (Haft et al., 2022). However, this assumption might overlook the need for these treatments to be effectively applicable to all racial, ethnic, and cultural groups, many of which were not represented in the original DBT studies.

Cultural adaptations involve cultural competence and sensitivity, emphasizing clinician awareness of cultural factors (see also Chapter 5; Benuto et al., 2021). While awareness is cognitive, delivering culturally adapted psychotherapy, particularly DBT, is primarily behavioral. Thus, a comprehensive conceptualization of cultural adaptations should integrate behavioral elements of treatment delivery, such as skill assignments and clinician–client interactions, alongside cognitive aspects like case formulations and cultural knowledge (Benuto et al., 2021). This approach is considered most beneficial to the field, ensuring that evidence-based treatments are systematically modified to align with individual cultural patterns, meanings, and values (Haft et al., 2022).

However, this definition leaves room for interpretation regarding what constitutes an adaptation. Adaptations can range from superficial changes, such as incorporating quotes from culturally significant figures to substantial adjustments, like omitting or replacing DBT skills to better fit the client's cultural environment. The use of therapist self-disclosure is not an adaptation specific to cultural contexts, as sharing personal information and engaging in personal interactions with clients is a common practice in DBT therapy.

Grasping what defines cultural adaptation within DBT is especially challenging, given that DBT is intrinsically designed to be adaptable to diverse cultural contexts. DBT is inherently *ideographically* (customized to the unique characteristics, needs, and situations) sensitive to clients (Haft et al., 2022). In contrast, the *nomothetic* approach seeks universal principles applicable to all (Haft et al., 2022). In essence, the complexity lies in distinguishing between standard personalization in DBT and adaptations specifically made for cultural considerations, given that DBT therapists are expected to integrate each client's cultural background into their therapy. This personalized approach makes it challenging to clearly define which modifications are solely due to cultural factors, as opposed to the broader goal of tailoring therapy to meet the client's individual needs and context.

DBT offers unique benefits that can be enhanced through adaptation, including accurate communication of emotional nuances that may be misinterpreted when seeking support. It is important to explicitly address historical and intergenerational trauma, acculturative stress, cultural differences, discrimination, and racism in treatment. This should also be considered in understanding maladaptive behaviors, such as disordered eating in Black adolescents, which may be a response to racial stressors rather than a desire for thinness as seen in their White counterparts (Kamody et al., 2020). Validating acculturative stress as a significant environmental stressor is essential (Cheng & Merrick, 2017).

Consider a Black client who is struggling with body image issues, emotion dysregulation, and feelings of invalidation. The client explores the dialectic between understanding how her eating disorder hurts her body and is a form of self-punishment, objectification, and oppression, while also identifying it as necessary, when in certain spaces her body helps to keep her safe. The client learns to recognize and verbalize the conflict between engaging in disordered eating behaviors to conform to certain beauty standards or to protect herself in environments where she feels unsafe, versus the long-term harm these behaviors cause.

For instance, the client might discuss how they feel pressured to maintain a certain body type to avoid negative judgments or to fit in with peers, while also understanding that these behaviors are detrimental to her health. Through DBT, the client develops a more compassionate relationship with her body and begins to challenge these harmful patterns. The therapist helps the client to find alternative, healthier ways to cope with her environment, reinforcing the importance of her long-term well-being and self-worth over short-term safety mechanisms.

What is required of a provider that practices DBT? How do they demonstrate an understanding of their Black client's cultural influences? What steps should a DBT provider take to incorporate cultural adaptations for Black clients? To integrate cultural adaptations to effectively address the unique cultural influences of their Black clients, the DBT provider might:

- Explore the client's dual perspectives on their eating disorder as both harmful and protective.
- Address cultural norms and stereotypes about body image, recognizing societal pressures on emotional distress.
- Validate the client's experiences while challenging unhelpful beliefs and behaviors.
- Help the client reconcile conflicting thoughts about their eating disorder, fostering self-awareness and acceptance.
- Adapt mindfulness and distress tolerance skills for the client's safety and coping needs.
- Collaborate with the client to create a treatment plan respecting their cultural values and autonomy.
- Use culturally sensitive language and examples when discussing body image and self-acceptance.
- Examine how racial and cultural identity intersect with the client's body image concerns, enhancing understanding of their experiences.

This culturally adaptive approach ensures that DBT interventions are not only effective but also responsive to the nuanced challenges faced by Black clients dealing with body image issues. By integrating cultural considerations into the therapeutic process, the provider can better support the client's journey toward healing and self-acceptance.

FAMILY-BASED THERAPY (FBT)

Family-based treatment (FBT) for eating disorders is a specialized, evidence-based approach designed for adolescents, where the family assumes a pivotal role in the therapeutic journey. The therapist in FBT is considered an expert consultant, while parents are viewed as the experts on their child and family (Rienecke & Le Grange, 2022). This collaborative method unfolds across three structured phases, integrating professional guidance with active familial participation. While initially designed for treating anorexia, FBT has also been adapted to treat bulimia.

Initially, therapists empower families to support their child's weight restoration, offering compassionate guidance and establishing boundaries tailored to observed family dynamics (Rittenhouse, 2021a). The goal is for parents to help their loved one establish healthy, normalized, non-diet eating habits and to monitor the period after meals to deter compensatory actions (Le Grange & Lock, 2007). For this to be effective, it is essential that the parents collaborate closely. The child or adolescent is encouraged to participate in this effort. If the client has siblings, it is recommended that they offer nonjudgmental support to the adolescent throughout this process.

As treatment progresses, families gradually transition control back to the adolescent, while therapists address and resolve any family dynamics that may exacerbate the disorder (Le Grange & Lock, 2007). The final phase emphasizes nurturing the adolescent's independence alongside sustained family support, essential for fostering recovery and cultivating a resilient adolescent identity (Rittenhouse, 2021a). By harnessing the family's strengths and commitment, FBT provides a flexible yet powerful framework to restore health and establish normalcy for adolescents navigating eating disorders.

Family-based therapy offers distinct advantages and disadvantages. A significant benefit is its inclusion of the family in the treatment process, which is less common in other approaches. FBT involves separating the illness from the adolescent and recognizing that the adolescent is not intentionally being difficult or stubborn, but rather is being influenced by a powerful disorder (Rienecke & Le Grange, 2022). This perspective helps parents to focus on fighting the illness rather than blaming or criticizing their child. Involving the family in treatment fosters ongoing familial support, potentially making it easier for the child or adolescent to rely on their family when urges increase or when they engage in behaviors. Extensive research indicates that family and caregiver involvement significantly enhance recovery and leads to better treatment outcomes (Rittenhouse, 2021a).

Additionally, FBT assists families in increasing effective communication, establishing healthy boundaries, and strengthening relationships during treatment. However, this approach may be less feasible for individuals requiring more intensive care. A limitation of FBT is that it is not easily applicable in higher levels of care, such as hospitalization or residential treatment.

There are several challenges associated with FBT. These include the significant time commitment required from both therapists and families and the absence of a dietitian on the treatment team. Additionally, FBT's strict protocols limit the ability to tailor treatment to the unique needs of each family. FBT prioritizes early behavioral change over exploring the underlying mechanisms that sustain an eating disorder. The primary objective is to achieve rapid symptom reduction and weight restoration, thereby minimizing long-term damage and preventing the disorder from becoming deeply ingrained in the adolescent's personality and identity (Rienecke & Le Grange, 2022).

Therapists focus on food-related behaviors and attitudes specific to the eating disorder, rather than delving into deeper psychological or cognitive factors. FBT recognizes that underlying psychological or cognitive factors may contribute to the development and persistence of an eating disorder, but it does not prioritize extensive exploration of these factors (Rienecke & Le Grange, 2022). Instead, the focus is on immediate behavioral changes, anticipating that improvements in physical health will positively influence emotional and psychological well-being over time. It is important to note that FBT does not overlook the importance of understanding the fundamental mechanisms that sustain eating disorders.

Treatment Efficacy

Family-based therapy often overlooks the socioeconomic status of clients. It relies on caregivers managing recovery at home, which may not be possible for clients who must work full time or who are single parents. For Black clients, it's important to distinguish between individualistic and collectivistic beliefs, as these can significantly influence parenting styles. Understanding these cultural dynamics is crucial because they affect how parents interact with their children and how family dynamics operate.

Providers can adjust by first acknowledging and respecting the cultural and racial beliefs of Black clients. This involves actively listening to their perspectives on parenting and family dynamics, recognizing the impact of systemic racism and socioeconomic factors on their experiences. Adjustments in therapy may include adapting interventions to align with cultural values, promoting communal support systems, and integrating culturally sensitive approaches such as incorporating rituals or traditions that are meaningful to the family. By incorporating these cultural considerations, therapists can ensure that their approach is inclusive and effective, enhancing the therapeutic process for Black families within the framework of family-based therapy.

UNIFIED TREATMENT MODEL

The Unified Protocol (UP) for Emotional Disorders, a form of cognitive behavioral therapy (CBT) (Barlow & Long, 2023), is a transdiagnostic treatment approach that addresses common underlying mechanisms of emotional disorders like anxiety and depression (Ayuso-Bartol et al., 2024). Transdiagnostic treatments emerged because traditional therapy, which addressed issues individually, didn't align with the reality of patients who had multiple concerns they wanted to address. The Unified Protocol (UP) was developed specifically to address these challenges. It is a single treatment designed to target a variety of problems, facilitating the delivery of evidence-based care by psychologists, psychiatrists, social workers, and mental health counselors. The UP equips therapists with a versatile tool to effectively support a diverse range of patients (Unified Protocol Institute, n.d.).

By focusing on shared processes rather than specific symptoms, the UP aims to improve emotion regulation strategies, reduce symptoms, and enhance overall quality of life and social adjustment (Ayuso-Bartol et al., 2024; Ferreres-Galan et al., 2024). The protocol is designed to apply across various diagnostic categories and can be administered in group settings, enhancing its flexibility and efficiency as a treatment option.

The Unified Protocol (UP) has several limitations that need consideration. Its generalizability may be limited across different populations and cultural contexts, necessitating further research to determine its effectiveness in diverse settings. While the UP uses a transdiagnostic approach, individual variations in symptom presentation and treatment response may require further tailoring or additional interventions. The success of the UP also depends on the expertise of therapists trained in delivering the protocol, which may pose challenges in settings with limited access to trained professionals. The UP focuses primarily on emotional disorders and may not address the unique aspects of specific diagnoses, indicating that some individuals might benefit more from specialized treatments tailored to their specific conditions (Ferreres-Galan et al., 2024).

The Unified Protocol (UP) acknowledges the importance of cultural adaptivity for marginalized populations (i.e., Black clients). The UP validates the need for therapists to deliver therapy that is both culturally sensitive and effective (Ferreres-Galan et al., 2024). It is important to consider cultural factors and tailor the treatment to meet the unique needs and experiences of Black individuals. The UP emphasizes building trust, addressing racial and ethnic stressors, recognizing intersectionality, empowering clients, and promoting cultural competence among therapists (Ayuso-Bartol et al., 2024; Barlow & Long, 2023). Additionally, ensuring responsiveness to diverse patient needs involves addressing stigma, remaining mindful of biases, and collaborating with other treating professionals. By incorporating these considerations, therapists can provide culturally responsive therapy that respects and supports the unique experiences and needs of Black clients.

Overview

With the support of eating disorder research and clinical experts, The Unified Treatment Model for Eating Disorders® (UTM) was developed by The Renfrew Center based on the Unified Protocol (UP), The UTM is a comprehensive and evidence-based approach to treating eating disorders. It integrates various evidence-based techniques and interventions to address common elements and symptoms associated with these disorders. The UTM focuses on and includes structured interventions for enhancing motivation, promoting emotion awareness and acceptance, cognitive appraisal and reappraisal, managing avoidance and emotion-driven behaviors, improving interoceptive awareness and tolerance, and conducting emotion exposures (Thompson-Brenner et al., 2021b). It aims to address both the symptoms and the underlying emotional difficulties associated with eating disorders.

The UTM conceptualizes eating disorders as largely driven by emotional intolerance, avoidance, and relational disconnection (Thompson-Brenner et al., 2021a). At its core, the UTM emphasizes the importance of relationships and community in psychological health, involving patients and their families in goal-setting and ongoing assessment to foster a supportive environment. The treatment is holistic and evidence-based, addressing the whole person and targeting both symptoms and diagnoses using best practices. With a focus on building resilience, the UTM explicitly targets underlying emotional factors driving symptoms and promotes emotional and relational resilience, aiming for sustainable recovery (Thompson-Brenner et al., 2021a).

While the UTM has several benefits—including its transdiagnostic approach, evidence-based interventions, focus on emotion regulation, comprehensive structure, and relational-cultural principles (see below)—it also has limitations. These include limited research, challenges with generalizability, difficulties addressing comorbid conditions, adaptation challenges, and limited guidance for adaptation (Thompson-Brenner et al., 2021a). Despite these limitations, the UTM's strengths lie in its ability to provide sustained therapeutic effects and offer structured, evidence-based care for individuals struggling with eating disorders.

Treatment Efficacy

Staff adherence to the treatment model is regularly evaluated and staff are provided recommendations and corrections to develop clinician competence and confidence with the manualized treatment. Given that membership in diverse racial, ethnic, and cultural groups is often associated with inequitable health and mental health outcomes for diverse populations, the UTM was intentionally developed to be inclusive in terms of materials used and programming offered. For example, the manual infuses culturally diverse examples throughout the modules and worksheets include representation from varying groups. The Renfrew Center also offers a variety of support groups so people from a variety of cultures and backgrounds can find a supportive community while they prioritize their eating disorder recovery.

In the spirit of contributing to eating disorder literature, The Renfrew Center has been collecting data to evaluate the effectiveness of the Unified Treatment approach applied to eating disorder patients and to help inform clinical changes to improve treatment outcomes. All patients at The Renfrew Center are given research surveys to complete (with patient/guardian consent) at admission, discharge, and six months following discharge from treatment. The surveys gather clinical information related to various concerns including eating disorder symptoms and severity, depressive symptoms, and anxiety symptoms. The outcomes have been published in several peer-reviewed journals (Thompson-Brenner et al., 2019; Thompson-Brenner et al., 2021a).

On average, patients who attended residential treatment for at least a week showed improvement in their eating disorder behaviors, depression, and emotional avoidance when they received the Unified Treatment. When comparing patient outcomes by race, there were minimal group differences between White and Black patients. While sample size was small (only 34 patients who identified as Black), there were no differences in level of eating disorder, anxiety, and depressive symptoms at time of discharge and six-months-following residential treatment. While more research is needed in this area, this may indicate that the UTM is equally effective for White and Black patients. In summary, The UTM facilitates patient progress during treatment, with those gains largely sustained after discharge.

ADDITIONAL TREATMENT APPROACHES OF INTEREST

Acceptance and Commitment Therapy (ACT)

Acceptance and commitment therapy (ACT) is a form of CBT that emphasizes mindfulness skills and the concept of *psychological flexibility.* This approach involves embracing the present moment without judgment, prioritizing long-term values and goals over short-term impulses and emotions (Rittenhouse, 2021a). ACT encourages individuals to accept reality and commit to adapting in ways that align with their values, even if they cannot change the situation. By fostering a compassionate relationship with negative beliefs, individuals can learn to let go of them.

ACT supports individuals in overcoming psychological challenges and promoting meaningful life changes by integrating mindfulness and acceptance strategies with commitment and behavior change techniques (Fogelkvist et al., 2021). Widely applied in treating conditions such as eating disorders, anxiety, depression, and substance abuse, ACT helps individuals enhance their well-being through adaptive coping and values-driven actions. It addresses underlying processes rather than specific symptoms, making it applicable across various mental health conditions (Fogelkvist et al., 2021). By integrating its principles into daily life, ACT enhances overall well-being through a holistic, transdiagnostic approach.

Exposure and Response Prevention Therapy (ERP)

Exposure and response prevention (ERP) is a therapeutic approach that deliberately involves exposing individuals to the stimuli that trigger distress or disordered behaviors (Rittenhouse, 2021a). Clients are guided to employ coping strategies to handle their emotional reactions, rather than falling back on disordered behaviors to escape or suppress these feelings.

For instance, a person with an eating disorder may be gradually exposed to fear foods, binge eating triggers, or asked to confront body image after weight restoration, all while learning and practicing skills to deal with the discomfort that arises, instead of relying on their eating disorder behaviors to cope. This approach can be effective because individuals are not simply taught skills and isolated from their triggers. Rather, they face those triggers head on and learn how to maintain recovery in their immediate environment that is activating.

Interpersonal Psychotherapy (IPT)

Interpersonal psychotherapy (IPT) is an effective cognitive therapy for eating disorders. By focusing on interpersonal issues and improving relationships, IPT addresses relationship conflicts, significant life changes, grief, and difficulties in maintaining supportive connections, all of which can trigger disordered behaviors (Russell et al., 2023). IPT reduces symptoms and enhances outcomes by developing coping strategies for life changes, conflict resolution, and improving communication and boundary-setting (Russell et al., 2023; Rittenhouse, 2021a). It can be applied independently or integrated with other therapies like CBT or FBT to support recovery efforts.

Medical Nutrition Therapy

All individuals diagnosed with eating disorders should receive nutrition therapy as part of their treatment. Nutrition therapy, which is based on the premise that malnutrition exacerbates both physical and mental health, is frequently combined with other cognitive therapies to address the effects of malnourishment on overall well-being (Rittenhouse, 2021b). As a reminder, all eating disorders, regardless of behavior or presentation, involve malnutrition that requires nutritional support. The treatment emphasizes educating individuals about nutrition interventions that promote optimal physical and cognitive performance. It encourages consistent engagement in these nutritional choices to sustain both physical and psychological well-being.

Relational Cultural Theory (RCT)

Relational cultural theory (RCT) is a psychological framework and therapeutic approach that emphasizes the pivotal role of relationships in human development and well-being (Jean Baker Miller Training Institute, 2024). It asserts that relationships are fundamental to personal growth, highlighting the importance of connection, mutual empathy, and authenticity. RCT promotes growth-fostering relationships characterized by empowerment and acknowledges the profound impact of connection and disconnection on well-being. Integrating principles from feminist, multicultural, and psychodynamic counseling approaches, RCT emphasizes the therapeutic relationship and relational tools in the healing process (Jean Baker Miller Training Institute, 2024; Russell et al., 2023). Supported by research, RCT enhances counseling practices by addressing power dynamics, privilege, oppression, and marginalization, fostering empathy and empowerment in therapeutic settings (Frey, 2013). RCT underscores how relational experiences shape individual development and psychological health.

Key principles include emphasizing connection, empathy, and mutual empowerment while addressing cultural and social contexts. RCT aims to nurture authentic relationships, tackle power dynamics and social inequalities, and facilitate healing and growth through resilience and transformative dialogue (Jean Baker Miller Training Institute, 2024). Widely applied in therapeutic contexts, RCT effectively treats various mental health issues, including eating disorders, depression, anxiety, trauma, and relationship challenges (Russell et al., 2023).

WORKING WITH OLDER ADULTS

Throughout this chapter, we have emphasized the need for cultural adaptations in treatment; similarly, age-specific adaptations are crucial. Targeted strategies are necessary to increase the inclusion of older people of color in mental health research. Cultural adaptations of mental health programs are vital for addressing the unique mental health needs of older people of color, ensuring that models of care consider their social and cultural contexts. Racism and discrimination stand as the leading causes of mental health care disparities among older people of color, underscoring the urgency of tailored approaches (Jimenez et al., 2022). Moreover, effective mental health care for ethnically diverse older adults in primary care requires consideration of their cultural beliefs and treatment preferences, thereby promoting better clinical outcomes.

Cynthia Bulik (2013) highlights the scarcity of evidence-based treatments for eating disorders in midlife and the complexities involved. As mentioned earlier in this chapter, evidence-based treatment does not guarantee effectiveness for everyone, it means that a treatment has been shown to be more effective than no treatment. As we seek culturally responsive treatments for Black individuals, we must also ensure the same consideration for older Black women (Bulik, 2013). In the realm of eating disorder treatment for older adults, there exists limited published information, primarily comprising case studies and clinical commentaries (Jimenez et al., 2022). Predominantly, cases involve anorexia nervosa, with fewer instances of bulimia nervosa or unspecified eating disorders. Treatment approaches currently lack consistency, though multidimensional methods show promise as the most effective. Persistent challenges include chronic illness, very low body mass index, and difficulties in treatment engagement, often hindering sustained improvement (Jimenez et al., 2022).

Additionally, comorbid mood disorders frequently influence treatment outcomes. Recognizing and addressing eating disorders among older adults is crucial, necessitating the development of tailored treatment approaches. While multimodal strategies generally yield positive outcomes, a standardized management approach remains elusive. Future research should concentrate on developing and executing trials to establish age-appropriate clinical guidelines for individuals aged 65 and older, ensuring these guidelines incorporate the diverse needs of older people of color (Jimenez et al., 2022).

Evidence-based treatments, when culturally and age-adapted, are highly effective in addressing the diverse needs of clients. Integrating cultural and age-related adaptations into treatment approaches is vital for improving the effectiveness and acceptance of interventions across diverse populations. By systematically modifying evidence-based treatments to align with clients' cultural backgrounds and age-specific needs, clinicians can ensure their practice is both inclusive and effective (Mishu et al., 2023). This approach upholds treatment fidelity while respecting and valuing the unique cultural and developmental contexts of each individual, leading to better clinical outcomes.

MOVING FORWARD

When selecting a treatment approach, it is crucial to be flexible and inclusive of your clients' cultural, ethnic, racial backgrounds, and age. Culturally and age-adapted interventions have shown to be effective in reducing symptoms of depression and anxiety, indicating that incorporating these factors into evidence-based therapies can uphold treatment fidelity, despite being a complex process (Mishu et al., 2023). Adaptations are essential for enhancing the acceptance and effectiveness of treatments among diverse racial, ethnic, cultural, and age groups. In collectivist cultures, which prioritize community and interconnectedness, adaptations should reflect these values, contrasting with individualist cultures that emphasize independence and uniqueness. Similarly, treatments should be adapted to the developmental stage of the client, addressing age-specific concerns and developmental milestones.

A comprehensive approach to adaptation incorporates both behavioral elements, such as skill assignments, psychoeducation, and clinician–client interactions; and cognitive elements, like case formulations and clinician cultural knowledge. One widely accepted definition of cultural adaptation is the systematic modification of an evidence-based treatment or intervention protocol to consider language, culture, context, and age, ensuring compatibility with the individual's cultural patterns, meanings, values, and developmental stage (Mishu et al., 2023; Reyes-Rodriguez & Franko, 2020). Adaptations can be classified into therapist-related adjustments (e.g., ethnic matching, provider language proficiency), content-related modifications (e.g., use of culturally sensitive terms, translation of materials), and organization-specific changes (Haft et al., 2022). These categories enable tailored approaches that respect and incorporate the cultural patterns, meanings, values, and developmental needs of individuals, enhancing the accessibility and effectiveness of interventions in clinical practice.

Chapter 7

HOW DO I HELP BLACK WOMEN REIMAGINE A HEALTHIER RELATIONSHIP WITH FOOD AND THEIR BODIES?

A group of Black women engaged in a conversation about body image, weight, and the desire to lose weight, among other topics. Their discussion flowed seamlessly, like a stream of shared consciousness, with their thoughts aligning so closely that it felt as though they were speaking with one voice.

My exact thoughts. Damn these kids f*cked me up! I probably wouldn't have this gut if it wasn't for them. . . . I need to go ahead and invest in getting my body done. It's so hard for me to eat right and exercise. I can go hard on one and lack the energy for the other. I need a balance, but I don't know how. I know high blood pressure and diabetes run in my family and I don't comply with meds so for my kids' sake I try to eat healthier or exercise to try to extend my lifespan. Also, my health plays a major role that helps me get on board with weight loss. Diets don't work for me, it's hard being pleasantly plump, and working out is so hard to stick to. I want to look better in my clothes and out of them. I want my body to be more muscular as opposed to flabby. Honestly, when I think about dieting and all that, I usually feel like it's such a balancing act. I know it's important to stay healthy, but sometimes it can feel like a lot of pressure. I just try to focus on feeling good and being active in a way that works for me, rather than obsessing over the scale. (Anonymous, personal communication, 2024)

The discussion illuminated the common challenges these women faced, subtly underscoring the pressures of diet mentality. Their shared experiences revealed the complex relationship they had with body image, weight, and health, highlighting the broader struggle between societal expectations and personal well-being.

GETTING RID OF THE DIET MENTALITY

Have you ever noticed that even if you are not following a specific diet plan, you allow yourself "cheat foods" or indulgences as a reward for eating well during the week? Have you ever opted for a lower-calorie dish while dining out, even though it wasn't what you truly desired? Do you restrict certain foods at home because you fear you won't be able to control your consumption? Many of us—Black women included—find ourselves caught up in dieting behaviors or influenced by diet culture, even when we are not on a diet.

Diet mentality refers to a deprivation mindset focused on restrictive eating patterns, often driven by the desire to lose weight or change one's body shape (Hooper et al., 2021). The diet mentality prioritizes short-term weight loss goals and narrow parameters for wellness over long-term health and well-being. It involves constant thoughts about food, calories, and weight, and may lead to cycles of restrictive eating followed by periods of overeating or bingeing. It relies on rigid adherence to external rules or guidelines regarding food intake and body weight rather than trusting one's body and internal cues.

I, Paula, have encountered numerous Black women who admit to having been on a diet or currently being on one at some stage in their lives. However, the persistent emphasis on "eating better," "eating healthier," or "getting fit" often obscures their recognition of these thoughts as part of a diet mentality. While they may acknowledge the presence of certain behaviors, they may not fully realize that their thoughts are consistently centered around dieting or disordered eating patterns. *Disordered eating* refers to irregular eating habits that, while not meeting the full criteria for a clinical eating disorder, still involve unhealthy patterns that can harm both physical and mental well-being (discussed in Chapter 2). These behaviors can include loss of control when eating, overeating in response to emotions, and restricting food intake. Individuals may experience episodes of binge eating, emotional eating, strict dieting, and the use of harmful weight control practices. These behaviors can have physical, emotional, and social consequences and may require professional help.

Disordered eating can also involve an obsessive focus on food, body weight, and shape, often leading to cycles of dieting followed by overeating.

Emotions, alongside hunger and satiety signals, play significant roles in driving eating disorder symptoms. Black adolescents and women may experience a sense of detachment from oneself, leading to an adverse connection with food, heightened preoccupation with dieting, a longing to alter one's identity, and a disconnect from one's own body (Bucchianeri et al., 2016). Eating disorders disrupt the ability to perceive hunger and fullness cues, resulting in the need for nutritional rehabilitation, which is critical to the treatment of eating disorders (Sonneville & Rodgers, 2019; Coelho et al., 2014). To assist Black women with reducing diet mentality, it is imperative to start by raising awareness and providing education about the harmful effects of restrictive eating patterns. This involves helping them recognize that what they perceive as healthy eating is a form of dieting. Encouraging them to challenge societal norms and question diet culture can also be beneficial. Listening to the body's hunger and fullness cues, rather than adhering to strict food rules, can help shift their mindset away from dieting. The work that you are doing will assist your client in adopting a healthier relationship with food and their body.

ALL FOODS FIT

The *all foods fit philosophy*, associated with *intuitive eating* (see below) and a non-diet approach to nutrition, promotes the idea that there are no "good" or "bad" foods. It emphasizes moderation, variety, and listening to one's body cues to foster a healthy relationship with food. This approach encourages individuals to eat when hungry, stop when full, and enjoy a diverse range of foods without guilt or shame (Tribole & Resch, 2020; Ralph-Nearman et al., 2019).

This philosophy is beneficial for promoting sustainable and balanced eating habits, particularly for those with a history of dieting or disordered eating. It's important to note that while "all foods fit" promotes inclusivity of all foods, it also supports mindful eating and the understanding that different individuals may have specific dietary needs or preferences that guide their food choices.

NORMALIZED EATING

Normalized eating refers to having a balanced and healthy relationship with food, where eating patterns are not driven by strict rules or emotional factors.

It involves listening to your body's hunger and fullness cues, eating a variety of foods in moderation, and enjoying meals without anxiety, guilt, or shame. Normalized eating also involves being flexible and eating when hungry and stopping when full, rather than adhering to rigid dieting practices or restrictive eating patterns. Overall, it promotes a sustainable and enjoyable approach to nourishing your body; and recognizing that occasional indulgences are a normal part of life.

Note: The foundational beliefs guiding nutrition and weight management counseling for Black women include the idea that motivation for health can provide the necessary drive to adopt new behaviors; that these behaviors will gradually become ingrained habits, thus reducing difficulty; and that the health advantages of these behaviors will contribute to their long-term maintenance (Baskin et al., 2009). Please be cautious to *not* embrace this perspective or adopt this belief. Cultural, psychosocial, and lifestyle factors strongly shape Black women's food and activity preferences and behaviors, which may persist *despite* efforts to change, even among highly motivated individuals. Black women striving to alter their dietary composition or food intake may experience a sense of deprivation, missing out on the enjoyment associated with eating. Food choices are predominantly influenced by taste and cost rather than nutrition or weight control concerns, even among Black women who prioritize health as a central aspect of their lifestyle (Baskin et al., 2009; Glanz et al., 1998).

INTUITIVE EATING

Providing information on the negative impacts of chronic dieting and promoting a more balanced and intuitive approach to eating, which should incorporate foods that are reflective of your client's culture, can be beneficial. Providers should encourage Black clients to embrace and honor their hunger cues as a natural and essential aspect of their body's needs (Barrada et al., 2020). By tuning into their body's signals and responding with mindful eating practices, they can foster a healthier relationship with food and better meet their nutritional needs.

Practical Tips: Encourage Your Client to Follow the Principles of Intuitive Eating

Evelyn Tribole and Elyse Resch (2020) developed the principles of intuitive eating, an approach to eating that encourages listening to one's body's hunger and fullness cues, rather than following external rules or diets. Cultural adaptations may be required such as recognizing and honoring cultural differences in food traditions, meal patterns, and dietary preferences. The essential principles of intuitive eating include:

1. Reject the diet mentality: Let go of dieting and restrictive eating habits.
2. Honor your hunger: Listen to your body's signals and eat when you are hungry.
3. Make peace with food: Give yourself permission to eat all foods without guilt.
4. Challenge the food police: Challenge the thoughts and beliefs that label foods as "good" or "bad."
5. Respect your fullness: Listen to your body's signals, and stop eating when you are satisfied.
6. Discover the satisfaction factor: Seek out foods that are satisfying and enjoyable.
7. Honor your feelings without using food: Find other ways to cope with emotions besides eating.
8. Respect your body: Accept and appreciate your body for its unique size and shape.
9. Exercise—feel the difference: Focus on how physical activity makes you feel rather than just burning calories.
10. Honor your health—gentle nutrition: Make food choices that honor your health and taste buds while making you feel good (Tribole & Resch, 2020).

Before embracing intuitive eating, providers are encouraged to work with their client on normalizing eating patterns, reconnecting with their body, increasing awareness of hunger and satiety, and reducing disordered eating behaviors. Without these foundational tools, clients may not be equipped to practice intuitive eating. Because clients with eating disorders are often disconnected from their body, their intuition may be influenced by diet culture and negative beliefs about their body and food. Thus, a reduction in eating disordered behaviors is required to work toward intuitive eating. To rebuild trust in their body's cues, especially when feeling disconnected or misaligned, clients should consider the following strategies:

- Practice mindful eating by focusing on the experience of eating without judgment.
- Establish regular mealtimes to regulate hunger cues over time.
- Keep a food journal to track eating patterns and emotions related to food intake.

ENCOURAGING BALANCED NUTRITION

Meal Plans That Reflect Culture

In Black families, food often serves as a source of joy and comfort (Talleyrand et al., 2017), providing opportunities for shared cultural experiences and connection through culinary traditions. To promote a more diverse and inclusive approach to meal planning and food choices for our Black clients, offer meals that reflect a variety of cultural backgrounds. This means moving beyond traditional American foods that are predominantly Eurocentric and incorporating dishes that are representative of your clients' diverse heritages. In my work with clients at both The Renfrew Center and in private practice, I have encountered individuals whose dietary practices often reflect diverse cultural backgrounds and communal eating traditions. However, during treatment, some clients faced dietary recommendations, such as peanut butter and jelly sandwiches, that were unfamiliar to them, as these foods were not part of their meal options. Recognizing these differences is crucial, as it allows us to explore tailored accommodations for each client. This process involves discussing meals at home and ensuring that both clients and their families receive the necessary support to navigate these dietary changes effectively.

It is essential to consider the cultural beliefs, preferences, and nutritional needs of your clients to ensure that all foods are seen as suitable and respectful of their backgrounds. By doing so, you honor their cultural identities and provide a more inclusive and supportive treatment environment. As many clients of color have mentioned, "I don't eat oatmeal or drink milk. Why not offer meals that are respectful of and reflect other cultures, even if they are not my own?" (Anonymous, personal communication, 2023). The belief that "all foods fit" for some means "all foods fit if they fall within the parameters set by providers," who are often White, in both treatment facilities and outpatient settings.

Variety

Adopting an all foods fit mentality promotes flexibility and variety in meals. Dietitians who create meal plans that reflect Black clients' food preferences, while also introducing opportunities to broaden their food choices, cultivate a more inclusive and culturally sensitive approach to nutrition. Considering variety and food choices for Black people involves recognizing and respecting their diverse culinary traditions and preferences. Incorporating traditional and culturally significant foods into meal planning not only honors cultural heritage but also promotes better engagement and satisfaction with nutritional guidance.

Offering a diverse array of food options helps to avoid the imposition of a homogeneous diet that may not resonate with personal and cultural preferences, thus supporting both physical health and cultural identity. It is also crucial for dietitians to educate themselves about different cultural cuisines and to be open to learning from their clients to provide the most relevant and respectful dietary recommendations.

Accessibility

Addressing food and dietary intake among Black Americans is quite complex. Food insecurity is more prevalent in Black communities due to systemic racism and economic disparities, leading to a higher likelihood of experiencing hunger. In 2022, food insecurity (i.e., the sense of not having enough to eat) among Black people was almost two and a half times the rate of White people, nearly 23%, or 1 in 5, Black people in the United States (Feeding America, 2022; Baskin et al., 2009).

Additionally, Black neighborhoods tend to have fewer full-service supermarkets than White neighborhoods, and Black individuals typically have to travel out of food deserts to access foods not readily available in their areas (Powell et al., 2007). These systemic issues, coupled with insufficient or few transportation options, can make it challenging for Black clients to follow common nutrition recommendations (Office of Disease Prevention and Health Promotion, n.d.).

Household food deprivation involves a lack of access to sufficient and nutritionally adequate food, as well as difficulties in acquiring food in a socially acceptable manner (Rasmusson et al., 2019). Obtaining food in a socially acceptable way typically refers to accessing food through conventional means, such as purchasing from grocery stores or receiving it from family, which align with societal norms and expectations. In contrast, obtaining food in an unacceptable manner may involve using food banks or pantries, which can carry stigma or shame for some individuals, or stealing food, an action that is generally socially unacceptable and illegal. For individuals experiencing food insecurity, navigating these distinctions can be quite complex. They may encounter difficulties in accessing food that is both sufficient and aligned with their social identity and cultural values, which can result in feelings of stigma, embarrassment, or exclusion.

Signs of food insecurity involve being unable to afford nutritious foods, worrying that food supplies will run out, and reducing meal sizes or skipping meals due to limited resources. More severe indicators include going an entire day without eating and deliberately restricting food intake because of limited access to food (Rasmusson et al., 2019). In a study of food-insecure Black women, over 50% reported unintentional fasting, reduced appetites leading to practiced restriction, and skipping meals despite having food available (Bernard, 2021; Becker et al., 2017).

A recent study discovered that within the population experiencing food insecurity in the United States, the severity of food insecurity correlated with the frequency of binge eating, along with other forms of eating disorder psychopathology and internalized weight bias (Becker et al., 2017). Understanding the intricate relationship between limited food resources and outcomes such as binge-eating disorder (BED) is crucial, considering the apparent influence of food insecurity on weight, dietary restriction, and binge-eating behaviors. An example of this complex relationship is encapsulated in a discussion I, Paula, had with a college counselor at a historically Black university a couple years after the COVID-19 pandemic lockdowns. The counselor shared that students were reportedly exhibiting binge-like behaviors due to food shortages during the COVID era. School staff noted that students who contracted COVID were quarantined in their rooms, with individual meal deliveries. However, students consumed the food quickly, as access to the cafeteria was restricted, and meal deliveries were limited to once or twice a week, exacerbating food insecurity concerns.

I have encountered situations where parents and foster parents have reported children exhibiting hoarding behaviors similar to binge tendencies. Many of these children came from impoverished areas where food insecurity was prevalent. Reflecting on my own upbringing, I recall that my grandparents, who fostered children, often dealt with similar issues. Despite living in a non-restrictive environment, some foster children would hide or even "steal" food, leading to disciplinary actions. This behavior stemmed from their past experiences of going without food for extended periods due to their family's socioeconomic status, driving them to consume and hoard food as a means of coping and fulfilling their needs.

The uncertainty about food availability and the timing of the next meal can commonly lead to overconsumption, mirroring the pattern seen in binge-eating disorder. This issue is compounded by environments that are often classified as food deserts frequently overlap with food swamps—areas characterized by an abundance of fast food and highly processed foods—which can further contribute to unhealthy eating behaviors and may increase the risk of binge-eating episodes (Becker et al., 2017). Inadequate food availability can result in poor nutrition and irregular meal patterns, ultimately affecting overall health and well-being.

Support from a team of providers is critical during times when Black clients are experiencing food insecurity. Assistance should focus on normalizing client eating patterns, finding ways to increase variety in their diet, and creatively incorporating as many food groups as possible based on availability. Community resources such as food pantries, the Women, Infants, and Children (WIC) program, and the Supplemental Nutrition Assistance Program (SNAP) should be discussed and normalized as part of the treatment process. Having a deeper understanding of these behaviors as a provider can aid in educating families and identifying solutions rather than resorting to disciplinary actions.

ENSURING EMOTIONAL HEALTH

Eating Disorders Are Not About Food

Eating disorders are emotional disorders characterized by unhealthy eating behaviors that stem from emotional distress. They often arise as a way for individuals to cope with intense feelings, manage internal conflicts, and regain a sense of control.

Consider the complex predicament often experienced by Black women, (referred to as the "Strong Black Woman" in Chapter 5), which entails feeling obligated to conceal emotions while prioritizing the care of others. This identity may be complicated for some. As Tracy Hopkins (2021) writes, "Black women have a complicated relationship with our superpowers . . . odes to Black girl magic make us feel seen and heard" (p. 90). Recognition and acknowledgment can empower Black women and girls who often feel overlooked, disregarded, or invisible. The desire to be seen as strong and resilient is often admired by others, but what is the impact on your Black client? Maintaining identities like this becomes unmanageable for anyone and often results in emotional suppression, prioritizing others over oneself, increased stress, and engaging in eating-related behaviors or exercise to address the conflict.

Black women are consistently mindful of how they are perceived, carefully considering their tone, choice of words, and pronunciation, as well as the oversexualization or underrepresentation of their bodies. They worry about maintaining healthy relationships, both romantic and peer—striving to be a supportive friend, managing their professional growth as they mature, and balancing the needs of their parents, children, and siblings (Hopkins, 2021; Burke et al., 2023).

One of my clients demonstrated a recurring narrative, experiencing a sense of obligation and inner turmoil, as she processed and grappled with the passing of her aunt, who died of an illness that she concealed from the family for a decade. Feeling accountable and torn, she believed she had betrayed her aunt by "choosing sides," and essentially ending their relationship. Overwhelmed with guilt, she took on the task of planning the funeral, despite others who were also capable. The relentless narrative in her mind only intensified her distress.

Uncover (Explore) the Emotional Components

Emotional connections to food for Black women can encompass a range of experiences and associations, reflecting cultural, social, and personal dimensions. Food serves as a source of joy and satisfaction within Black families, providing opportunities for shared cultural experiences and connection through culinary traditions. These Black culinary traditions are often associated with the term *soul food*. Soul food embodies the culinary linkage between African heritage and the Southern United States, reflecting a deep-rooted history in the African American diet (Baskin et al., 2009; Dirks & Duran, 2001). For some, it takes on a more spiritual meaning reflecting the struggles, sacrifices, and ingenuity taken to prepare the food (McMillan, 2021; Liburd, 2003).

Eating in the Black community has been considered a ritual, conveying cultural traditions and a multitude of meanings. The association between being Black and dietary intake carries specific connotations, highlighting the social significance of food (Baskin et al., 2009; Liburd, 2003). Food preparation is often regarded as an expression of love, with generous servings shared with loved ones as a gesture of affection.

Consequently, making significant changes to dietary practices may prove challenging, as some may perceive altering traditional foods or cooking methods as a devaluation of their Black identity (Liburd, 2003). A few Black women shared that they have always associated food with love, stating, "It is about connection and love. Food demonstrates the sacrifices that were made and how we (Black slaves) made something delicious out of the scraps they were given. The traditions that we have as Black people were born out of suffering, we didn't have anything as a people in this country" (Anonymous, personal communication, 2023).

Black women report higher levels of stress in comparison to women of other ethnic and racial backgrounds (Hopkins, 2021; Salami et al., 2019; Talleyrand, 2006). Black women facing race-related stress may turn to disordered eating as a coping mechanism due to feelings of depression. Despite the stereotype of Black women as superwomen or magical, they still experience psychological distress.

Spiritual beliefs, community support, and a sense of collectivism have been considered protective factors against mental health issues. It is important to remember that your Black clients are individuals with their own struggles and vulnerabilities. The treatment setting that you create with your client may be the only opportunity for Black women and girls to show up as their authentic self—vulnerable and emotionally expressive.

ADDRESSING STRESSORS AMONG BLACK WOMEN

Black women can experience a considerable amount of stress, including general, minority, and racial stress. Black individuals constantly navigate life's demands. It is common to hear Black people express their inability to hide their racial identity; they can never escape being Black. Unlike others who can conceal their marginalized identities, Black people are always identified as such. The burden of navigating both racial and gendered identities can amplify their stress levels. A strategy that contributes to and maintains stress is *code-switching*.

Code-switching: A strategy employed by Black women to adeptly navigate diverse environments, involving the adjustment of language, dialects, speech patterns, and cultural expressions to fit in. (Williams & Lewis, 2021)

Black women may code-switch to avoid negative stereotypes or to gain acceptance in predominantly White spaces. Code-switching is a complex and nuanced practice that reflects the intersectional experiences of Black women (Williams & Lewis, 2021; Stitham, 2021; Washington Harmon, 2020). Code-switching is such a common occurrence that Black people often engage in this behavior instinctively. The dominant culture may view this as adaptive and believe it is a strength that your patient possesses. Although your client may appear to be managing their distress, some Black women are constantly in survival mode, and they may also demonstrate patterns of excessive commitment and maladaptive coping mechanisms, leading to higher levels of stress.

Black women face a myriad of challenges throughout life, spanning from adolescence through adulthood and into their senior years. Combined with their responsibilities and other stressors, Black women experience a heightened risk and vulnerability to both mental and physical health problems (Taylor & Braithwaite Holden, 2009). Physiological, psychological, sociocultural, interpersonal, and spiritual factors further compound the challenges experienced by Black women (Fuller, 2021). The expectation for Black women to maintain composure during crises often leads them to disregard, suppress, or conceal symptoms of both physical and mental distress.

Identity Crisis

How do you define your identity? What informs your sense of self? Black women's racial and gender identities are complex and multifaceted. Understanding the significance of identity development is essential for grasping disordered eating behaviors in Black adolescents. It illuminates how both gender and racial identities influence adolescents' perceptions of self-image, behavior, and appearance (Blazek & Carter, 2019). Black adolescents not only navigate the exploration of their racial identity but may also delve into their gender identity—a process that extends into adulthood. *Gender identity* pertains to the degree to which individuals feel or embrace masculine and feminine gender identities and traits. *Racial identity* refers to the significance and interpretation that individuals attribute to being part of their racial group. Analyzing intersecting social identities may provide a more insightful understanding of disordered eating patterns in this demographic. Adolescents' body ideals and their susceptibility or resilience to disordered eating behaviors (DEB) are influenced by their gender and racial identity development.

Black women and adolescent girls must strategically navigate gendered racial oppression, stereotypes, and biases across multiple settings, including work, school, and home, to effectively cope with these challenges (Williams & Lewis, 2021; see Chapter 3). They navigate to survive oppressive environments, prioritizing their identity over conforming to European beauty standards. Black women often feel burdened as they strive to fulfill numerous roles dictated by gender norms. Gender norms can significantly influence one's sense of identity, shaping perceptions of self-expression, roles, and expectations, not only as a woman, but as a Black woman, within society. Black women navigating the intersection of racial and gender biases often find their decision-making influenced by the challenges they face. Melissa Harris-Perry (2011) explores this dynamic in her book *Sister Citizen*, using the metaphor of crooked rooms to depict the psychological toll of being overlooked or misunderstood despite their contributions.

To fully understand eating disorders within diverse groups of women, cultural factors like ethnic identity and acculturation levels must be considered. Therefore, if eating pathology is viewed as a culturally bound syndrome heavily influenced by sociocultural factors (e.g., media, peers, parents), the extent to which diverse populations adhere to Eurocentric mainstream values could impact the pathways leading to maladaptive eating behaviors in response to experiences of racial stress (Salami et al., 2019).

Williams and Lewis (2021) demonstrate that "throughout their identity development, Black women become increasingly more critically aware of their intersectional identity through integrating their gendered racial socialization, rejecting the influence of oppression on their identity, navigating when necessary, and personally redefining what it means to be a Black woman" (p. 224).

Have you considered the impact of your client's identity and experiences on what they present when they walk into your office?

Rejection of Self

Is it easier to reject oneself when others reject you? Undermining oneself is highly detrimental, as it negates any positive thoughts we have about ourselves (Edwards-Gayfield, 2021). Imagine the significant challenges Black women face as they navigate a world that idolizes Whiteness and maleness. Black women have been overlooked, underrepresented, forgotten, ignored, not given credit for their work—erased for years (Bernard, 2021; Walker-Barnes, 2017). However, this practice has become increasingly easier with social media. Black women report internalizing body image concerns and experiencing dysphoria due to exposure to social media messages and images promoting thinness. Acceptance of mainstream values undermines cultural expression, leading to increased body dissatisfaction and disordered eating.

As mentioned earlier in this chapter and in Chapter 5, society imposes the Strong Black Woman ideal as the benchmark for defining "good" Black womanhood. Despite its divergence from their true selves, Black women are pressured to conform to this standard, risking their physical, emotional, social, and spiritual welfare. When Black women strive to distance themselves from this ideal and articulate their need for support, they may encounter condemnation for appearing "weak" and be urged to "get it together" (Walker-Barnes, 2017).

Black women and girls may also encounter issues that harm their self-image, making them feel invisible, inferior, and unhealthy; ultimately increasing the possibility of rejecting oneself. Because strength is viewed as essential to racial and gender authenticity, women who embody the Strong Black Woman ideal may see their suffering as a failure to live up to this standard if they begin to break down (Walker-Barnes, 2017). This perceived failure is often accompanied by feelings of shame, guilt, low self-esteem, and depression (Harrington et al., 2010).

Familial Conflict

Villatoro and Aneshensel (2014) found that psychiatric disorders, negative self-evaluation of mental health, family history of treated disorder, and living arrangements are significant factors influencing utilization of mental health services with Black individuals. Some of these factors may be negative family interactions, as well as how the client views their family. Family dynamics among Black clients can induce stress and contribute to disordered behaviors and psychological issues. Additionally, family conflict may arise from different roles individuals play, particularly among Black women and adolescent girls.

It is important to explore the concept of family with the client and determine who is included in that definition. Alongside exploring family dynamics, addressing coping mechanisms is crucial for navigating family conflicts effectively. This could include setting boundaries, enhancing communication skills, and seeking support from other sources if needed. Navigating the rules around conflict resolution within the family dynamic can be challenging for clients, but it is an important aspect of their growth and well-being. Providing support and guidance in developing effective communication and problem-solving skills can empower clients to navigate these challenges successfully.

Discrimination

Race-based discrimination hinders Black individuals' access to employment, housing, and essential resources, affecting their overall well-being (Downer, 2021; Salami et al., 2019; Becker et al., 2017). For Black American women, stress related to racial discrimination is linked to maladaptive eating behaviors, as discussed in Chapter 3. This stress may elevate the risk of eating pathology, as it correlates with depressive symptoms (Burke et al., 2023; Kinkel-Ram et al., 2023). When working with Black women, providers are encouraged to explore the complex relationship between stress, negative emotions, and eating disorders.

When confronted with racial discrimination, individuals may employ helpful and unhelpful coping strategies. These strategies may involve substance use, seeking social support, embracing racial identity, praying, and engaging in unhealthy eating behaviors (Burke et al., 2023; Kinkel-Ram et al., 2023). Chronic exposure to discrimination and racial stress can deplete psychological resources, leading to increased health issues (Williams & Lewis, 2021). Maladaptive eating behaviors, like overeating or restrictive eating, may emerge as a response to racial stress, serving as unhealthy coping mechanisms.

Body Shame

How have you been taught to perceive your own body and the bodies of others? Black women have often been subjected to messages suggesting that their bodies are undesirable, unattractive, or inadequate. These harmful beliefs stem from societal pressures regarding body size and perpetuate negative stereotypes. Furthermore, some Black women and adolescents endure these negative messages based on their skin tone, hair texture, and racial identity. Body image is well addressed in Chapter 4, but it is such an important and complex topic that a few points bear repeating here:

- Black women are both admired and criticized for displaying similar behavioral and physical attributes, particularly those that are often associated with cultural stereotypes such as curvy body shapes or fuller lips; and Black girls are often scrutinized in ways usually reserved for adults.

- Body dissatisfaction, which involves critiquing and feeling negatively about one's body, stands as one of the most firmly established risk factors contributing to the onset of eating disorders and associated health complications.
- Racial and ethnic disparities are evident in the way weight-based stigma is experienced, particularly for Black women who may encounter additional challenges stemming from intersecting racial and gender prejudices (Ciciurkaite & Perry, 2018).
- Stigma serves as a significant stressor, impacting both physical and mental well-being.

Inequality in Health Care

Racial disparities in health care are pervasive in the United States, particularly between Black and White Americans (Muscatell et al., 2022). The history of the U.S. medical establishment demonstrates a pattern of distrust and marginalization toward Black individuals, further fueling apprehension to seek treatment within marginalized communities (Thomas, 2022; Ho et al., 2022); see also Chapter 3. Black individuals encounter substantial health challenges and disparities compared to other ethnic groups. Muscatell et al. (2022) provides insight into the factors that contribute to the marginalization, discrimination, and distrust of Black individuals.

- Health care distrust: Black individuals often encounter systemic and interpersonal racism within the health care system, leading to medical mistrust and can result in delays in seeking preventive care, especially among Black men (Powell et al., 2019).
- Structural racism: U.S. laws and institutional policies often favor dominant groups, which can restrict economic mobility and contribute to health disparities among Black Americans (Braveman et al., 2022).
- Cultural racism: The notion that the cultural creations of the dominant group are superior to those of marginalized groups can result in the internalization of negative stereotypes about Black individuals, both within the Black community and from external perspectives.

- Interpersonal racism: Implicit or explicit interpersonal racism is widespread and reinforces distrust of Black individuals.
- Vicarious racism: Black individuals may experience racism indirectly by witnessing or learning about racist incidents that affect members of their racial community (Chac et al., 2021; Heard-Garris et al., 2018).
- Media representation: Media often portrays Black people negatively, which can shape public perception and exacerbate existing distrust.

These factors collectively affect the health and well-being of Black people. The distrust they face is not due to any inherent traits, but rather stems from systemic, cultural, and interpersonal racism that sustains negative stereotypes and biases. Limited access to health care imposes a considerable burden on the social and economic circumstances crucial for survival and well-being (Taylor & Braithwaite Holden, 2009).

Two notable examples of medical maltreatment of Black women highlight the historical trauma that has contributed to medical mistrust within the Black community (Ho et al., 2022). Perhaps most well-known, in 1951 Henrietta Lacks underwent a minor procedure at Johns Hopkins and had cancerous cells collected without her knowledge or consent, which were later used for biomedical research. Additionally, in 1961 Fannie Lou Hamer, a Black female civil rights leader (and my great-great-aunt) was given a hysterectomy in Mississippi without her knowledge or consent. Forced sterilization of Black women to prevent reproduction was so common it was named "the Mississippi appendectomy" (Ho et al., 2022; Michals, 2017). Her experience highlights the deep mistrust between the Black community and the medical system, shaped by a history of abuse and exploitation. Medical mistrust has been described in various ways, including:

- Distrust in the health care system due to past experiences of discrimination when receiving care (Ellis et al., 2019);
- Suspicion of the treatment provided to an individual's racial or ethnic group by conventional health care systems and professionals (Sheppard et al., 2014);
- Distrust toward health care organizations and medical professionals (Sutton et al., 2019);
- Distrust in the health care system and skepticism toward the motives and actions of medical practitioners (Tekeste et al., 2019); and

- A tendency to be wary of medical systems and personnel perceived to embody the mainstream culture (Thompson et al., 2004).

Many Black women that I have met—clients, colleagues, friends, and family—expressed frustration at feeling excluded from important information, both concerning their own care and that of their loved ones. Some Black individuals remarked that doctors never communicated their observations during or after appointments. They believe that some health care professionals failed to engage clients in their plan of care, which they perceived as an implicit belief by providers of Black people as inferior, incompetent, or too ignorant to understand. Culturally sensitive and trauma-informed approaches in health care are needed to address the unique experiences of individuals who have experienced racism (Muscatell et al., 2022).

Practical Tips: How to Cultivate Equitable Care

There are many things we as providers can do to combat inequities in the field and ensure more culturally sensitive, trauma-informed, antidiscriminatory, bias-free experiences for our Black clients. Here is a brief but important list of things we can do:

- Acknowledge Black women as authorities on their own bodies and health stories.
- Prioritize genuine empathy, active listening, and cultural competence.
- Acknowledge that Black women often face perilous circumstances during their interactions with health care providers. Trusting medical systems alone is insufficient for historically marginalized groups if patient blame and decentering persist.
- Create a safe and nonjudgmental space for clients to express themselves openly.
- Appreciate that Black women seek health care providers who understand their cultural background and share similar identities. If you are a non-Black provider, realize that your client may be hesitant and uncomfortable, and do what you can to put them at ease.
- Establish a therapeutic alliance with your Black client by actively listening to their personal narratives and refraining from pathologizing their experiences.

- Involve clients in shared decision-making; this empowers them and fosters a sense of agency in their own care.
- Continue your own education in interpersonal skills and cultural sensitivity.
- Advocate for sustainable and fair social justice within the health care system.
- Promote population health, conduct research, and develop policies with the goal of enhancing the health of the Black community and diminishing disparities compared to White populations (Baskin et al., 2009).

BUILDING A TEAM

Eating disorders necessitate comprehensive treatment that encompasses the diverse impacts on overall well-being. The participation of a multidisciplinary team adheres to best practice in the treatment of eating disorders; and ensures holistic care that addresses the physical, mental, and emotional needs of individuals with eating disorders. The team typically includes:

- a physician
- a mental health provider
- a dietitian
- family members or support persons
- other professionals as needed

Effective teams maintain regular communication to ensure coordination of care among all members, ensuring a collaborative approach to successfully design a treatment plan and to enhance treatment outcomes for Black women. Recognizing the importance of a treatment team, each member may hold crucial information to address not only eating disorders but also body image and co-occurring concerns. Individually, these details provide an incomplete picture, but collectively, they reveal the severity of the eating disorder and its impact on the client's health, well-being, and psychological functioning (Churchill, 2021).

Your Black client grappling with an eating disorder is at the heart of the treatment team. Treatment plans should be created using a person-centered, culturally sensitive, and recovery-oriented approach (National Eating Disorders Collaboration, 2018). The composition of the treatment team may vary depending on factors such as the type and severity of the eating disorder, the treatment environment, and the need to address the individual's psychological, physical, nutritional, and psychosocial requirements (National Alliance For Eating Disorders, n.d.). Providers are encouraged to explore opportunities for eating disorder specific training.

MOVING FORWARD

It is crucial to recognize that Black women face not only similar stressors and difficulties with food and body image as other women but also unique challenges. Understanding these nuances is vital for your work with them. While this chapter does not delve into all aspects of training, it's essential to acknowledge your own biases and how they affect your perception of Black women. Labels like "superwoman" or "Black girl magic," although embraced by some as strengths, can harm their psychological well-being, as they imply an expectation to endure and persevere without complaint, which is overwhelming.

Establishing a collaborative team is important. If you haven't already, reach out to providers, explore available resources, and continue to learn from various disciplines. Remember, your client is the expert on their own life. Black individuals may hesitate to seek necessary treatment due to historical and ongoing medical mistrust. They need your support, but more importantly, they need you to listen, be present, and ask the necessary questions to fully understand their experience. This will enable you to truly show up for them and provide the care they seek.

A consideration for future research is to increase the participation of Black health care professionals who would have increased rapport with, empathy for, and understanding of the concerns of Black women (Gary et al., 2015). Crafting impactful research and translating its findings into practical strategies and programs can be enhanced by cultural insights unique to Black researchers (Baskin et al., 2009). This process necessitates collaboration between social science and medical researchers, alongside community partners.

Chapter 8

WHICH MEDICAL COMPLICATIONS SHOULD I BE AWARE OF?

Eating disorders are serious mental illnesses that can have severe consequences if left untreated. As mentioned in earlier chapters, eating disorders can affect anyone, regardless of gender, age, socioeconomic status, ethnicity, or body shape. They require timely recognition, understanding, and proper treatment to address the complex psychological and physical factors involved. Eating disorders are not only associated with significant psychiatric comorbidities but also impact various organ systems, leading to serious and potentially life-threatening medical complications.

It is common for individuals to have misconceptions about the severity of their eating disorder, often comparing themselves to others or relying on medical tests for validation. Providers not specialized in eating disorders might inadvertently reinforce these beliefs by focusing on one set of data or misunderstanding the medical risks that eating disorders pose. This underscores the importance of comprehensive treatment approaches that address both the psychiatric and medical aspects of eating disorders to improve outcomes and ensure the well-being of individuals affected by these conditions. Dedication to seeking education and support are crucial for professionals to understand the true impact of these disorders.

Medical conditions associated with eating disorders can vary in severity, ranging from mild to life threatening. Complications can affect multiple body systems, including the cardiac, metabolic, gastrointestinal, and reproductive systems (Hambleton et al., 2022; Mehler & Rylander, 2015). Eating disorders can have serious and potentially fatal consequences, with anorexia nervosa (AN) often receiving more attention even though all eating disorders are equally serious. Complications such as liver dysfunction, gastrointestinal issues, respiratory failure, and heart disease can arise, and despite treatment, some may result in death.

The mortality risk for individuals with eating disorders surpasses that of the general population, particularly in anorexia nervosa due to its profound effects on the cardiovascular system and heightened risk of suicide (Hambleton et al., 2022). Elevated mortality rates are also observed in bulimia nervosa (BN) and other specified feeding and eating disorder (OSFED) (Hambleton et al., 2022). Suicide rates are heightened across all eating disorders, with even greater risks seen in individuals with accompanying psychiatric conditions. Suicide ranks as the second most common cause of death for individuals with anorexia nervosa, and rates of suicidal behavior are higher in bulimia nervosa and binge-eating disorder compared to the general population (Smith et al., 2018).

EATING DISORDERS AND MEDICAL COMPLICATIONS

The purpose of this chapter is to equip clinicians with a basic understanding of both the medical concerns that Black women endure and the medical complications associated with eating disorders and co-occurring conditions. A significant topic of discussion in the field of behavioral medicine and health psychology is the impact of mental health on physical health (Bell, 2017). Despite Black women consistently ranking high in rates of heart disease, high blood pressure, and HIV, the connection between mental health and these conditions is often overlooked.

Unhealthy habits such as overeating (Blue & Berkel, 2010), paranoia in relationships, overworking (Jones & Shorter-Gooden, 2003), and the stereotype of the Black woman attitude or Angry Black woman are all indicative of deeper issues affecting Black women's health. Identifying medical concerns for lesser-known signs of disordered eating, often overlooked due to weight stigma, can aid Black women in promptly recognizing and addressing disordered eating behaviors. Some of these signs may include dental problems, electrolyte imbalances, digestive issues like constipation and irritable bowel syndrome (IBS), bone health concerns, irregular menstrual cycles, and changes in skin and hair health.

Black women experience distinct ongoing stressors that elevate the risk of numerous chronic health conditions, including hypertension, diabetes, lupus, preterm birth, and maternal morbidity (Uzogara, 2019). On average, Black women have a higher prevalence of various health conditions, including heart disease, stroke, cancers, fibroids, anemia, higher body weight, and stress, despite being younger than White women at onset (Chinn et al., 2021). Health outcomes are influenced by the social conditions in which they are situated. This discrepancy arises due to a combination of genetic, environmental, social, and economic factors. The compounded effects of sexism and racism can also lead to significantly worse health outcomes for Black women (Berdahl & Moore, 2006; Uzogara, 2019).

A client shared her experience of recent physical pain and questioned when she should seek medical attention. She noted that her cousin frequently sought medical care for health concerns, whereas she and many others she knew often did not. She wondered if her cousin was overly cautious or if she herself minimized concerns, believing they weren't serious enough for a doctor's visit. This led her to question whether this behavior reflects a general reluctance among Black women to seek medical attention, possibly stemming from experiences of being dismissed or their symptoms being minimized.

Do Black women tend to normalize or ignore symptoms instead of seeking medical treatment? This pattern raises concerns about how cultural and historical factors might influence health-seeking behaviors and highlights the importance of addressing these issues to improve health outcomes in the Black community. Efforts to address the disparities (Oh et al., 2022) often focus on improving health care access, enhancing health education, and addressing the social determinants of health (Mikhail & Klump, 2021; Belgrave & Abrams, 2016) that contribute to these outcomes. The aim of this book, and our aspiration, is to confront systemic inequalities and advocate for health equity within the Black community, with your invaluable assistance.

ANOREXIA NERVOSA

Anorexia nervosa deprives the body of essential energy, leading to a decline in normal function. This can result in serious health issues, including heart problems (low blood pressure, slow heart rate, irregular heartbeat, heart attack, and sudden death), anemia, kidney failure, bone density loss (osteopenia or osteoporosis), and amenorrhea, which can impact reproductive health (Office on Women's Health, HHS, 2022a). The resulting medical complications can be severe, affecting nearly every organ system, all stemming from prolonged malnutrition. Some of the most significant complications include (Gaudini, 2019; Office on Women's Health, HHS, 2022a; National Eating Disorders Association, n.d.):

Cardiovascular System
> *Bradycardia*: Slow heart rate
> *Hypotension*: Low blood pressure
> *Arrhythmias*: Irregular heartbeats, which can be life-threatening
> *Heart Failure*: Due to weakened heart muscles from malnutrition

Gastrointestinal System
> *Gastroparesis*: Delayed stomach emptying, causing bloating and nausea
> *Constipation*: Common due to reduced food intake and slowed metabolism
> *Pancreatitis*: Inflammation of the pancreas

Endocrine System
> *Amenorrhea*: Absence of menstruation due to low body fat and hormonal imbalances
> *Hypoglycemia*: Low blood sugar levels
> *Thyroid Dysfunction*: Leading to cold intolerance, fatigue, and hair loss

Skeletal System
> *Osteoporosis*: Loss of bone density, increasing the risk of fractures

Hematologic System
> *Anemia*: Reduced red blood cells, causing fatigue and weakness
> *Leukopenia*: Low white blood cell count, leading to heightened susceptibility of infection
> *Thrombocytopenia*: Low platelet count, which can cause bleeding issues

Renal System
> *Dehydration*: Due to inadequate fluid intake
> *Electrolyte Imbalance*: Such as low potassium, which can cause heart problems
> *Kidney Failure*: A result of prolonged dehydration and electrolyte imbalances

Neurological System
> *Cognitive Impairment*: Difficulty concentrating, poor memory, and decision-making issues

Peripheral Neuropathy: Numbness and tingling in extremities
Muscular System
Muscle Wasting: Loss of muscle mass and strength
Dermatologic System
Lanugo: The body grows fine hair in an attempt to retain warmth
Dry Skin and Hair: Resulting from malnutrition
Brittle Nails: Weak and easily breakable nails
Psychological Effects
Severe Depression and Anxiety: Common comorbid conditions
Increased Risk of Suicide: A result of severe mental and physical distress (Udo et al., 2019).
General Complications
Severe Malnutrition: Resulting in a weakened immune system and heightened susceptibility to infections
Multi-Organ Failure: Can occur when an organ fails to work at full capacity, which may develop gradually or suddenly and potentially impact other interconnected organs.

The severity and life-threatening nature of the medical complications arising from anorexia nervosa emphasize the crucial role of early intervention and holistic treatment approaches.

TABLE 8.1

HOW ANOREXIA NERVOSA AFFECTS YOUR BODY	
Blood	Anemia and other blood cell problems
Body electrolytes	Low glucose, phosphorus and sodium, prealbumin
Brain and nerves	Anxious/obsessive thoughts, difficulty concentrating, poor memory and decision-making issues, fear of gaining weight, sad, moody, fainting, changes in brain chemistry, numbness and tingling in extremities
Hair	Hair thins, falls out
Heart	Low blood pressure, slow heart rate, fluttering of the heart (palpitations), heart failure

Hormones	Periods stop; bone loss; problems growing; fertility concerns; increased risk of miscarriage, c-section, low birth-weight baby, and postpartum depression
Intestines	Constipation, bloating, liver failure, delayed stomach emptying, obstruction
Kidneys	Kidney stones, kidney failure, dehydration, low potassium
Muscles, joints, and bones	Weak muscles, fractures, osteoporosis
Skin	Bruise easily, dry skin, growth of fine hair all over body, get cold easily, yellow skin, brittle nails, blue fingertips

Credit: Office on Women's Health, U.S. Department of Health and Human Services, 2022a

BULIMIA NERVOSA

Bulimia nervosa presents a range of medical complications, influenced by the method and frequency of purging. These complications can be severe and lead to lasting adverse effects due to significant physical and psychological stress. Individuals engaging in purging behaviors may experience potassium loss through vomiting, laxative use, or diuretic abuse, resulting in low levels of potassium (hypokalemia) and chloride (hypochloremia) in the blood (Nitsch et al., 2021; Mehler & Rylander, 2015). In otherwise healthy young women with unexplained hypokalemia, covert purging should be suspected. While mild hyponatremia may resolve with the discontinuation of purging behaviors and oral rehydration, severe cases may necessitate hospitalization (Nitsch et al., 2021).

The medical complications of bulimia nervosa encompass Type 2 diabetes, hypertension, nonalcoholic fatty liver disease, metabolic syndrome, nutritional deficiencies, gastrointestinal complaints, gastric perforation, and gastric outlet obstruction (Nitsch et al., 2021; Physiopedia, 2021).

A colleague shared that one of her former patients in her twenties needed veneers because several of her front teeth had eroded significantly from over a decade of purging. She noted that the individual's teeth resembled baby teeth due to the severe erosion. This is an example of a medical complication related to dental health that is often overlooked.

Dentists often detect bulimia first due to tooth erosion from repeated vomiting. Teeth become permanently damaged, discolored, and weakened, with thinning, chipping, and sensitivity to temperature changes. Gums and soft tissues also suffer, with lesions from purging devices causing pain and swelling. Immediate brushing after vomiting worsens damage, but rinsing the mouth helps mitigate decay (Nitsch et al., 2021). Bulimia behaviors lead to dry mouth, cavities, periodontal disease, and overall poor oral hygiene (Nitsch et al., 2021: Mehler & Rylander, 2015).

The following highlights some of the major health concerns linked to bulimia nervosa (Nitsch et al., 2021; Gaudiani, 2019; Forney et al., 2016):

Cardiovascular System
  Electrolyte Imbalances: Frequent vomiting and laxative use can lead to imbalances in potassium, sodium, and chloride levels, causing arrhythmias and even sudden cardiac arrest
  Hypotension: Low blood pressure due to dehydration and electrolyte disturbances
Gastrointestinal System
  Esophagitis: Inflammation of the esophagus from repeated vomiting
  Esophageal Tears (Mallory-Weiss tears): Small tears in the esophagus that can cause significant bleeding
  Gastroesophageal Reflux Disease (GERD): Chronic acid reflux and heartburn
  Gastric Rupture: A rare but life-threatening complication where the stomach ruptures from overdistension during binge eating
  Constipation: Often due to laxative abuse leading to dependence and subsequent bowel dysfunction
Dental and Oral Health
  Dental Erosion: Stomach acid from vomiting erodes tooth enamel, leading to sensitivity, decay, and gum disease
  Swollen Salivary Glands: Particularly the parotid glands, causing a "chipmunk cheeks" appearance
  Mouth Sores: Chronic exposure to stomach acid can cause sores and ulcers in the mouth
Endocrine System
  Menstrual Irregularities: Including amenorrhea (absence of menstruation) or irregular periods due to hormonal imbalances

Thyroid Dysfunction: Potential disruption of thyroid hormones, affecting metabolism

Renal System

Dehydration: Due to vomiting and laxative or diuretic abuse

Electrolyte Imbalances: Leading to renal dysfunction and possible kidney stones

Musculoskeletal System

Muscle Weakness: Due to malnutrition and electrolyte imbalances, particularly low potassium levels

Skin and Hair

Russell's Sign: Calluses or scars on the knuckles from self-induced vomiting

Dry Skin and Brittle Hair: Due to malnutrition and dehydration

Psychological and Psychiatric Effects

Depression and Anxiety: High prevalence of mood disorders co-occurring with bulimia nervosa

Substance Abuse: Increased risk of alcohol and drug abuse

Neurological System

Cognitive Impairment: Issues with concentration and memory due to malnutrition and electrolyte imbalances

Seizures: Electrolyte disturbances can lower the seizure threshold

General Health

Fatigue and Weakness: Due to malnutrition, dehydration, and electrolyte imbalances

Immune System Suppression: Increased susceptibility to infections and slower healing due to poor nutrition

Bulimia nervosa has profound and diverse medical complications, impacting nearly every organ system in the body. The physical and psychological toll of the disorder highlights the importance of early detection and comprehensive treatment, which should address both the physical health concerns and the underlying psychological issues driving the behavior. Proper intervention can prevent many of these complications and significantly improve the quality of life for those affected.

TABLE 8.2

HOW BULIMIA NERVOSA AFFECTS YOUR BODY	
Blood	Anemia
Body electrolytes	Dehydration, low potassium, magnesium, chloride, and sodium
Brain	Depression, anxiety, dizziness, shame, low self-esteem, cognitive impairment
Cheeks, face	Swelling, soreness, nosebleeds
Heart	Irregular heartbeat, heart failure, palpitations, low blood pressure
Hormones	Irregular or absent periods
Intestines	Constipation, irregular bowel movements, bloating, diarrhea, abdominal cramping
Kidneys	Problems from diuretic abuse
Mouth	Cavities, tooth enamel erosion, gum disease, sensitivity to hot/cold foods, swollen salivary glands, mouth sores
Muscles	Fatigue, weakness
Skin	Abrasion of knuckles, dry skin, brittle hair
Stomach	Ulcers, pain, possible rupture, delayed emptying
Throat and esophagus	Sore, irritated, possible tear and rupture, blood in vomit, heartburn, acid reflux

Credit: Office on Women's Health, U.S. Department of Health and Human Services, 2022c

BINGE-EATING DISORDER

Binge-eating behaviors, often dismissed as "emotional eating," can be perilous if untreated, leading to various medical complications arising from the physical and psychological effects of overeating and subsequent weight gain (Rittenhouse, 2012). These medical complications include electrolyte imbalances, metabolic disturbances, gastrointestinal problems, nutritional deficits, and increased risk of conditions like Type 2 diabetes and hypertension. These, and the following complications can significantly impact the health and mortality rates of individuals with binge-eating disorder (Physiopedia, 2021; Gaudiani, 2019; Rittenhouse, 2012; Taylor & Braithwaite Holden, 2009).

Cardiovascular System
  Hypertension: High blood pressure because of excessive weight and poor diet
  Heart Disease: Increased risk of coronary artery disease, heart attack, and stroke
Metabolic System
  Type 2 Diabetes: Higher risk of insulin resistance associated with excessive weight
  Dyslipidemia: Elevated cholesterol and triglyceride levels, contributing to cardiovascular risks
  Metabolic Syndrome: A cluster of conditions that increase the likelihood of heart disease, stroke, and diabetes
Gastrointestinal System
  Gastroesophageal Reflux Disease (GERD): Increased stomach acid and heartburn due to overeating
  Gallbladder Disease: Higher risk of gallstones and gallbladder inflammation
  Irritable Bowel Syndrome (IBS): Binge eating can exacerbate symptoms of IBS, causing abdominal pain, bloating, and changes in bowel habits
Endocrine System
  Hormonal Imbalances: Including issues with reproductive hormones, potentially affecting menstrual cycles and fertility in women
  Polycystic Ovary Syndrome (PCOS): Common condition in women with BED, characterized by irregular periods and metabolic complications (Ottey, 2021; PCOS Challenge, Inc., n.d.)
Musculoskeletal System
  Osteoarthritis: Increased wear and tear on joints due to excessive weight, particularly in the knees and hips
  Chronic Pain: Ongoing, generalized body pain often caused by the strain of excess weight
Psychological and Psychiatric Effects
  Depression and Anxiety: High prevalence of co-occurring mood disorders
  Low Self-Esteem: Guilt or shame about eating behaviors and poor body image

Substance Abuse: Increased risk of substance use disorders

Respiratory System

Sleep Apnea: Breathing interruptions during sleep

Asthma: Excess weight can exacerbate respiratory issues, leading to more severe asthma symptoms

Renal System

Kidney Disease: Elevated risk due to hypertension, diabetes, and metabolic syndrome

General Health

Excess Weight: A common consequence of BED, leading to health issues

Fatigue: Chronic tiredness due to poor sleep quality, excessive weight, and nutritional imbalances

Nutritional Deficiencies: Lack of essential nutrients due to poor dietary choices

Binge-eating disorder has wide-ranging medical complications, affecting nearly every bodily system. These complications underscore the importance of early intervention and comprehensive treatment approaches that address both the physical and psychological aspects of the disorder. Proper management can help mitigate these risks and improve overall health outcomes.

TABLE 8.3

HOW BINGE-EATING DISORDER AFFECTS YOUR BODY	
Brain	Increased risk for depression, anxiety, low self-esteem
Breath	Shortness of breath, obstructive sleep apnea
Heart	High blood pressure, high cholesterol, heart disease
Hormones	Irregular periods, fertility concerns, PCOS
Intestines	Acid reflux, heartburn, IBS
Metabolism	Metabolic syndrome, Type 2 diabetes
Muscles and joints	Osteoarthritis, generalized body pain, decreased mobility due to joint degeneration
Weight	Often associated with obesity

Credit: Office on Women's Health, U.S. Department of Health and Human Services, 2022b

COMMON MEDICAL COMPLICATIONS IN BLACK INDIVIDUALS

Black individuals contend with notable medical complexities that may intersect with those observed in eating disorders. It is essential to recognize that certain medical conditions may impact Black women more than other demographics, with factors like genetics, socioeconomic status, and health care disparities playing significant roles (Parker et al., 2023; Mikhail & Klump, 2021; Sonneville & Lipson, 2018). Prevalent health issues among Black women include:

1. Cardiovascular disease: Black women face an elevated risk of cardiovascular diseases, including hypertension, heart disease, and stroke attributed to factors such as higher rates of obesity, diabetes, and high blood pressure within the Black community (Parker et al., 2023). Cardiovascular disease disproportionately affects Black women, with 22.6% of deaths among Black non-Hispanic women attributed to heart disease in 2021, representing a higher percentage compared to other racial and ethnic groups (CDC, 2024).

2. Breast cancer: Black women exhibit a higher mortality rate from breast cancer compared to other racial/ethnic groups. Factors contributing to this disparity include delayed diagnosis, limited health care access, and inequalities in treatment options (Parker et al., 2023; Chinn et al., 2021).

3. Maternal health: Black women experience elevated rates of maternal mortality and morbidity, influenced by factors like inadequate prenatal care, higher rates of pre-existing conditions, and racial biases in the health care system (Bailey-Straebler & Susser, 2023; Parker et al., 2023; Chinn et al., 2021).

4. Fibroids: Black women are more prone to developing uterine fibroids, noncancerous growths in the uterus that can cause symptoms like heavy menstrual bleeding, pelvic pain, and fertility issues (Parker et al., 2023).

5. Mental health: Black women confront distinct mental health challenges, including heightened rates of depression, anxiety, and postpartum depression, stemming from systemic racism, discrimination, and limited access to mental health care (Parker et al., 2023; Bell, 2017).

Although these medical concerns can affect individuals of any race or ethnicity, they are particularly prevalent among Black women and must be acknowledged. Black women frequently need to assertively advocate for themselves to secure consistent and high-quality health care. Addressing health care disparities and advocating for equitable access to quality health care is pivotal in tackling these issues and enhancing health outcomes for Black women.

Eating disorder specialists, or providers familiar with eating disorders, are imperative in exploring differential diagnoses. Here are several major medical issues affecting Black women that parallel complications seen in eating disorders (Mikhail & Klump, 2021; de Dios et al., 2020; Taylor & Braithwaite Holden, 2009):

Cardiovascular Disease
> *Hypertension* (High Blood Pressure)
> *Heart Disease*
> Similarities to eating disorders: Eating disorders can also lead to cardiovascular problems like heart arrhythmias, heart failure, and hypotension due to malnutrition and electrolyte imbalances.

Diabetes
> *Type 2 Diabetes*
> Similarities to eating disorders: Both conditions can result in substantial metabolic disruptions. For example, individuals with eating disorders might experience hypoglycemia (low blood sugar) or misuse insulin, mirroring the glucose regulation issues observed in diabetes.

Obesity
> *Higher Rates of Obesity and Related Complications*
> Similarities to eating disorders: Both obesity and eating disorders can result in gastrointestinal problems, cardiovascular complications, and endocrine disturbances. Binge-eating disorder, specifically, is closely linked to obesity.

Chronic Kidney Disease
> *Higher Prevalence of Kidney Issues*
> Similarities to eating disorders: Both conditions can cause renal complications. In eating disorders, dehydration and electrolyte imbalances can lead to kidney damage like chronic kidney disease.

Mental Health Disorders
> *Higher Rates of Depression and Anxiety*
> Similarities to eating disorders: Depression and anxiety often coexist

with eating disorders, contributing to considerable psychological distress that impacts overall health in both populations.

Sickle Cell Disease

A Genetic Blood Disorder

Differences from eating disorders: This condition is specific to individuals of African descent and presents unique complications such as pain crises and organ damage, which are distinct from those associated with eating disorders.

Similarities in Medical Complications

Cardiovascular Issues: Both populations may encounter significant heart-related issues, whether stemming from hypertension and heart disease in Black individuals or malnutrition and electrolyte imbalances in eating disorders.

Metabolic Disruptions: Diabetes and the metabolic effects of eating disorders, like hypoglycemia and insulin manipulation, underscore a mutual susceptibility in managing glucose and metabolic health.

Kidney Problems: Dehydration, electrolyte imbalances, and chronic kidney damage are shared concerns in both eating disorders and chronic kidney disease, which is prevalent among Black individuals.

Mental Health: Both populations experience heightened rates of depression and anxiety, emphasizing the necessity of comprehensive mental health support in addressing these conditions.

Medical complications faced by Black individuals, including cardiovascular disease, diabetes, and chronic kidney disease, exhibit notable similarities to those observed in eating disorders. Both groups encounter complex and multifaceted health challenges, highlighting the need for comprehensive, culturally sensitive, and multidisciplinary approaches to treatment and care.

HIDDEN IN PLAIN SIGHT

Eating disorders are among the deadliest mental health disorders (Goldstein & Gvion, 2019), second only to opioid overdose in recent years. However, what many people fail to realize is that death certificates often do not list the eating disorder as the cause of death. Instead, it may list the immediate medical cause. This can lead to underreporting the impact of eating disorders on mortality rates (Udo et al., 2019) and may obscure the need for resources and attention to these conditions. The mortality associated with eating disorders can be due to various direct and indirect complications, including:

Medical complications: These can arise from malnutrition, electrolyte imbalances, gastrointestinal problems, cardiovascular issues, and other organ damage.

Metabolic complications: Severe eating disorders can lead to metabolic disturbances that can be fatal if not treated promptly and effectively.

Suicide: Individuals with eating disorders have a higher risk of suicidal ideation and suicide attempts.

Early screening and detection are critical for improving outcomes for individuals with eating disorders. This is particularly important for populations that may be underdiagnosed or undertreated, such as Black women and girls. Research has shown that eating disorders affect individuals across all ethnic and racial groups, but there can be disparities in who gets diagnosed and receives treatment (National Eating Disorders Association, n.d.; Sonneville & Lipson, 2018). Additionally, socioeconomic disadvantage and age can increase the incidence of many health conditions, highlighting the need for comprehensive medical evaluation. Some of the laboratory and medical tests recommended (Gaudiani, 2019) include:

- Orthostatic vital signs
- Basic metabolic panel (BMP)
- Dual Energy X-Ray Absorptiometry (DEXA, or DXA) scan
- Complete blood count (CBC) with differentials
- Physical examination to assess overall health and signs of physical complications
- Electrocardiogram (EKG or ECG)

Testing protocols may differ based on the individual's symptoms, medical history, and the health care provider's clinical judgment. The objective of testing is to evaluate the individual's physical and psychological well-being and to guide appropriate treatment planning.

Musculoskeletal System

Eating disorders, notably anorexia, profoundly impact bone and muscle health. Stringent dietary limitations and malnourishment impede the growth of bone density, increasing the likelihood of developing osteoporosis and experiencing bone fractures later in life (Eating Disorder Hope, 2024). Diminished muscle mass may result in cardiac complications such as heart failure. Bone density loss is usually diagnosed through a DEXA scan (Gaudiani, 2019). As we age, bone production slows, but eating disorders can accelerate this process through malnutrition and stress, which hampers the body's ability to receive adequate nutrition (Clarke et al., 2021). *Osteopenia*, a reversible condition, is a warning sign of insufficient nutrition. *Osteoporosis*, characterized by weakened bones, occurs when the body cannot produce new bone quickly enough, leading to injuries, fractures, and chronic pain (Eating Disorder Hope, 2024; Bothwell, 2022). Osteoporosis is a lifelong condition that can be difficult to manage without medical treatment. Recommended medical tests include (Gaudiani, 2019):

- Dual Energy X-Ray Absorptiometry (DEXA or DXA) scan
- Serum estradiol
- Calcitonin
- Type 1 procollagen carboxy-terminal propeptides
- Serum type 1 collagen carboxy-terminal telopeptide

Central Nervous System

Mimura et al. (2021) recommend that health care providers closely monitor patients with severe anorexia nervosa undergoing refeeding therapy for neurological symptoms, which can sometimes be overlooked or underestimated in clinical settings. These symptoms include cognitive impairments such as brain fog, concentration difficulties, headaches, memory problems, and issues with executive functions which may result from cerebral atrophy due to starvation, poor nutrition, and weight loss.

Renal System (Urinary System)

Kidney Failure. While not medical professionals in the traditional sense, Dr. Small and I have delved into understanding the medical complexities associated with eating disorders. Reflecting on personal experiences, I recall my grandmother's daily use of laxatives, a practice I once innocently thought was simply her way of managing constipation; I thought it was normal! With a deeper understanding of eating disorders, I now recognize the potential implications of laxative abuse. Excessive laxative use can potentially lead to electrolyte imbalances and dehydration, which can put a strain on the kidneys and potentially lead to kidney failure in severe cases. Additionally, it highlights how easily such behaviors can be normalized without recognizing their disordered nature, particularly among Black women who might misuse laxatives for weight control.

In her book *Sick Enough* (2019), Dr. Jennifer Gaudiani discusses the significance of bicarbonate and chloride levels, revealing how imbalances can indicate severe issues like chronic diarrhea or dehydration from laxative abuse. It is essential for health care providers to recognize the dual impact of laxative abuse on bicarbonate levels and not overlook potential serious abnormalities that could lead to kidney failure. Laxative abuse may lead to nausea, cramps, and diarrhea; it can also cause pancreatitis and kidney stones (Gaudiani, 2019). Daily laxative use can have detrimental effects on the body. Some possible outcomes of prolonged laxative use include:

- Laxative dependency: Repeated use of laxatives can lead to dependence, making it difficult for the body to have bowel movements naturally without their aid.
- Dehydration: Laxatives can result in excessive water loss, leading to dehydration and electrolyte imbalances.
- Nutrient deficiencies: Persistent laxative use can interfere the absorption of nutrients from food, potentially causing deficiencies in essential vitamins and minerals.
- Bowel damage: Excessive laxative use can harm the muscles and nerves in the digestive system, culminating in chronic constipation and other gastrointestinal complications.
- Disruption of gut flora: Laxatives have the potential to disturb the balance of beneficial gut bacteria, resulting in digestive problems and a compromised immune system.

While laxative use may initially seem like a harmless means to aid bowel movements, particularly when observed within familial contexts, deeper professional insight reveals a more complex reality. Among Black women and girls, laxative use often serves as a method to control or prevent weight gain; weight loss may not be the intended outcome. Many clients have recounted discovering a historical pattern of laxative use or abuse among their grandparents and even their parents, despite it not being openly discussed. This silent presence of laxative use often perpetuated a diet mentality within the family, further influencing subsequent generations.

Hyponatremia. Hyponatremia is a potentially life-threatening condition characterized by low sodium levels in the blood. Sodium is crucial for maintaining water balance and supporting nerve and muscle function throughout the body. Causes include excessive water intake, medications, hormonal issues, kidney problems, heart failure, liver disease, or conditions causing fluid retention. Symptoms vary based on severity rate of onset. Mild cases may have no symptoms at all, but as the condition becomes more severe, symptoms can include:

- Nausea and vomiting
- Headache
- Confusion
- Loss of energy and fatigue
- Restlessness and irritability
- Muscle weakness, spasms, or cramps
- Seizures
- Coma

Endocrine System

The endocrine system, responsible for regulating metabolism, energy levels, and reproduction through hormone secretion, is profoundly affected by eating disorders due to malnourishment (Rittenhouse, 2021b). This disruption causes hormonal imbalances and interferes with vital bodily processes. Specifically, the hypothalamus, located at the brain's base, is impacted, affecting cues for nourishment, sleep patterns, and reproductive function. Ovarian functioning can also be compromised, leading to menstrual irregularities and conditions like hypothalamic amenorrhea and polycystic ovarian syndrome (PCOS) (Yasmin et al., 2022; Rittenhouse, 2021b).

Diabetes. Black women are disproportionately impacted by both Type 1 and Type 2 diabetes with the latter being the most prevalent. In a 2022 National Diabetes Surveillance System, the CDC reports that this disease remains prevalent among this demographic and ranks as the fourth leading cause of death (Office of Minority Health, HHS, 2023). Diabetes is almost twice as common in Black women compared to White women, and having a family background of African American (Black) is a risk factor (Office of Minority Health, HHS, 2023, 2015a). Type 2 diabetes typically emerges later in life and disrupts the production or function of insulin regulation of blood glucose levels, impacting metabolism and growth in the body (Wilcox, 2005).

Given that 90–95% of diabetes cases are Type 2 diabetes, national estimates as compiled by the Centers for Disease Control and Prevention (CDC) do not differentiate by diabetes type (Encinosa, 2021). In our diet-focused society, many attribute Type 2 diabetes and other medical conditions to the lifestyles and the types of food (diet) that Black women eat. It may be surprising to some to learn that malnutrition and stress contribute to Type 2 diabetes and may be passed on through *epigenetic* (the study of how environmental factors and behaviors can alter gene expression without changing the DNA sequence; these changes can influence gene activity and may be passed down to future generations [Chinn et al., 2021]) mechanisms (Encinosa, 2021). A colleague would frequently say, "It's not always about the food, but the impact (of stress) on the soul."

A former client received a Type 2 diabetes mellitus (T2DM) diagnosis at the age of 30. Reflecting on her past, she recalled her primary care physician frequently emphasizing the importance of her health, suggesting dietary changes, and starting diabetic medications to regulate her glucose levels. However, her doctor never delved into her eating behaviors, focusing solely on the types of foods she consumed. She admitted that she never brought up her binge-eating behaviors, she also was never prompted to discuss them. She revealed a history of binge eating spanning a decade, with half of that time predating her diabetes diagnosis. The client began to question whether her diabetes diagnosis could have been prevented if her binge-eating behaviors had been identified and addressed earlier by health care providers or if she had disclosed those behaviors. This raises concerns about the potential impact of untreated binge eating on overall health outcomes and underscores the importance of early detection and intervention for eating disorders.

A 2017 study found most of the Type 2 diabetes patients felt stigmatized, most commonly citing perceptions that Type 2 diabetes is a character flaw or personal failure due to "overeating, poor diet, inactivity, laziness, or being overweight or obese" (Liu et al., 2017). When negative stereotypes surrounding Type 2 diabetes intersect with preexisting biases against minority communities, it perpetuates the pathologization of minority cultures. Stress related to weight stigma and oppression can contribute to the development of Type 2 diabetes, not just eating behaviors.

Type 1 Diabetes. Type 1 diabetes is a chronic autoimmune disorder where the pancreas produces little or no insulin, which is essential for glucose to enter cells and provide energy (Tarcin et al., 2023; Strayhorn, 2009). The immune system mistakenly attacks and destroys insulin-producing cells in the pancreas. While the exact cause is unknown, it is believed to result from a combination of genetic and environmental factors, like viral infections. Symptoms, which can develop rapidly, especially in children, include increased thirst, frequent urination, hunger, weight loss, fatigue, and blurred vision (Tarcin et al., 2023). Typically diagnosed in children and young adults, Type 1 diabetes has no cure and requires lifelong management. Disordered eating behaviors frequently occur among adolescents with Type 1 diabetes, potentially harming their metabolic control and overall health (Tarcin et al., 2023).

Some clients misuse insulin to lose weight, a disordered eating behavior like diabulimia, involving the intentional manipulation of insulin doses (Tarcin et al., 2023; Nitsch et al., 2021). This practice, known as insulin manipulation, is a significant issue in the Black community and other groups, where individuals intentionally underdose or omit insulin to induce hyperglycemia to control weight or blood sugar levels. Such behavior is complex and can lead to serious consequences like uncontrolled blood sugar, diabetic ketoacidosis, and long-term diabetes complications (Nitsch et al., 2021). Health care providers must be aware of this potential issue in their diabetic patients (Tarcin et al., 2023).

Providers should diligently screen for signs of insulin manipulation, such as unexplained blood sugar fluctuations or reluctance to discuss insulin management. Open, nonjudgmental conversations about insulin use and any challenges patients face are essential. Health care providers need to be informed about the prevalence of insulin manipulation in the Black community and actively support patients struggling with this issue. Recognizing insulin manipulation for weight loss as a serious manifestation of disordered eating is crucial for implementing comprehensive treatment strategies. This understanding within the broader eating disorder spectrum allows for tailored interventions and support systems, ultimately fostering improved health outcomes for affected individuals.

Diabetic Ketoacidosis (DKA)

Diabetic ketoacidosis (DKA) is a severe complication of diabetes where the body, lacking insulin, breaks down fat too rapidly, causing a buildup of acidic ketones in the blood. This condition is more common in Type 1 diabetes but can also occur in Type 2 during severe illness or stress. Symptoms include nausea, vomiting, abdominal pain, rapid breathing, fruity breath, confusion, and coma. Black individuals may be at higher risk for DKA due to disparities in health care and socioeconomic factors. Treatment involves insulin, fluids, and electrolytes, typically in a hospital. Certain diets like intermittent fasting or low carb/high protein can also induce ketoacidosis, as can alcoholic and starvation conditions.

Symptoms of ketoacidosis can include:

- Excessive thirst
- Frequent urination
- Nausea and vomiting
- Abdominal pain
- Weakness or fatigue
- Shortness of breath
- Fruity-scented breath
- Confusion

Lymphatic System

The immune system plays a vital role in defending the body against infections, comprising components such as white blood cells, antibodies, and lymphatic organs (Oh et al., 2022). However, eating disorders can impair immune function, leaving individuals vulnerable to infections and other health complications (Bothwell, 2022; Oh et al., 2022). For instance, anorexia nervosa may lead to malnourishment and bone marrow failure and may exacerbate infection risks (Bothwell, 2022). Bulimia, characterized by binge-purge cycles, can swell parotid glands and lead to recurrent tonsillitis (Bothwell, 2022). Given the serious medical consequences of eating disorders and their impact on various aspects of life, seeking treatment is imperative.

Reproductive System

Polycystic ovarian syndrome (PCOS), the most common endocrine disorder in women, is characterized by a complex interplay of hormones, metabolism, and reproduction (Yasmin et al., 2022; PCOS Challenge, Inc., n.d.). Diagnosis typically involves identifying at least two out of three key criteria: irregular menstrual cycles or ovulation, signs of hyperandrogenism like excess hair growth or acne, and the presence of multiple immature follicles in the ovaries (Ottey, 2021). Additionally, it is crucial to rule out other conditions with similar symptoms.

PCOS can lead to various challenges, including fertility issues, mental health concerns, insulin resistance, and metabolic syndrome. Sasha Ottey (2021) highlights that Black women with PCOS are more prone to higher body weights, hypertension, and a heightened risk of cardiovascular disease. Additionally, over half of women with PCOS develop Type 2 diabetes or prediabetes by age 40, and they face a 4 to 7 times higher risk of heart attack compared to women without PCOS of the same age (PCOS Challenge, Inc., n.d.). Despite these risks, PCOS remains poorly understood, with an estimate of up to 70% of affected women going undiagnosed, leaving them vulnerable to associated health complications (Yasmin et al., 2022).

A former client expressed frustration during treatment as she shared her struggle with fertility. Despite efforts with her partner, she faced uncertainty and frustration as to why conception remained elusive. Along the way, she discovered she had PCOS, a condition she knew little about. Reflecting on her medical history, she recognized symptoms dating back to high school, including excess facial hair, persistent acne, and indications of insulin resistance. She felt disappointed that her provider hadn't identified PCOS earlier, given the symptoms she experienced. Women with bulimia nervosa and binge-eating disorder may be at higher risk of developing PCOS, which also compromises fertility (Nitsch et al., 2021).

Eating disorders and reproductive health are closely connected, as nutritional deficits and disordered eating patterns can greatly impair fertility. Eating disorder behaviors, like calorie restriction, avoiding specific nutrients, or purging, may not always result in noticeably low weight but can still cause significant hormonal imbalances that lead to irregular or absent menstrual cycles (*amenorrhea*) and reduced ovulation (*anovulation*) (Bailey-Straebler & Susser, 2023).

Hormonal disruptions from eating disorders occur as the body's adaptive response to perceived starvation, conserving energy by reducing nonessential functions like reproduction. These changes are highly individualized, restrictive eating doesn't always result in clinically low weight but rather a weight insufficient for the body's physiological needs (Thomas, 2022). Dietary restriction can markedly impair fertility. Higher maternal weights during pregnancy can elevate the risk of gestational diabetes and hypertensive disorders, conditions that Black women are particularly susceptible to (Bailey-Straebler & Susser, 2023). Detecting eating disorders in women of reproductive age is crucial to mitigate obstetric risks associated with both high and low maternal weight (Thomas, 2022).

It is important to understand that the impact on reproductive health is due to internal stress and hormonal changes, not necessarily the extent of weight loss (Bailey-Straebler & Susser, 2023). Chronic stress from racism, rather than race itself, is a significant risk factor for maternal mental health disorders. This ongoing stress and higher lifetime exposure to trauma exacerbates adverse health and mental health outcomes among Black women, perpetuating even higher stress levels (Policy Center for Maternal Mental Health, 2023).

This persistent intergenerational stress cycle, known as *weathering*, refers to a series of biological processes that deteriorate Black women's physical and mental health (Policy Center for Maternal Mental Health, 2023). Black individuals are more likely to experience birth trauma compared to White individuals and face three to four times higher mortality rates from pregnancy-related causes than White women, with many of these deaths being preventable (CDC Office of Health Equity, 2024; Black Mamas Matter Alliance, 2020). Addressing these issues requires a holistic approach that focuses on restoring nutritional health, achieving a healthy weight, and treating the underlying psychological aspects of the eating disorder.

A former client experienced several miscarriages, and her partner's mother questioned what might be wrong, which led the client to wonder if she was at fault. The client later realized that her partner's mother was unaware of how common miscarriages were because their family didn't discuss such topics. In contrast, the client grew up in a family where her mother, aunts, and grandmother openly talked about female-related issues like miscarriages, menopause, and bodily changes. This open communication helped her understand and cope with these experiences, while families that don't discuss them often leave Black women confused and self-blaming. She felt grateful for the supportive and informative environment provided by her maternal relatives.

Cardiovascular System

Black individuals exhibit a higher prevalence of cardiovascular risk factors, including hypertension and diabetes, which poses a serious threat as hypertension is a significant risk factor for heart disease and stroke (Cooper et al., 2023). Black women exhibit higher rates of hypertension, often developing it at younger ages compared to White women or men, yet they are less likely to receive adequate treatment to manage it (Taylor & Braithwaite Holden, 2009). Black women are disproportionately underserved in health care, experiencing lower rates of referral for diagnostic procedures and limited access to lifesaving therapies for heart attacks compared to other demographic groups (Taylor & Braithwaite Holden, 2009).

Stroke, closely linked to heart disease and hypertension, is exacerbated by stress. As the burden of stress increases, the physical responses of the body can make an individual more prone to injuries and illnesses. Therefore, it is unsurprising that stress stemming from experiences of discrimination correlates with poorer psychological well-being and worse physical health outcomes, particularly among Black individuals who report experiencing greater degrees of discrimination. Psychosocial stressors like discrimination, hostility, diet, socioeconomic status, and sleep patterns contribute significantly to these conditions (Davis et al., 2009).

Stroke is the third leading cause of death for all women and is particularly severe in Black women (CDC, Heart Disease Facts, 2024; Davis et al., 2009). This heightened severity is partly due to the overrepresentation of Black women in lower socioeconomic groups. Improving outcomes for Black women may be achieved by increasing awareness of these conditions and developing tailored interventions that address their specific needs and circumstances.

Orthostatic Changes or Intolerances. Orthostasis refers to a drop in blood pressure that occurs when standing up from a sitting or lying position (Gaudiani, 2019). This sudden change can lead to dizziness or lightheadedness. During the check-in process, some of our patients have felt lightheaded or dizzy when moving from sitting to standing, known as orthostatic symptoms. These orthostatic symptoms result from a drop in blood pressure or heart rate as the body adjusts to the change in position. Patients often dismiss these symptoms, underestimating their significance for overall physical health. Additional cardiac concerns include (National Center for Health Statistics [NCHS], 2019):

Tachycardia: A condition where the heart is beating faster than normal, typically defined as a resting heart rate of over 100 beats per minute in adults.

Bradycardia: Defined as a resting heart rate that is below 60 beats per minute.

Postural Tachycardia Syndrome (PoTS): Defined by the inability of the body to adequately control blood circulation and blood pressure, leading to a marked rise in heart rate when an individual transitions from a reclining to an upright stance. The word *postural* pertains to the position or stance of the body, while *tachycardia* denotes an accelerated heart rate.

Hypertension (High Blood Pressure): A medical condition where there is elevated pressure in the arteries. It is diagnosed when blood pressure consistently measures 130/80 mmHg or higher (Davis et al., 2023). This condition poses a significant risk factor for various cardiovascular diseases, including heart attack, stroke, heart failure, and kidney disease (National Center for Health Statistics [NCHS], 2019).

High blood pressure is commonly referred to as the *silent killer* and may not present noticeable symptoms but can lead to serious health conditions and other complications. Regular blood pressure checks and management by health care professionals are crucial steps in maintaining health and preventing related complications. While dietary factors like high-fat, salty, and fried foods are often implicated in the diagnosis of high blood pressure among Black individuals, other significant contributors exist. Stress plays a substantial role, encompassing minority stress, historical trauma, racism-induced trauma, and general stress (Adams & Allwood, 2023; Hopkins, 2021). These factors contribute to the elevated prevalence of high blood pressure and other health issues among Black women.

High Cholesterol: Refers to elevated levels of cholesterol in the blood. Cholesterol is a crucial substance for hormone production, vitamin D synthesis, and digestion (National Center for Health Statistics [NCHS], 2019). While the body produces cholesterol, it is also obtained from animal products. While genetic factors may contribute to elevated blood levels of cholesterol, it is largely preventable and treatable.

Other Diseases Impacting Black Individuals

Sickle cell disease (SCD) is a life-threatening genetic blood disorder affecting over 100,000 individuals in the United States, with 90% of them being Black (Hood et al., 2022). Those with SCD face unpredictable pain episodes and frequent health care needs, often encountering health-related stigma due to physical limitations, social isolation, and discrimination (Hood et al., 2022). This stigma is linked to higher levels of depressive symptoms, fatigue, and anxiety.

Refeeding Syndrome. Refeeding syndrome is a serious, potentially fatal condition that occurs when malnourished individuals begin eating again, causing dangerous shifts in fluids and electrolytes within the body (Gaudiani, 2019). This can lead to various complications, even in individuals with different body sizes and histories of restrictive eating behaviors. To prevent refeeding syndrome, health care providers must closely monitor patients to prevent dangerous imbalances that could lead to the syndrome. Symptoms of refeeding syndrome may include:

- Muscle weakness
- Confusion
- Respiratory distress
- Cardiac failure
- Seizures
- Arrhythmias
- Hypophosphatemia (low phosphate)
- Hypokalemia (low potassium)
- Hypomagnesemia (low magnesium)

Gastrointestinal/Digestive System

Thyroid disease has varied impacts on Black women, influenced by factors such as genetic predisposition, health care access, and socioeconomic status (Office on Women's Health, HHS, 2015b). These disorders, which disproportionately affect women, can disrupt menstrual cycles, impair fertility, and pose pregnancy risks like premature delivery and preeclampsia.

When coupled with eating disorders, thyroid issues further complicate health outcomes by affecting hormonal balance, metabolism, and overall well-being (Office on Women's Health, HHS, 2015b). Addressing these intertwined challenges requires culturally sensitive approaches in diagnosis, treatment, and support tailored specifically for Black women, considering cultural factors and societal pressures related to body image and health norms.

Gastroesophageal reflux disorder (GERD) occurs when the muscles between the stomach and the esophagus weaken, allowing stomach acid and partially digested food to travel back up through the esophagus. This condition can result from disordered eating behaviors, notably those associated with bulimia, which weakens the muscles and contributes to GERD. GERD manifests through symptoms such as heartburn, acid regurgitation, nausea, diarrhea, and constipation. It is essential to recognize that while GERD is a significant digestive issue linked to purging, it's not the only complication that may arise from such behaviors.

Severe malnourishment can lead to electrolyte imbalances, cardiac complications, bone density loss, hormonal disturbances, impaired immune function, organ damage, cognitive and neurological effects, and delayed gastric emptying or *gastroparesis*—slowed or delayed stomach emptying. Individuals experience feelings of fullness quickly, bloating and may report "belly" distension. Consistent food intake and/or weight restoration, if warranted, typically resolves gastroparesis. These consequences underscore the importance of early intervention and proper treatment to mitigate potential complications arising from disordered eating behaviors.

MEDICAL COMPLICATIONS IN OLDER BLACK WOMEN

Triple jeopardy describes the unique challenges faced by low-income Black women at retirement age (Taylor & Braithwaite Holden, 2009). These women are particularly susceptible to a wide range of health disparities. While advanced age brings health challenges for all racial and gender groups, Black women remain particularly vulnerable. Their socioeconomic status exacerbates this vulnerability, making older Black women especially susceptible to health issues. Menopause contributes to the heightened vulnerability to heart disease among older Black women. Menopause increases the risk for heart disease as estrogen, which provides some protection against heart disease, decreases after menopause (Sellers et al., 2009). Cultural taboos around menopause discussions have led many Black women to grow up without essential knowledge about reproductive health, causing unnecessary anxiety about normal changes (Gary et al., 2015). This discomfort with the topic continues into adulthood for some, making it difficult for them to express concerns and seek appropriate care.

MOVING FORWARD

To advance health equity for Black women, we must deepen our understanding of the complex health disparities they face, enabling us to implement targeted strategies and policies that address systemic barriers and promote equitable access to health care. However, identifying the next steps is challenging, particularly given the lack of representation of Black women in research, which contributes to these disparities and limits access to care. Adopting an intersectional approach that considers how race, gender, class, and other factors intersect to shape experiences and influence health outcomes can lead to more equitable and effective health policies and interventions (Harris et al., 2022). This involves recognizing the impact of discrimination, resource access, and societal structures, as well as the interplay of various forms of oppression and privilege. By emphasizing health equity, we can bridge the gap between the goal of eliminating health disparities and the strategies needed to achieve it. As we work to elevate Black women's narratives and dismantle blame, we must challenge conventional research practices, promote cultural competence, address historical injustices, and advocate for systemic changes within the health care system.

Chapter 9

WAIT . . . BLACK MEN GET EATING DISORDERS TOO?

Several years ago, Carlton, a young man from Atlanta, enrolled as a freshman at a large university on the East Coast, known among other great things, for its successful sports programs. His family moved to Atlanta from Jamaica when he was three. Carlton had always been very popular at school and in his community. He was friendly and was considered quite good looking because of his smooth, dark skin and muscular physique. People often admired his long, natural, locked hair. Friends loved his Jamaican patois. He played several musical instruments, spoke two languages (English and Spanish) and was learning a third (Portuguese). In college, Carlton excelled academically with relative ease.

However, although it seemed he was liked well enough by others at his new school, he had a difficult time connecting with a core group of friends. He often felt uncomfortable or out of place. He felt this way a lot in classes, which were much larger than he was used to, or had expected. Professors and some students, perhaps not meaning to be offensive in their delivery, often did offend him with queries about his ethnic background. He often felt alone. Socially, he thought things could be better and wondered how to make that happen. Although he entered college on an academic scholarship, Carlton was also an athletic standout, exceling in three different high school sports (basketball, football, and track). Looking for greater opportunities to socialize, he decided to try out for the football team in college and did make the team.

Carlton quickly found that college football was different than high school football. He was surprised to see human beings so large. And while quite fit himself, at 6'5", 290 pounds, he thought his muscular frame seemed pretty lean compared with others. He decided that as an offensive lineman, he had better bulk up. He began counting calories and binge eating expressly to gain weight. He often ate until he was uncomfortably full. As planned, his increased weight did provide some advantages on the field. And soon, as in high school, Carlton became recognized for his skill and ability on the field. He also found greater success socially and even began spending time with a particular young lady. But even as his popularity grew, Carlton continued to feel on the periphery of friend groups. He began to feel awkward, as if he just didn't quite fit in. He became anxious in certain situations. To reduce anxiety and feel less awkward in social settings, he began drinking.

Meanwhile, Carlton continued to overeat. Between-meal snacks became meals themselves. His girlfriend noticed that he seemed almost obsessive about eating. He could easily eat an entire ham at one sitting. She guessed something was wrong because he started weighing himself after meals. And depending on what he saw on the scale, he would add another meal to his day in an effort to achieve and maintain his weight goal. He never tried to hide this behavior or his reasoning for it, thinking that this was just all part of college sports. Though he never said so, his girlfriend suspected that Carlton (and others) was encouraged by his training staff to eat those hefty portions.

After some time, Carlton became aware that he had begun bingeing and purging (. . . he didn't tell his girlfriend about that part). He remembered with crystal clarity the first time he did it. He had such indigestion and felt painfully bloated. He thought if he only threw up *a little*—because he didn't want to lose his caloric intake—that he'd feel better. And he did. Initially, Carlton only did it once or twice a month. Gradually he did it with greater frequency, often after drinking, which provided a convenient explanation for the behavior.

Though not at first, and not wanting to admit it to himself, he did come to the realization that this was something he should not be doing, although he was not exactly sure why. He continued to maintain secrecy about it. Because he was able to exercise a modicum of control over purging, reducing the number of times he did it each week, he believed that control over whether and when he purged was something he could maintain. However, he quickly discovered that as the frequency of bingeing and purging decreased, his drinking increased. The converse was also true.

More than a year passed before Carlton visited the counseling center for help. This was not so much because of any stigma around seeking treatment for mental health concerns, but because he was embarrassed about seeking help for doing something he had heard only women did.

CAUSES OF EATING DISORDERS IN BLACK MEN

Black men and women are both exposed to the same events that could and have served as mediating factors in the development of eating disorders (EDs). However, not everyone develops an ED. A number of factors account for why one may or may not develop an ED, including one's temperament, biology, environment, and culture. These factors can influence the way events are experienced by individuals, impacting particular outcomes. For instance, in terms of temperament, children who have anxiety or express obsessive tendencies are at an increased risk for developing anorexia nervosa (AN) (APA, 2022). Similarly, individuals who experienced weight issues, problems with self-esteem, depressive symptoms, and social anxiety as children are at a greater risk for developing bulimia nervosa (BN) (APA, 2022). It is not unusual for EDs to occur among first-degree biological family members (APA, 2022). In addition, persons with EDs are at greater risks for experiencing one or more co-occurring mental disorders (i.e., substance abuse), which could impact the expression of ED behaviors.

Many of the environmental events we're exposed to affect us similarly, while other events have had a slightly different, or even opposite effect on us, yet the outcome can be the same—an eating disorder. Colorism, racism, subtle racism, acculturative stress, microaggressions, macroaggressions, trauma, adverse childhood experiences (ACEs), health care disparities, violence and injustice, and inequity in pay are examples of some of those events.

SYMPTOM MANIFESTATION IN BLACK MEN

While ED symptom presentation in men may differ in some aspects from those presented in women, symptomology of the three most prevalent conditions can be seen in both men and women. With AN, for instance, both men and women restrict energy intake yielding significantly lower body weight than expected in various contexts (*DSM-5*, APA, 2022). Both men and women with binge-eating disorder (BED) can be observed to eat larger amounts of food than what others would eat under similar circumstances and feel negatively about themselves as a result. Similarly, persons with BN can be observed to eat large amounts, followed by engagement in compensatory behaviors with the intention of preventing weight gain (*DSM-5*, APA, 2022).

There may be some variations in the way these behaviors manifest in individuals, particularly if there are co-occurring conditions present (as noted above, and below). For example, some persons with AN may skip meals, while others may cut out whole food groups. Some may weigh themselves excessively and scrupulously monitor their food intake, careful to not exceed their calorie budget. Still others adhering to strict plans or strategies weigh their food and are cautious to not add a fraction of an ounce more than is allotted.

In the above case study, Carlton's bingeing behavior differed from what might ordinarily be seen in women, as perhaps did the reasons his symptoms arose initially. In Carlton's case, he began binge eating and quickly met *DSM-5* criteria for BED. And while he did often eat until he was uncomfortably full, as in the case of many persons who engage in binge eating, Carlton did not *always* do so. Most of the time his excessive eating was planned, occurring between meals, even when he wasn't feeling physically hungry. Recall, he began adding extra meals to bulk up in order to improve his performance as a member of the offensive line. He was eating for an express purpose.

Also, regarding the etiology of his concerns, while there is an element of muscularity-oriented disordered eating, the focus is not so much on muscle dysmorphia and body dissatisfaction in the sense of being unhappy with his image (e.g., in terms of attractiveness), as it is on being powerful enough to help his team advance toward the goal line. And as his behavior gradually migrated from BED to BN, which is not uncommon, particularly as one behavior decreases or increases in frequency, Carlton began misusing alcohol, sometimes drinking more as an excuse to purge by vomiting. And while many women with BN also purge by vomiting, as well as engaging in other compensatory behaviors including overexercising or using laxatives, the purpose of the behavior is likely different than in Carlton's case.

PREVALENCE OF EATING DISORDERS IN BLACK MEN

If I, Charlynn, didn't know better, I might believe after a review of the literature, that Black men were somehow spared from experiencing the awfulness of grappling with eating disorders. An article from 1987 was the first scholarly work I found that focused on a young Black man with problematic eating patterns. There were one or two other earlier articles in which a few Black cases were presented, or where racial influences on women with EDs were discussed. However, Burket et al.'s (1987) study was the first I saw addressing the subject of Black men expressly. They presented the case of a 14-year-old Black adolescent boy who was transferred from a pediatric hospital unit to the psychiatric unit after results of a comprehensive examination for episodes of vomiting were completely within normal limits. While the person in the case presented some classic symptoms of anorexia nervosa, with features of both restricting and binge-eating/purging type, the authors did not make that diagnosis. Instead, they ". . . classified" the young person ". . . as having an atypical eating disorder," (Burket et al., 1987) because, well, after all, it was 1987 and they were using the *DSM-III*.

Approximately 40 years later, we still can't talk with any measure of accuracy about the prevalence of EDs in Black men, due in part to a relatively small number of well-controlled or other research studies on EDs and Black men (Payton, 2014), or that even include Black men. For example, in Sangha et al.'s (2019) comprehensive scoping review designed expressly to identify gaps in evolving or emerging topics in the discipline, they give attention to many aspects concerning EDs and males including stigma, risk factors, body dissatisfaction, clinical presentation, treatment recommendations, and gender. However, there is no mention of the impact of race on EDs as an evolving topic. Nor is there a definitive statement indicating that Black men are an underrepresented or underserved segment of persons affected by this phenomenon.

In another recent review of the literature, Nagata et al. (2020) offers a few important observations about Black boys, but lumps them together under the heading *Special Populations*, which doesn't seem quite right either. Unfortunately, Harris's (2015) statement, that references to race and cultural factors in these regards are made as an afterthought, still seems true. As was historically the case with Black women in the ED literature, when there are only scant references to Black men in this literature, it can lead to the misconception that in general they don't grapple with these concerns. I never understood why these assumptions weren't challenged more often. Especially when you consider that for myriad reasons, Blacks have almost always experienced greater risks for a number of deadly or potentially deadly conditions and illnesses including heart disease, diabetes, and stroke (Office of Minority Health, HHS, 2019).

It begs the question, "Why would Black people be exempt from EDs?" For example, Black people have the highest mortality rate for all forms of cancer combined, compared with any other racial or ethnic group (American Cancer

Society, 2024); the cancer mortality rates in Black men are twice as high as Asian men, who have the lowest mortality rates (American Cancer Society, 2024); they suffer kidney failure at 3 times the rate of White persons (National Kidney Foundation, 2018), though they are 37% less likely than Whites to be preemptively referred for transplant evaluations (Gander et al., 2018); and the death rate for Black babies is twice that of those born to non-Latinx, White mothers (CDC, 2022a). Given these dreadful health statistics, it seems unlikely that Black men would be exempt from EDs, particularly given that EDs emerged as ways Black persons coped with racism and acculturative stress (Thompson, 1994) (see Chapter 3). Yet, the misconception that these groups have escaped EDs persists.

TREATMENT CENTER LEVELS OF CARE AND MULTIDISCIPLINARY EATING DISORDERS

ED treatment options for men were relatively limited until recent years, given that these disorders continue to be seen as issues concerning females. Still, levels of care provided and treatment team composition would perhaps be similar for Black men as for Black women, with the exception of a very few, if any, changes. As stated earlier (see Chapter 1 for greater detail), the level of care assigned for treatment is determined by a number of different factors including but not limited to the type of medical treatment required, specific manifestation or constellation of symptoms, frequency of presenting behaviors, existing coping skills and other protective factors, trauma history, co-occurring conditions, acuity of symptoms, suicidality, and available treatment modalities (CBT, DBT, IPT, FBT, etc.).

What bears mentioning however, is that through no one's fault in particular, certain aspects of the treatment process continue to exist in ways that are not as accommodating to men with eating disorders. For example, many group treatment formats as we currently know them, include mostly women, who at some point tend to feel comfortable enough to begin working through their issues in that format. Good luck getting one or two men—or two *Black* men—to sit with a group of women and be vulnerable about their eating disorders. Adjustments would need to be made to make groups more palatable to men. Although more attention is given to men with eating disorders now, the creation of large numbers of centers for men with EDs may still take a little more time. However, all-gender facilities seem to be trending. This may be a step in a positive direction.

MEDICAL COMPLICATIONS AND THE IMPACT OF EATING DISORDERS ON BLACK MEN

Anorexia Nervosa

Medical complications of eating disorders are well-detailed in Chapter 8, and there are many similarities between women and men in these regards. For example, as with women, eating disorders can cause medical complications that affect every organ and system in the body. For instance, findings of a recent study showed adolescent boys and young adults with AN were found to have significant cardiovascular abnormalities including bradycardia, orthostatic heart rate changes, abnormal cholesterol levels, and electrolyte problems including low potassium, phosphorus, and calcium (Vo et al., 2016) among other serious concerns associated with malnutrition. Gastroenterology problems included liver and other electrolyte abnormalities (Vo et al., 2016). Osteoporosis and related spinal injury without trauma or falls have been reported in younger males with AN, resulting in decreased height (Mehler & Andersen, 2010).

Bulimia Nervosa

Again, like women, men's bodies are similarly impacted by BN. For instance, women and men can both be affected by bowel disease and constipation, hypertension, diabetes mellitus, and high cholesterol. In men, BN can result in low testosterone which affects libido, and may also impact sperm count.

Binge-Eating Disorder

Research has well-documented that living in larger bodies, which can be the result of BED, can be associated with poor physical and mental health outcomes, leading to a reduced quality of life for many Black persons. And all of the same organ systems adversely impacted by behaviors associated with AN and BN can be impacted by BED. See Table 9.1.

TABLE 9.1

HOW EATING DISORDERS AFFECT MEN	
Bone health	Osteoporosis, low bone density, fractures
Breath	Shortness of breath, obstructive sleep apnea

Cardiovascular issues	High/low blood pressure, anemia, slow heart rate, heart palpitations, heart failure, heart disease
Electrolyte imbalances	Dehydration, low prealbumin, and low potassium, magnesium, phosphorus, chloride, sodium
Face, cheeks, and mouth	Swelling, soreness, tooth enamel erosion, gum disease, sensitivity to hot/cold foods, swollen salivary glands, mouth sores
Gastrointestinal problems	Chronic constipation, bloating, delayed stomach emptying, obstruction, irregular bowel movements, diarrhea, abdominal cramping, acid reflux, heartburn, irritable bowel syndrome
Hair and skin	Thinning and brittle hair, hair loss, abrasion of knuckles, bruise easily, dry skin, get cold easily, yellow skin, brittle and nails
Hormonal imbalances	Reduced testosterone levels, infertility, muscle wasting
Kidneys	Kidney stones, kidney failure, dehydration, low potassium, complications from diuretic abuse
Mental health	Anxious/obsessive thoughts, cognitive impairment, increased risk of suicidal ideation, higher levels of shame and stigma
Metabolism	Metabolic syndrome, Type 2 diabetes
Muscle atrophy and weakness	Muscle wasting, overall physical weakness, osteoarthritis, generalized body pain, decreased mobility due to joint degeneration, fatigue,
Throat and esophagus	Sore, irritated, can tear and rupture, blood in vomit, heartburn, acid reflux

Credit: Office on Women's Health, U.S. Department of Health and Human Services, 2022a, 2022b, 2022c; Physiopedia, 2021; Rosen, 2015

ASSESSMENT OF EATING DISORDERS IN BLACK MEN

In an examination of the assessment of measures of EDs in Black persons, Harris (2015) summarized the major points of some of the most frequently used assessment measures. Though all of the measures described are designed for the assessment of disordered eating symptomology and the diagnosis of EDs, she makes subtle distinctions between clinical interviews and self-report instruments.

Harris (2015) notes that because clinical interviews usually assess for a wider range of symptomology, they tend to be more comprehensive and detailed, and place greater emphasis on the clinical judgment of the evaluator compared with most self-report instruments. Information obtained from self-report measures is often helpful in tracking improvement or regression in behaviors or symptoms over time, as well as aiding in clinical decision-making. Harris also notes that one helpful, built-in feature of self-report measures is that they allow respondents to endorse items semi-privately. Completing an instrument in this manner is advantageous because the client often feels less shame, embarrassment, or anxiety and can therefore feel freer to respond more candidly and reliably, which should aid in diagnosing and treatment (Harris, 2015).

Harris (2015) evaluated several clinical interview measures, including the Eating Disorder Examination (EDE; Fairburn et al., 2014) semistructured, clinical interview, which is used to assess the range and severity of EDs. The 17th edition of the diagnostic instrument is the current version. A respondent's attitudes, cognitions, and behaviors relating to their eating patterns are assessed. Harris (2015) notes that the EDE has been dubbed "the gold standard of ED assessment." Initially, the lowest reliability had been reported in samples of persons with BED, suggesting caution should be taken when using the EDE with Black persons with BE or BED (Harris, 2015). However, recent studies, i.e., Burke et al. (2017) have shown a brief, 3-factor version of the EDE measured disordered eating symptomology similarly across samples of Black and White (non-Latinx ethnicity) girls and boys.

The Child Eating Disorder Examination (ChEDE; Bryant-Waugh et al., 1996) is a similar semistructured, clinical interview adapted from the EDE for use with adolescents and younger children. The ChEDE was also used in the Burke et al. (2017) study and showed similar results. Of approximately 11 self-report measures evaluated, only the Bulimia Test–Revised (BULIT-T; Thelen et al., 1991) was reported to have comparability for different racial or ethnic groups (Harris, 2015). Mixed results were reported for the measures that included Black samples in subsequent studies.

Because body image concerns in men are often linked to issues of muscularity, which many believe are not adequately captured by many of the extant measures, Murray et al. (2019) developed the Muscularity-Oriented Eating

Test (MOET). The self-report measure was designed to assess eating-related attitudes and behaviors associated with a drive to increase muscle mass. Fifteen items assess the drive to increase muscularity, as well as the drive to decrease body fat. A total of 511 participants (26 were Black) were included in the validation study. Adequate psychometric properties were reported for the MOET and for several other measures of muscularity-oriented eating concerns.

Harris (2015) wrote that Black persons' invisibility from the EDs literature has contributed to their exclusion from the norming and standardization of most of the extant measures for assessing ED risk factors and symptoms. Indeed, the converse is true as well. Their exclusion from the norming and standardization samples impacts their representation in the literature, as well as the accuracy of the reported prevalence of disordered eating patterns in Black men. Results of assessment measures normed on groups from which Black men were excluded would not reliably predict disordered eating behaviors of Black men (Harris, 2015), given their different cultural view of the world and their experience of it.

Because their experience would likely not be captured by items on any of the extant measurement instruments, results might not represent valid assessments of the construct being measured. In other words, a false-negative or type II error occurs. Specifically, assessment results would indicate no ED is present, when there is one present. These inaccurate results lead to the false conclusion that Black men do not experience EDs, perhaps accounting in part for the few cases presented in the literature and a reported prevalence that is likely lower in another than the actual prevalence rate.

Conversely, in a recent review of the literature, the U.S. Preventative Services Task Force (2022) discussed obtaining false-positive outcomes as a potential harm when using some screening questionnaires. They note that with false-positive results, there is an increased risk of seeking unnecessary referrals and treatment, labeling, anxiety, and stigma. Their discussion of race and ethnicity was minimal. While any faulty results are undesirable, it seems likely that erring on the side of an omission presents the greater concern in the case of Black men, because if an ED is present then further treatment isn't likely to be sought or recommended based on interpretation of the faulty findings.

Part of what makes successful treatment so difficult for these groups is that the illness has gone unrecognized and thus undiagnosed and untreated for so long, that the body is impacted both emotionally and physically. Until clinicians routinely ask about the existence of any disordered eating behavior, chances are that such a discussion may not occur, and they will continue failing to recognize EDs in Black men. Just as with Black women, the issue of internal consistency leads to the bigger question of whether these extant measures for assessing disordered eating are psychometrically adequate for use with Black men.

The virtual absence of Black men from the extant literature contributes to our limited understanding of the impact of eating disorders on these groups and hinders development of effective interventions (Luther et al., 2021). However, from Taylor et al.'s (2007) seminal research examining the prevalence of EDs among Black persons in the National Survey of American Life (NSAL), we learned that Black women had higher lifetime prevalence rates of any episodes of binge eating (5.82), and a higher 12-month prevalence of BN (1.04) and BED (1.11) than Black men. Lifetime prevalence rates of EDs for Black men were 0.20% (AN), 0.97 (BN), 0.78% (BED), and 4.14% for any episodes of binge eating. The NSAL also showed that BED was the most prevalent eating disorder among Black people, with a lifetime prevalence of 1.66%, although 5.08% had reported some problems with binge eating whether or not they met criteria for a disorder.

Age of Onset

The prevalence of AN in Black populations is generally low as gleaned from the scant extant research in the literature. Taylor et al. (2007) found consistent results and reported a mean age of onset for AN in their NSAL study occurred during middle adolescence (14.89) in Black groups, while other studies, i.e., Hudson et al. (2007) reported a late adolescent onset (18.9) in their National Comorbidity Survey Replication (NCS-R). For BN, Taylor et al. (2007) found a mean age of 19.44 in the NSAL compared with 19.7 in the NCS-R, with episodes of binge eating having the highest age of onset at 22.75 in the NSAL study and 25.4 for the NCS-R.

In a review of the literature on eating disorders and men of color, Payton (2014) lists underreporting of ED symptoms in communities of color, inadequate mental health care outreach in these communities, as well as high attrition rates for those who do seek treatment, a lack of culturally competent practitioners, and an adaptive mistrust of health care related to systemic racism as reasons for the knowledge gaps on prevalence and mortality rates of EDs among these groups.

BARRIERS TO CARE

It can be extremely difficult to get some men to seek health care. There are numerous barriers to care, more so for Black men in particular. Not only are there a multiplicity of barriers to treatment and care for men, but some of them often intersect and overlap. The types of barriers encountered are themselves often deeply rooted in various complex systems that can obstruct treatment access for illnesses, some of which have far fewer complexities and intricacies than eating disorders. With this in mind, it is just as important to consider whether and which barriers may be present, as it is to consider which illnesses need to be treated.

Cultural Mistrust

Unfortunately, the origins of this mistrust are factually based following the occurrence of numerous, unethical experimentation and sacrifice of Black bodies at someone else's will. The resulting damage to the psyche of Black persons has led to mistrust of the medical community and continues to be a hinderance to health care seeking in Black men.

In addition to the examples of heinously and egregiously experimenting with Black bodies mentioned in Chapter 3, perhaps the most notorious event involving Black men without their consent during the twentieth century is one perpetrated by the U.S. government. The U.S. Public Health Service (USPHS) Untreated Syphilis Study at Tuskegee, originally called the USPHS Tuskegee Study of Untreated Syphilis in the Negro Male, was an attempt to track and record the full progression of the disease (CDC, 2022b). Unfortunately, tracking its natural history meant withholding treatment or intervention from participants even as they experienced the physical pain of life-threatening problems including multiple organ failure, dementia, and death (Nix, 2023; CDC, 2022b). It also meant collecting postmortem data (Nix, 2023).

Part of what made this "study" so heinous and so abominable was its potential catastrophic impact. Hundreds of impoverished Black men, some with and some without syphilis were led to believe that spinal taps and other experimental procedures they endured were treatments for their benefit. Participation came at the expense of not only the participants, but also of family members and other people close to them, giving credence to the notion in the eyes of some, that Black people were absolutely disposable.

This supposition seemed easily plausible if you consider that in addition to free medical exams and meals as compensation for their livelihoods (probably unbeknownst to them), participants also received burial insurance. Despite the significantly higher death rate in the men with syphilis compared with those without the disease, what participants did not receive was penicillin, which had been found to be a lifesaving treatment in the mid-1940s.

The 40-year-long study began in 1932 and ended in 1972 after a news story by the Associated Press which sparked public disgust and outrage, setting off a series of events resulting in a government Ad Hoc Advisory Panel's recommendation to discontinue the study. It was determined that the study was "ethically unjustified" from its inception, and that the conduct of the study was judged to be scientifically unsound, and its results disproportionately meager compared with known risks to human participants (CDC, 2022b). These events led to initiatives in 1974 designed to protect human research participants. The National Research Act of 1974 required that U.S. research involving human participants must be reviewed and approved by an entity's Institutional Review Board (IRB). A primary tenet of the IRB process is that participants must give their voluntary, informed consent to participate in any study conducted at any research facility being granted federal monies, and consent must be secured prior to assignment, even to a treatment condition (LaMorte, 2016).

In February 1994, a symposium was held in Charlottesville, VA, to revisit the Syphilis Study and its legacy. Symposium participants formed the Tuskegee Syphilis Study Legacy Committee. Among its primary purposes were development of an adroit, comprehensive plan for providing answers, referrals, treatment, or care in response to the psychological distress left behind in the wake of the infamous study, and an apology from then-President Bill Clinton (Tuskegee University, n.d.). On May 16, 1997, President Bill Clinton delivered a formal apology to the eight surviving study participants, and the family members of all of the study participants (White House Office of the Press Secretary, 1997). The last study participant died in January 2004 (CDC, 2022b).

My purpose with this discussion is not in retrying these awful events, but to summarize with more clarity some of the reasons for the reluctance of Black men (and many Black persons in general) to seek medical treatment when necessary. In his apology, President Clinton stated that the Syphilis Study helped to sow distrust of U.S. medical institutions and most notably with regard to research. He talked about the small number of Black people who participate in medical research and organ donation, and described the IRB process and its purpose before sharing a new initiative to increase participation of underrepresented communities in research and to seek health care (White House Office of the Press Secretary, 1997).

It's Not Manly to Ask for Help. As stated, not only does it seem that Black men are not first in line to ask for health care, it appears that it doesn't matter whether it's for preventative care (Thorpe, 2020), intervention, or follow-up care. For example, I have a close friend whose brother once experienced excruciating dental pain and required extensive dental work to remediate it. The beginning stages of the work were completed in three visits and required the application of three temporary crowns. After several pain-free weeks had passed, the dental patient determined that the temporary crowns he had in place were satisfactory, and he chose not to return to complete the work which would have included adding an implant and replacing the temporary crowns with permanent crowns. To my knowledge, he never returned. Strong evidence suggests that regular, preventative care would have precluded the severity of his concerns initially.

Many Black men just do not seek preventative care. It is not unusual for them to minimize, deny, dismiss, or otherwise neglect signs and symptoms of illness, alleging exhaustion (Reddy Medical Group, 2023). My oldest brother once told me that men believe that a nap will cure whatever ails them. Well, perhaps that's true in some instances, until it isn't. This seemed to be the case with my other brother, whose blood sugar level had risen above 900 by the time he decided to seek care for his diabetes symptoms. The doctor walked into his hospital room and asked, "What are you still doing alive?"

In addition to the reluctance to seek health care treatment, for many men the increased risk for various medical issues and their potential lethality compared with women is also factored into barriers to care. Vaidya et al. (2012) reported that myriad studies document the disparities that exist in health care utilization between men and women. There are as many reasons for this lopsided gender condition as there are reasons for men not seeking health care. So great are the barriers to health care that they have been studied systematically to include models of health behavior, categories of influence, societal and organizational level perspectives, and gender norms (Novak et al., 2019).

Much of the notoriety surrounding men's reluctance to seek medical care is rooted in the widely held, and generally accepted, notion—right or wrong—

that there's some type of weakness or unmanliness connected to asking for help (Novak et al., 2019). Any help. I've known men who wouldn't even ask for directions. From a very young age, boys have been socialized to "Shake it off . . . ," "Rub some dirt on it . . . ," "Suck it up . . . ," "Be a man about it . . . ," whenever they get hurt or experience any type of discomfort, whether physically or emotionally. And above all, for goodness sake, they're admonished "Don't cry."

Another mentality encapsulating these very sentiments is an idiom being used with increased frequency from hip-hop parlance, especially among millennials and Gen Zer's, is "Thug it out." The phrase, which can be heard often in rap music in particular, is defined by the wildly popular crowdsourced video hosting social media app TikTok, as to persevere or endure negative circumstances. These expectations, which can be observed to operate in many cultures and societies, are grounded in a set of hegemonic values established by men in power, with the express purpose of organizing society into gender unequal segments (Jewkes & Morrell, 2012) or castes, which maintain the power dynamic by design. In addition to a structure designed to dominate and oppress women, a hierarchy of masculinity exists by which some men are also denied access to power. This linchpin of hegemonic masculinity is the assumption of heterosexuality (Jewkes et al., 2015).

Still, one might surmise that there would be a few particular instances when men would be more inclined to make exceptions and quickly seek the care of health experts. For instance, in the case of the other ED—erectile dysfunction. However, in a large, cross-national survey of men designed to identify factors that resulted in both treatment-seeking behavior and barriers to seeking treatment in men with erectile dysfunction, Shabsigh et al. (2004) found that most respondents with the disorder had not sought treatment. Men in the study were from six different countries (USA, France, Germany, Italy, Spain, and the UK) and ranged in age from 20–75. Survey analyses showed that factors most predictive of respondents seeking help for their erectile dysfunction was a desire to have sex or when there was urging from their sex partner (Shabsigh et al., 2004). Further analyses showed that the youngest respondents (20–39 years) in the study were least likely of all participants to seek care for erectile difficulties, choosing as it were to "thug it out," believing that symptoms would remit without intervention. Older participants often did not seek care because they believed these issues were associated with the aging process. The beliefs of persons in these two demographics worked as barriers to seeking care for erectile difficulties (Shabsigh et al., 2004).

Paulsen et al. (2020) reported similar findings in another larger cross-sectional health care, population-based study of 48,910 men. Participants aged 20–29 were least likely to seek care for their erectile difficulties. Researchers offered embarrassment to discuss the issue or the belief that the symptoms would remit on their own as possible reasons for not seeking the consult of a healthcare practitioner (Paulsen et al., 2020). As with other studies, older participants (70 and above) in this sample were least likely to consult a physician for these concerns believing this was to be expected in their declining years (Paulsen et al., 2020; Rahman et al., 2011). Reluctance to seek care for intimate concerns may also be viewed as taboo compared with other symptoms such as cardiovascular, orthopedic, etc. (Paulsen et al., 2020).

Rahman et al. (2011) reported that even persons currently under a doctor's care for other health concerns remained reticent to disclose such issues and ask for help. Still, because of these types of barriers, the prevalence of erectile dysfunction is probably underestimated (Paulsen et al., 2020), and it would behoove practitioners to raise the issue during visits at some determined point. Maybe in this way, perhaps a few more men would be helped. Perhaps raising the issue of eating disorders in men during routine (or other) doctor visits might aid in the detection of men who grapple with these concerns, resulting in treatment. Still, maybe not.

Employment Status. Schlicthorst et al. (2016) reported that in addition to manliness and gender concerns, there are a number of other reasons and factors associated with men seeking health care—or not seeking health care—including socioeconomic status (i.e., cost, access), age, maturity, marital status, and level of education. One particularly important, and perhaps overlooked, factor, which is related to level of education and serves as a bona fide predictor of men not seeking health care, is employment status.

In researching this chapter, I spoke with a number of men who encouraged me to explore this line of inquiry. Among those offering their perspectives on employment status and men not seeking health care—Black men in particular—is my son. Chuck presented a pretty unique and particularly apropos example of how employment status can impact one's decision to seek health care either as necessary or routinely. My son is a college senior and a licensed Federal Aviation Administration (FAA) pilot. He called my attention to some recent literature he was assigned that focused on the issue of pilots choosing whether to hide or disclose mental health challenges. In a recent examination of Veteran's Affairs (VA) disability claims, Rein and Whitlock (2023) state that nearly 5,000 military veterans who reported to the FAA that they were healthy enough to fly did not report collecting veterans' benefits for health issues. Self-disclosing that they had received health benefits could quite possibly lead to having to provide details about their health concerns. And while many health concerns do not impact the ability to fly, there is no question that some do. In fact, only about 0.1% of medical certificate applicants who disclose health issues are denied (U.S. Department of Transportation; DOT, 2023). However, because earning those wings is quite an expensive, emotional and labor-intensive, time and energy consuming process, the chance of losing them through self-disclosure simply is not a chance that some are willing to take. And in cases where certificates have been denied, and ultimately obtained or reobtained, that process is so arduous (as I explain in the paragraphs that follow), again, some persons simply are not willing to take the risk.

Nondisclosure of health issues is not a new industry problem. However, it remains one that has the potential to significantly impact the mitigation of safety risks. For instance, while the FAA relies on its members to self-disclose any physical (Sachs, 2023) or mental health diagnoses that could negatively affect their ability to safely operate an aircraft, the FAA's ability to prevent or guard against safety hazards in our nation's airspace is greatly reduced when its members do not self-disclose (DOT, 2023). These self-disclosures are mandated by law. Failure to report mental health conditions that could render a pilot unfit to fly can result in severe penalties including fines, imprisonment, or both (Sachs, 2023). The DOT (2023) study lists several possible reasons for pilots' non-disclosure of mental health diagnoses, including stigma, financial concerns, and the "potential impact on their careers." However, stated more plainly, many pilots are not disclosing their mental health issues because of the threat of losing their wings.

An FAA-directed exam performed by an aviation medical examiner (AME) is required every 6 months to every 5 years depending on the type of flying the pilot does (commercial, private, etc.) and their age (DOT, 2023). AMEs are physicians who evaluate pilots for the purpose of determining their medical and mental fitness to fly. That determination is based in part on a review and consideration of all self-reported health information (Sachs, 2023; DOT, 2023). Such information includes any visit during the previous 3 years with a mental health practitioner, any diagnoses given, and a listing of all medications taken (DOT, 2023; Sachs, 2023). An admission to any of these criteria can result in an AME passing, denying, or deferring an application (Sachs, 2023), triggering a pilot's removal from the flight deck and an ensuing investigation that can take as long as 2 years to resolve (DOT, 2023). However, such an investigation is only one phase of the process.

My son explained to me that a pilot must also maintain currency and proficiency. Currency refers to a pilot's flight control skills—daytime take-off and landing ability in particular. These skills must be demonstrated in accord with federal aviation requirements for having performed the maneuvers a certain number of times over a prescribed period of time (DOT, 2023; Aircraft Owners and Pilots Association [AOPA], 2024). Conversely, proficiency means being competent in performing the maneuvers, as well as being knowledgeable about emergency procedures for the particular aircraft one flies, and also the type of flying done (DOT, 2023; AOPA, 2024). Proficiency requires adeptness with multiple skill sets. Although a mental health diagnosis (i.e., depression, anxiety, adjustment disorder) may not necessarily deem a pilot unfit automatically (Rein & Whitlock, 2023), it does carry that potential. And while being grounded is also not necessarily a permanent status, the road back to the flight deck can be an arduous, nebulous, very expensive journey (Sachs, 2023).

MOVING FORWARD

It has been said that EDs are among the most gendered mental health illnesses (Lavender et al., 2017), which seemed plausible given that at one time, the absence of menses was one of the criteria for the diagnosis of AN. This condition seemed to exempt males from the disorder. Further support for the supposition of EDs as gendered health conditions is possibly due to persons being generally more familiar with AN than BN. In addition, because BED has only recently been recognized as an ED in the *DSM-5*, AN was the extent of most persons' knowledge of EDs. With amenorrhea being an indicator of EDs, and males never having had a cycle, they were much less likely to be diagnosed as such. Fortunately, with amenorrhea no longer a criterion for diagnosis, BN being recognized more frequently, and BED now a *DSM-5* diagnosis, men's issues with EDs are now receiving the attention they should. And as a result, men can receive the care they deserve.

Conclusion

This book is part of our ongoing commitment to help facilitate centering and amplifying the voices of Black women so they will be heard by greater numbers of persons well-positioned to help them move from out of the shadows of eating disorders. Unfortunately, there is still a misconception that Black women don't experience eating disorders. Since Dr. Fuller and I sounded our clarion call for attention to the needs of these women, some of our colleagues in the discipline have found from their systematic reviews of the empirical literature that even while Black women remain underrepresented in ED clinical trials (Parker et al., 2023; Acle et al., 2021; Goode et al., 2020), there is evidence suggesting that ED prevalence is rising in this group (Acle et al., 2021; Goeree et al., 2011). For example, Goode et al. (2018) report that Black women in the U.S. have the highest rates of obesity and engage in frequent binge eating behaviors. It is difficult to accurately estimate the number of Black women in the United States who are impacted by EDs. Possible reasons for this include provider characteristics that may impact assessment and recognition of the disorders in these women, such as a limited knowledge about factors that mediate EDs in Black women, a lack cultural competence or sensitivity, and a lack of awareness of one's own implicit racial biases.

Because Black women with EDs have unique problems, the disorders manifest in ways differently than might be expected, and they often require different and/or additional ways to address them. In order to provide the most effective quality of care, practitioners have a responsibility to embrace a cultural humility approach to care, which includes seeking out resources tailored to these clients' needs. From young to old, Black women are sicker than their peers, for an overwhelming number of reasons including trauma, environmental racism, injustice, overt and covert racism, inequity, targeted marketing practices, food deserts, mistrust of the health care system, poor living conditions, and stress. Therefore, as mental health care practitioners, we must be vigilant about inquiring about our clients' histories, experiences, and environments. Treatment of these disorders is quite challenging and recovery looks different for each person. And while it's not unusual for clients to relapse at some point during the course of treatment, please remember that full recovery is possible. As health care practitioners, it is incumbent upon us to use our expertise to help facilitate the recovery process. Clients benefit from providers that are dedicated to their personal growth and development, enhancing their effectiveness as treating professionals.

Providers who approach their work with Black clients from a place of humility and empathy are actively nurturing a commitment to cultural awareness and prioritizing the therapeutic alliance. Culturally-adapted interventions have been shown to be effective in reducing symptoms of depression and anxiety, which indicates that incorporating these factors into evidence-based therapies can be quite effective. Adaptations are essential for enhancing the acceptance and effectiveness of treatments among diverse racial, ethnic, cultural, and age groups. Finally, we want to underscore that a practitioner's unexamined biases can affect their perception of Black women, impacting them in adverse ways. For instance, labels like "the strong Black woman" or similar monikers, while ostensibly offered as complimentary, often suggests a superhuman ability to endure pain and to tolerate the most distressing situations, while pressing toward the mark—and to do so without complaint or help. We can't. This is far too overwhelming for anyone to live up to. As Zora Neale Hurston said so clearly, "If you are silent about your pain, they'll kill you and say you enjoyed it." Culturally-informed providers create a more supportive and empathetic therapeutic environment, allowing for a more effective and relevant approach to treatment and support.

References

ABC News. (2022, June 25). Supreme Court overturns Roe v. Wade in landmark case on abortion rights. Retrieved from https://abcnews.go.com/Politics/supreme-court-overturns-roe-wade-landmark-case-abortion/story?id=85160781

Abhyankar, R. S., & Jessop, K. M. (2022). From craft to profession: The development of modern anesthesiology: Part II. *Missouri Medicine: The Journal of the Missouri State Medical Association. 119*(1), 14–20.

Acle, A., Cook, B., Siegfried, N., & Beasley, T. (2021). Cultural considerations in the treatment of eating disorders among racial/ethnic minorities: A systematic review. *Journal of Cross-Cultural Psychology 52*(2), 468–488. http://doi:10.1177/00220221211017664

Adams, S. W., & Allwood, M. A. (2023, December 21). Parallel processes of posttraumatic stress and cardiometabolic dysfunction: A systemic illness of traumatic stress. *Health Psychology. Advance online publication.*

Addiction Center. (2023). Is vaping addictive? https://www.addictioncenter.com/nicotine/vaping-addictive/

Adolescent Brain Cognitive Development Study [ABCD]. (2018). U.S. Department of Health & Human Services.

Ahmed, S., & Ashfaq, A. (2013). Impact of advertising on consumers' buying behavior through persuasiveness, brand image, and celebrity endorsement. *Global Media Journal, 6*(2), 149.

Aircraft Owners and Pilots Association. (2024). Currency vs. Proficiency: Pilot: Currency vs. proficiency. https://www.aopa.org/training-and-safety/active-pilots/safety-and-technique/currency-vs-proficiency

American Cancer Society. (2019). Cancer facts & figures for African Americans 2019–2021.

American Cancer Society (2023, January 12). Big tobacco targets people with limited incomes. Retrieved from https://www.fightcancer.org/policy-resources/big-tobacco-targets-people-limited-incomes

American Cancer Society. (2024). Cancer disparities in the Black community. https://www.cancer.org/about-us/what-we-do/health-equity/cancer-disparities-in-the-black-community.html#:~:text=African%20Americans%20have%20the%20highest,who%20have%20the%20lowest%20rates

American Lung Association. (2023). State of tobacco control: 10 really bad things the tobacco industry has done—and is doing—to entice kids to start smoking.

REFERENCES

American Psychiatric Association. (2022). *Diagnostic and statistical manual of mental disorders (5th ed., text rev.).* Retrieved October 2023, from American Psychiatric Association: https://doi.org/10.1176/appi.books.9780890425787

American Psychological Association, Presidential Task Force on Evidence-Based Practice. (2006). Evidence-based practice in psychology. *American Psychologist, 61*(4), 271–285.

American Psychological Association. (2024). Report of the APA Task Force on Advertising and Children. https://www.apa.org/pubs/reports/advertising-children

Amos Doss, Harriet E. (2017). The Enslaved Women Surgical Patients of J. Marion Sims in Antebellum Alabama, in ed. Ashmore, Susan Youngblood & Dorr, Lisa Lindquist. *Alabama Women: Their Lives and Times*, The University of Georgia Press.

Apfelbaum, E. P., Norton, M. I., & Sommers, S. R. (2012). Racial color blindness: Emergence, practice, and implications. *Current Directions in Psychological Science, 21*(3), 205–209. https://doi: 10.1177/0963721411434980

The Association of Black Psychologists. (2013). *On dark girls.* Retrieved July 30, 2023, from: https://www.abpsi.org

Awad, G. H., Norwood, C., Taylor, D. S., Martinez, M., McClain, S., Jones, B., . . . Chapman-Hilliard, C. (2015, December 1). Beauty and body image concerns among African American college women. *Journal of Black Psychology, 41*(6), 540–564.

Ayuso-Bartol, A., Gomez-Martinez, M., Riesco-Matias, P., Yela-Bernabe, J., Crego, A., & Buz, J. (2024). Systematic review and meta-analysis of the efficacy and effectiveness of the Unified Protocol for Emotional Disorders in Group Format for Adults. *International Journal of Mental Health Addiction*, https://doi.org/10.1007/s11469-024-01330-z

Bailey-Straebler, S. M., & Susser, L. C. (2023, August 31). The impact of eating disorders on reproductive health: Mitigating the risk. *The Primary Care Companion for CNS Disorders, 25*(4).

Bardone-Cone, A. M., Harney, M. B., Maldonado, C. R., Lawson, M. A., Robinson, D.P., Smith, R., & Tosh, A. (2010). Defining recovery from an eating disorder: Conceptualization, validation, and examination of prosocial functioning and psychiatric comorbidity. *Behaviour Research and Therapy, 48*(3), 194–202. https://doi.org/10.1016/j.brat.2009.11.001

Barlow, D. H., & Long, L. L. (2023). The Unified Protocol: Current status, future directions. *Clinical Psychology: Science and Practice, 30*(2), 222–225. https://doi.org/10.1037/cps0000152

Barrada, J., Cativiela, B., van Strien, T., & Cebolla, A. (2020). Intuitive eating: A novel eating style? Evidence from a Spanish sample. *European Journal of Psychological Assessment, 36*(1), 19–31.

Bartel, S., McElroy, S. L., Levangie, D., & Keshen, A. (2024). Use of glucagon-like peptide-1 receptor agonists in eating disorder populations. *International Journal of Eating Disorders, 57*(2), 286–293. https://doi.org/10.1002/eat.24109

Baskin, M. L., Odoms-Young, A. M., Kumanyika, S. K., & Ard, J. D. (2009). Nutrition and obesity issues for African Americans. In R. L. Braithwaite, S. E. Taylor, & H. M. Treadwell (Eds.), *Health issues in the Black community* (3rd ed., pp. 431–460). Jossey-Bass.

The Beck Institute for Cognitive Behavior Therapy. (2024). *Understanding CBT.* Retrieved February 2024, from: https://rb.gy/cg5iyh

Becker, A. E., Franko, D. L., Speck, A., & Herzog, D. B. (2003). Ethnicity and differential access to care for eating disorder symptoms. *International Journal of Eating Disorders, 33,* 205–212.

Becker, C. B., Middlemass, K., Taylor, B., Johnson, C., & Gomez, F. (2017). Food insecurity and eating disorder pathology. *The International Journal of Eating Disorders, 50,* 1031–1040. https://doi.org/10.1002/eat.22735

Belgrave, F. Z., & Abrams, J. A. (2016). Reducing disparities and achieving equity in African American women's health. *American Psychologist, 71*(8), 723–733.

Bell, K. (2017). Sisters on sisters: Inner peace from the Black woman mental health professional perspective. In S. Y. Evans, K. Bell, & N. K. Bur (Eds.), *Black women's mental health balancing strength and vulnerability* (pp. 23–41). SUNY Press.

Benuto, L. T., Singer, J., Gonzalez, F., Casas, J., & Ruork, A. (2021). How do clinicians define cultural sensitivity?: A mixed methods study. *International Journal of Mental Health, 50*(20), 151–167. https://doi.org/10.1080/00207411.2020.1830611

Berdahl, J. L., & Moore, C. (2006). Workplace harassment: Double jeopardy for minority women. *Journal of Applied Psychology, 91*(2), 426–436.

Bernard, C. (2021). Social desirability among Black women. In C. Small & M. Fuller (Eds.), *Treating Black women with eating disorders* (pp. 57–66). Routledge Press.

Berry, Daina Ramey, & Parker, Nakia D. (2018). Women and slavery in the nineteenth century. In E. Hartigan-O'Connor & L. G. Materson (Eds.), *The Oxford handbook of American women's and gender history*, (pp. 153–170). Oxford University Press. https://doi.org/10.1093/oxfordhb/9780190222628.013.9

Black Mamas Matter Alliance. (2020, September). *Issue brief: Black maternal health.* Retrieved January 2024, from Black Mamas Matter Alliance: https://blackmamasmatter.org/wp-content/uploads/2022/04/0322_BMHStatisticalBrief_Final.pdf

Blake, J. J., Butler, B. R., & Smith, D. (2015). Challenging middle-class notions of femininity: The cause of Black females' disproportionate suspension rates. In D. J. Losen (Ed.), *Closing the school discipline gap: Equitable remedies for excessive exclusion* (pp. 75–87). Teachers College, Columbia University.

Bland, R. (2007). Depression and its management in primary care. *Canadian Journal of Psychiatry, 52*(2), 75–76. http://doi.10.1177/070674370705200201

Blazek, J. L., & Carter, R. (2019). Understanding disordered eating in Black adolescents: Effects of gender identity, racial identity, and perceived puberty. *Psychology of Men & Masculinities, 20*(2), 252–265.

Blount, T. N., Prosek, E. A., King, K., Brookins, C., & Fitzpatrick, D. C. (2024). The lived experiences of African American women in natural recovery: Re-envisioning the role of counselors. *International Journal for the Advancement of Counseling, 46*, 567–585. https://doi.org/10.1007/s10447-024-09553-4.

Blue, E. L., & Berkel, L. A. (2010). Feminist identity attitudes, negative affect, and eating pathology in African American college women. *Journal of Black Psychology, 36*(4), 426–445.

Bothwell, S. (2022). Eating disorders and the musculoskeletal system. Retrieved December 2023, from Eating Disorder Hope. https://www.eatingdisorderhope.com/long-term-effects-health/musculoskeletal-system

Bounds, D. T., & Posey, P. D. (2022). A resistance framework for racially minoritized youth behaviors during the transition to adulthood. *Journal Of Research on Adolescence, 32*(3), 959–980. https://doi.org/10.1111/jora.12792

Boyland, E. J., Nolan, S., Kelly, B., Tudur-Smith, C., & Jones, A. (2016). Advertising as a cue to consume: A systematic review and meta-analysis of the effects of acute exposure to unhealthy food and nonalcoholic beverage advertising on intake in children and adults. *The American Journal of Clinical Nutrition, 103*(2), 519–533.

Braveman, P. A., Arkin, E., Proctor, D., Kauh, T., & Holm, N. (2022). Systemic and structural racism: Definitions, examples, health damages, and approaches to dismantling. *Health Affairs, 41*(2), 171–178. https://doi.org/10.1377/hlthaff.2021.01394

Bray, B., Bray, C., Bradley, R., & Zwickey, H. (2022). Binge eating disorder is a social justice issue: A cross-sectional mixed-methods study of binge eating disorder experts' opinions. *International Journal of Environmental Research and Public Health, 19*(10), 6243. https://doi.org/10.3390/ijerph19106243

Briere, J., & Scott, C. (2007). Assessment of trauma symptoms in eating-disordered populations. *The Journal of Treatment & Prevention, 15*(4), 347–358, doi:0.1080/10640260701454360

Brooks, G. (2014). *Multicultural perspectives . . . Why should I care?* The 24th Annual Renfrew Center Foundation Conference for Professionals–Feminist Relational Perspectives and Beyond: The "Practice" of Practice, Philadelphia, Pennsylvania.

Broskey, N. T., Marlatt, K. L., Most, J., Erickson, M. L., Irving, B. A., & Redman, L. M. (2019). The panacea of human aging: Calorie restriction versus exercise. *Exercise Sport Science Review, 47*(3), 169–175. https://doi.org/10.1249/jes.0000000000000193

Brown-Johnson, C. G., England, L. J., Glantz, S. A., & Ling, P. M. (2014). Tobacco industry marketing to low socioeconomic status women in the USA. *Tobacco Control, 23*(e2), e139–e146. https://doi.org/10.1136/tobaccocontrol-2013-051224

Brownell, K. D., & Warner, K. D. (2009). The perils of ignoring history: Big tobacco played dirty and millions died. How similar is big food? *Milbank Quarterly, 87*(1), 259–294. https://doi.org/10.1111/j.1468-0009.2009.00555.x

Bryant-Waugh, R. J., Cooper, P. J., Taylor, C. L., & Lask, B. D. (1996). The use of the eating disorder examination with children: A pilot study. *International Journal of Eating Dis-*

orders, 19(4), 391–397. https://doi.org/10.1002/(sici)1098-108x(199605)19:4<391::aid-eat6>3.0.co;2-g

Bucchianeri, M. M., Fernandes, N., Loth, K., Hannan, P. J., Eisenberg, M. E., & Neumark-Sztainer, D. (2016). Body dissatisfaction: Do associations with disordered eating and psychological well-being differ across race/ethnicity in adolescent girls and boys? *Cultural Diversity and Ethnic Minority Psychology, 22*(1), 137–146.

Buchanan, T. S., Fischer, A. R., Tokar, D. M., & Yoder, J. D. (2008). Testing a culture-specific extension of objectification theory regarding African American women's body image. *The Counseling Psychologist, 36*, 699–718.

Bulik, C. (2013). *Midlife eating disorders: Your journey to recovery.* Walker Publishing Company.

Burke, L. A., Chijioke, S., & Le, T. P. (2023). Gendered racial microaggressions and emerging adult Black women's social and general anxiety: Distress intolerance and stress as mediators. *Journal of Clinical Psychology, 79*, 1051–1069.

Burke, Natasha L., Tanofsky-Kraff, Marian, Crosby, Ross Mehari, Rim D., Marwitz, Shannon E., Broadney, Miranda M., & Shomaker, Lauren B. (2017). Measurement invariance of the Eating Disorder Examination in Black and White children and adolescents. *International Journal of Eating Disorders.* https://doi.org/10.1002/eat.22713

Burket, Roger C., Hodgin, Jon A., & Lawlor, Brian A. (1987). Eating disorders in Black men. *Journal of the National Medical Association, 79*(9).

Burton, N. K. (2017). Representations of Black women's mental illness in HTGAWM and being Mary Jane. In S. Y. Evans, K. Bell, & N. K. Burton (Eds.), *Black women's mental health: Balancing strength and vulnerability* (pp. 57–74). State University of New York Press.

Byrd, A. S., Toth, A. T., & Stanford, F. C. (2018). Racial disparities in obesity treatment. *Current Obesity Reports, 7*(2), 130–138. https://doi.org/10.1007/s13679-018-0301-3

Capodilupo, C. M., & Kim, S. (2014). Gender and race matter: The importance of considering intersections in Black women's body image. *Journal of Counseling Psychology, 61*(1), 37–49.

Carbado, D. W., Crenshaw, K. W., Mays, V. M., & Tomlinson, B. (2013). Intersectionality: Mapping the movements of a theory. *Du Bois Review: Social Science Research on Race, 10*(2), pp. 303–312.

Carter, M. M., & Sbrocco, T. (2018). Cognitive behavioral models, measures, and treatments for anxiety disorders in African Americans. In E. C. Chang, C. A. Downey, J. K. Hirsch, & E. A. Yu (Eds.), *Treating depression, anxiety, and stress in ethnic and racial groups: Cognitive behavioral approaches* (pp. 179–202). American Psychological Association.

Cassidy, O., Sbrocco, T., & Tanofsky-Kraff, M. (2015). Utilizing non-traditional research designs to explore culture-specific risk factors for eating disorders in African American adolescents. *Advances in Eating Disorders: Theory, Research and Practice, 3*(1), 91–102.

REFERENCES

Centers for Disease Control and Prevention (CDC). Adverse Childhood Experiences. (1997). https://www.cdc.gov/violenceprevention/aces/about.html

Centers for Disease Control and Prevention (CDC). (2007). HIV/AIDS surveillance report, 2005. *17(1)*, 1–46.

Centers for Disease Control and Prevention (CDC). (2021). Smoking and Tobacco Use. https://www.cdc.gov/tobacco/index.html

Centers for Disease Control and Prevention (CDC). (2022a). Infant mortality statistics from the 2020 period linked birth/infant death [Data set]. *National Vital Statistics Reports*. Table 2. https://stacks.cdc.gov/view/cdc/120700

Centers for Disease Control and Prevention (CDC). (2022b). The US Public Health Service untreated syphilis study at Tuskegee timeline. Public Health Service Study of Untreated Syphilis at Tuskegee and Macon County, AL - Timeline - CDC - OS. https://www.cdc.gov/tuskegee/about/index.html

Centers for Disease Control and Prevention (CDC). *Heart disease facts*. (2024, May 15). Retrieved from Heart Disease: https://www.cdc.gov/heart-disease/data-research/facts -stats/index.html#cdc_facts_stats_resources-resources

Centers for Disease Control and Prevention (CDC), Office of Health Equity. (2024, April 8). *Working together to reduce Black maternal mortality*. Retrieved May 2024, from Health Equity: https://www.cdc.gov/healthequity/features/maternal-mortality/index .html

Cerdeña, J. P., Plaisime, M. V., & Tsai, J. (2020). From race-based to race-conscious medicine: How anti-racist uprisings call us to act. *Lancet, 396*(10257), 1125–1128. doi: 10.1016/S0140-6736(20)32076-6

Chae, D. H., Yip, T., Martz, C. D., Chung, K., Richeson, J. A., Hajat, A., Curtis, D. S., Rogers, L. O., & LaVeist, T. A. (2021). Vicarious racism and vigilance during the Covid-19 pandemic: Mental health implications among Asian and Black Americans. *Public Health Reports, 136*(4), 508–517. https://doi.org/10 .1177/00333549211018675

Chao, Y. M., Pisetsky, B. A., Dierker, L. C., Dohm, F., Rosseli, F., May, A. M., & Striegel Moore, R. H. (2008). Ethnic differences in weight control practices among U.S. adolescents from 1995–2005. *International Journal of Eating Disorders, 41*, 124–133.

Chaves, E., Jeffery, D. T., & Williams, D. R. (2023). Disordered eating and eating disorders in pediatric obesity: Assessment and next steps. *International Journal of Environmental Research and Public Health, 20*(17), 6638. https://doi.org/10.3390/ijerph20176638

Cheng, P. H., & Merrick, E. (2017). Cultural adaptation of dialectical behavior therapy for a Chinese international student with eating disorder and depression. *Clinical Case Studies, 16*(1), 42–57. https://doi.org/10.1177/1534650116668269

Chinn, J. J., Martin, I. K., & Redmond, N. (2021). Health equity among Black women in the United States. *Journal of Women's Health, 30*(2).

Choo, H. Y., & Ferree, M. M. (2010). Practicing intersectionality in sociological research: A critical analysis of inclusions, interactions, and institutions in the study of inequalities. *Sociological Theory, 28*, 129–149.

Churchill, M. M. (2021). Who should be at the treatment table? College students with eating disorders and body image issues. In C. Small, & M. Fuller (Eds.), *Treating Black Women with Eating Disorders* (pp. 188–194). Routledge Press.

Ciciurkaite, G., & Perry, B. L. (2018). Body weight, perceived weight stigma and mental health among women at the intersection of race/ethnicity and socioeconomic status: Insights from the modified labelling approach. *Sociology of Health & Illness, 40*(1), 18–37.

Clarke, J., Peyre, H., Alison, M., Bargiacchi, A., Stordeur, C., Boizeau, P., . . . Delorme, R. (2021). Abnormal bone mineral density and content in girls with early-onset anorexia nervosa. *Journal of Eating Disorders, 9*(1), 9.

Claudat, K., Brown, T. A., Anderson, L., Bongiorno, G., Berner, L. A., Reilly, E., & Kaye, W. H. (2020). Correlates of co-occurring eating disorders and substance use disorders: A case for dialectical behavior therapy. *Eating Disorders, 28*(2), 142–156. https://doi.org/10.1080/10640266.2020.1740913

Coelho, J. S., Wilson, S., Winslade, A., Thaler, L., Israel, M., & Steiger, H. (2014). Over-evaluation of thoughts about food: Differences across eating-disorder subtypes and a preliminary examination of treatment effects. *International Journal of Eating Disorders, 47*, 302–309.

Conley, J. (2021). Creative training approaches for clinicians-in-training working with African American women with eating disorders. In C. Small, & M. Fuller (Eds.), *Treating Black women with eating disorders* (pp. 165–173). Routledge Press.

Cooper Owens, D. (2018). *Medical bondage: Race, gender, and the origins of American gynecology.* The University of Georgia Press.

Cooper, J., Nirantharakumar, K., Crowe, F., Azcoaga-Lorenzo, A., McCowan, C., Jackson, T., . . . Haroon, S. (2023). Prevalence and demographic variation of cardiovascular, renal, metabolic, and mental health conditions in 12 million English primary care records. *BMC Medical Informatics and Decision Making, 23*(1), 220.

Crawford Mann, W. (2021). The skin I'm in: Stereotypes and body image development in women of color. In C. Small, & M. Fuller (Eds.), *Treating Black Women with Eating Disorders* (pp. 67–74). Routledge Press.

Crenshaw, K. (1991). Mapping the margins: Intersectionality, identity politics, and violence against women of color. *Stanford Law Review, 43*(6), 1241–1299.

Crenshaw, K. (2000). Demarginalizing the intersection of race and sex: A Black feminist critique of antidiscrimination doctrine, feminist theory, and antiracist politics. In J. James, & T. D. Sharpley-Whiting (Eds.), *The Black Feminist Reader* (pp. 57–80). Wiley-Blackwell.

Cross, T. L., Bazron, B. J., Dennis, K. W., & Isaacs, M. R. (1989). Towards a culturally competent system of care volume I: A monograph on effective services for minority children who are severely emotionally disturbed. Washington, DC: Georgetown University Child Development Center, Child and Adolescent Service System Program Technical Assistance Center.

The Crown Act. (2023). *Creating a respectful and open world for natural hair.* Retrieved November 18, 2023, from: https://www.thecrownact.com/about

Davis-Coelho, K., Waltz, J., & Davis-Coelho, B. (2000). Awareness and prevention of bias against fat clients in psychotherapy. *Professional Psychology: Research and Practice, 31*(6), 682–684.

Davis, K. (2008). Intersectionality as a buzzword: A sociology of science perspective on what makes a feminist theory successful. *Feminist Theory, 9,* 67–85.

Davis, K. M., Knauft, K., Lewis, L., Petriello, M., Petrick, L., Luca, F., . . . Zilioli, S. (2023). The heart of Detroit study: A window into urban middle-aged and older African Americans' daily lives to understand psychosocial determinants of cardiovascular disease risk. *BMC Psychiatry, 23*(766), 1–11.

Davis, S. K., Collins Quarells, R., & Gibbons, G. H. (2009). Hypertension in African American communities. In R. L. Braithwaite, S. E. Taylor, & H. M. Treadwell (Eds.), *Health issues in the Black community* (3rd ed., pp. 233-258). Jossey-Bass.

de Dios, M. A., Childress, S. D., Cano, M. A., McNeill, L. H., Reitzel, L. R., & Vaughan, E. (2020). Elevated cholesterol among African American adults: The role of fatalistic attitudes about health. *Ethnicity & Health, 25*(6), 835–842.

Deloitte Study Press Conference. (2020). Social and economic cost of eating disorders in the United States. https://vimeo.com/aedweb/review/432476890/ac610ec6fd

Dirks, R. T., & Duran, N. (2001). African American dietary patterns at the beginning of the 20th century. *Journal of Nutrition, 131*(7), 1881–1889.

Downer, G. (2021). Considerations in the treatment of African American women with eating disorders. In C. Small, & M. Fuller (Eds.), *Treating Black women with eating disorders* (pp. 123–132). Routledge Press.

Duarte, C., Pinto-Gouveia, J., & Ferreira, C. (2017). Ashamed and fused with body image and eating: Binge eating as an avoidance strategy. *Clinical Psychology and Psychotherapy, 24,* 195–202.

Dunn, C. E. (2018). *Blacker the berry to darker the flesh: Gendered racial microaggressions, ethnic identity, and Black women's sexual behaviors.* Retrieved 2023, from https://scholarscompass.vcu.edu/etd/5641

Durham, A. (2024, May 30). Black voices, Black bodies: Life in the age of Ozempic. *STAT.* https://www.statnews.com/2024/05/29/ozempic-black-voices-black-bodies-weight-stigma/

Dutchen, S. (2021). Field correction. *Harvard Medicine,* Racism in Medicine Issue (Winter 2021). https://magazine.hms.harvard.edu/racism-medicine

Eating Disorder Hope. (2024). *Bone loss from eating disorders*. Retrieved January 12, 2024, from Eating Disorder Hope: https://www.eatingdisorderhope.com/information/eating-disorder/osteoporosis-bone-density-loss

Edwards-Gayfield, P. (2021). The weight of shame. In C. Small, & M. Fuller (Eds.), *Treating Black women with eating disorders: A clinician's guide* (pp. 150–157). Routledge Press.

Egan, S. J., Wade, T. D., Watson, H. J., Öst, L.-G., Cuijpers, P., & Shafran, R. (2023). Towards high standards of evidence for cognitive behaviour therapy for perfectionism: A critique of Smith et al. (2023). *Canadian Psychology / Psychologie canadienne, 64*(4), 377–381. https://doi.org/10.1037/cap0000369

Ellis, J. L., Kovach, C. R., Fendrich, M., Olukotun, O., Baldwin, V. K., Ke, W., & Nichols, B. (2019). Factors related to medication self-management in African American older women. *Research in Gerontological Nursing, 12*(2), 71–79.

Encinosa, M. (2021). Embodied injustices: COVID-19, race, and epigenetics. *PANDION: The Osprey Journal of Research and Ideas, 2*(1), 1–35.

Epstein, R., Blake, J., & Thalia, G. (2017). *Girlhood interrupted: The erasure of Black girls' childhood*. Washington, D.C.: Georgetown Law, Center on Poverty and Inequality.

Fahs, B. (2023). Psychological kinship between fat therapists and fat patients: Healing and solidarity around stigma, family relationships, and body image. *Fat Studies, 12*(2), 243–259.

Fairburn, C. G. (2008). *Cognitive behavior therapy and eating disorders*. Guilford Press.

Fairburn, C. G., Cooper, Z., & O'Connor, M. (2014). Eating Disorder Examination (EDE, 17th ed.).

Fairburn, C. G., Cooper, Z., & Shafran, R. (2003). Cognitive behaviour therapy for eating disorders: A "transdiagnostic" theory and treatment. *Behaviour Research and Therapy, 41*(5), 509–528. https://doi.org/10.1016/s0005-7967(02)00088-8

Feeding America. (2022). *Hunger in America*. Retrieved February 10, 2024, from: https://rb.gy/46k7av

Fernandes, N. H., Crow, S. J., Thuras, P., & Peterson, C. B. (2010). Characteristics of Black treatment seekers for eating disorders. *International Journal of Eating Disorders, 43*(3), 282–285.

Ferreres-Galan, V., Peris-Baquero, O., Moreno-Perez, J. D., & Osma, J. (2024). Is the Unified Protocol for transdiagnostic treatment of emotional disorders equally effective for men and women? *Current Psychology*, https://doi.org/10.1007/s12144-024-06159-2

Finch, Jody E., Xu, Ziqian, Girdler, Susan, & Baker, Jessica H. (2023). Network analysis of eating disorder symptoms in women in perimenopause and early postmenopause. *Menopause, 30*(3), 275–282. https://doi.org/10.1097/gme.0000000000002141

Fleming, S. (2024, June 3). *Racism and African American mental health: Using cognitive behavior therapy to empower healing*. Retrieved June 2024, from The Beck Institute for Cognitive Behavior Therapy: https://rb.gy/rb6v4u

Fogelkvist, M., Parling, T., Kjellin, L., & Gustafsson, S. (2021). Live with your body—

participants' reflections on an acceptance and commitment therapy group intervention for patients with residual eating disorder symptoms. *Journal of Contextual Behavioral Science, 20*, 184–193. https://doi.org/10.1016/j.jcbs.2021.04.006

Forney, K., Buchman-Schmitt, J. M., Keel, P. K., & Frank, G. K. (2016). The medical complications associated with purging. *International Journal of Eating Disorders, 49*(3), 249–259.

Frey, L. (2013). Relational-cultural therapy: Theory, research, and application to counseling competencies. *Professional Psychology: Research and Practice, 44*(3), 177–185. https://doi.org/10.1037/a0033121

Fuller, M. (2021). Black women "showing up" for therapeutic healing. In C. Small, & M. Fuller (Eds.), *Treating Black Women with Eating Disorders* (pp. 33–38). New York: Routledge Press.

Gander, Jennifer C., Zhang, X., Plantinga, L., Paul, S., Basu, M., Pastan, S., Gibney, E., Hartmann, E., Mulloy, L., Zayas, C., & Patzer, R. E. (2018). Racial disparities in pre-emptive referral for kidney transplantation in Georgia. *Clinical Transplantation, 23*(9), e13380. https://doi.org/10.1111/ctr.13380

Gary, F., Still, C., Mickels, P., Hassan, M., & Evans, E. (2015). Muddling through the health system: Experiences of three groups of Black women in three regions. *Journal of National Black Nurses Association, 26*(1), 22–28.

Gaudiani, J. (2019). *Sick enough: A guide to the medical complications of eating disorders.* Routledge.

Gay, R. (2017). *Hunger: A memoir of (my) body.* Harper Collins.

Georgetown University National Center for Cultural Competence. (n.d.). *Conscious & unconscious biases in health care.* https://nccc.georgetown.edu/bias/

Glanz, K., Basil, M., Maibach, E., & Goldberg, J. (1998). Why Americans eat what they do: Taste, nutrition, cost, convenience, and weight control concerns as influences on food consumption. *Journal of the American Dietetic Association, 98*(10), 1118–1126.

Glantz, S. (2019). Cigarette giants bought food companies, used cartoon characters, colors, flavors to boost sales of sweetened beverages. University of California San Francisco Center for Tobacco Control Research and Education. https://tobacco.ucsf.edu/cigarette-giants-bought-food-companies-used-cartoon-characters-colors-flavors-boost-sales-sweetened-beverages

Goeree, M. S., et al. (2011). Race, social class, and bulimia nervosa. *Health Economics eJournal.* http://dx.doi.org/10.2139/ssrn.1877636

Goldstein, A., & Gvion, Y. (2019). Socio-demographic and psychological risk factors for suicidal behavior among individuals with anorexia and bulimia nervosa: A systematic review. *Journal of Affective Disorders, 245*, 1149–1167.

Goode, R. W., Cowell, M. M., Mazzeo, S.E., Cooper-Lewter, C., Forte, A., & Olayia, O. I. (2020). Binge eating and binge-eating disorder in Black women: A systematic review. *International Journal Eating Disorders, 53*(4), 491–507. https://doi.org/10.1002/eat.23217

Goode, R. W., Kalarchian, M. A., Craighead, L., Conroy, M. B., Wallace, J., Eack, S. M., & Burke, L. E. (2018). The feasibility of a binge eating intervention in Black women with obesity. *Journal of Eating Behavior, April*(29), 83–90. https://doi.org/10.1016/j.eatbeh.2018.03.005

Goode, R. W., Watson, H. J., Masa, R., & Bulik, C. M. (2021). Prevalence and contributing factors to recurrent binge eating and obesity among Black adults with food insufficiency: Findings from a cross-sectional study from a nationally representative sample. *Journal of Eating Disorders, 9*(1), 154. https://doi.org/10.1186/s40337-021-00509-2

Goode, R. W., Webster, C. K., & Gwira, R. E. (2022). A review of binge eating disorder in Black women: Treatment recommendations and implications for healthcare providers. *Current Psychiatry Reports, 24*(12), 757–766. https://doi.org/10.1007/s11920-022-01383-8

Gordon, K. H., Brattole, M. M., Wingate, L. R., & Joiner, T. E. (2006). The impact of client race on clinician detection of eating disorders. *Behavior Therapy, 37*(4), 319–325. Retrieved from: https://www.nationaleatingdisorders.org/statistics-research-eating-disorders

Gordon, K. H., Castro, Y., Sitnikov, L., & Holm-Denoma, J. M. (2010). Cultural body shape ideals and eating disorder symptoms among White, Latina, and Black college women. *Cultural Diversity and Ethnic Minority Psychology, 16*(2), 135–143.

Gordon, S. E. (2013). Recovery constructs and the continued debate that limits consumer recovery. *Psychiatric Services, 64*(3), 270–271. https://doi.org/10.1176/appi.ps.001612012

Gray, A. (2019). *The care and feeding of ravenously hungry girls.* Berkley.

Haddad, C., Khoury, C., Salameh, P., Sacre, H., Hallit, R., Kheir, N., Obeid, S., & Hallit, S. (2021). Validation of the Arabic version of the eating attitude test in Lebanon: A population study. *Public Health Nutrition, 24*(13), 4132–4143. https://doi.org/10.1017/S1368980020002955

Haft, S. L., O'Grady, S. M., Shaller, E. A., & Liu, N. H. (2022). Cultural adaptations of dialectical behavior therapy: A systematic review. *Journal of Consulting and Clinical Psychology, 90*(10), 787–801. https://doi.org/10.1037/ccp0000730

Hambleton, A., Pepin, G., Le, A., Maloney, D., National Eating Disorder Research Consortium, Touyz, S., & Maguire, S. (2022). Psychiatric and medical comorbidities of eating disorders: Findings from a rapid review of the literature. *Journal of Eating Disorders, 10*(1), 132. https://doi.org/10.1186/s40337-022-00654-2

Hammond, W. P. (2010). Psychosocial correlates of medical mistrust among African American men. *American Journal of Community Psychology, 45*, 87–106.

Harlow, S.D., Burnett-Bowie, S. M., Greendale, G. A., Avis, N. E., Reeves, A. N., Richards, T. R., & Lewis, T. T. (2022). Disparities in reproductive aging and midlife health between Black and White women: The study of women's health across the nation (SWAN). *Women's Midlife Health, 8*(1), 3. https://doi.org/10.1186/s40695-022-00073 -y

Harrington, E. F., Crowther, J. H., & Shipherd, J. (2010). Trauma, binge eating, and the "strong Black woman." *Journal of Consulting and Clinical Psychology, 78*, 469–479.

Harris, L. K., Berry, D. C., & Cortés, Y. I. (2022). Psychosocial factors related to cardio-vascular disease risk in young African American women: A systematic review. *Ethnicity & health, 27*(8), 1806–1824. https://doi.org/10.1080/13557858.2021.1990218

Harris, S. M. (2015). Assessing eating pathology in African Americans. In L. T. Benuto & B. D. Leany (Eds.), *Guide to psychological assessment with African Americans* (pp. 195–215). https://doi.org/10.1007/978-1-4939-1004-5_13

Harris-Perry, M. V. (2011). *Sister citizen: shame, stereotypes, and Black women in America.* Yale University Press.

Harvard School of Public Health. (n.d.). Global obesity trends in children. Retrieved from https://www.hsph.harvard.edu/obesity-prevention-source/global-obesity-trends -in-children/

Hazzard, V. M., Hahn, S. L., Bauer, K. W., & Sonnerville, K. R. (2019). Binge eating-related concerns and depressive symptoms in young adulthood: Seven-year longitudi-nal associations and differences by race/ethnicity. *Eating Behavior, 32*, 90–94. https:// doi.org/10.1016/j.eatbeh.2019.01.004

Heard-Garris, N. J., Cale, M., Camaj, L., Hamati, M. C., & Dominguez, T. P. (2018). Transmitting Trauma: A systematic review of vicarious racism and child health. *Social Science & Medicine, 199*, 230–240. https://doi.org/10.1016/j.socscimed.2017.04.018

Heller, J. (1972). Syphilis Victims in US Study Went Untreated for 40 Years. *New York Times.*

Hewitt, J., & Murray, K. (2024). Negative body image mental health literacy in women: Exploring aesthetic and functional concerns and the role of self-objectification. *Body Image, 48*, 1–14.

Ho, I. K., Sheldon, T. A., & Botelho, E. (2022). Medical mistrust among women with intersecting marginalized identities: A scoping review. *Ethnicity & Health, 27*(8), 1733–1751.

Hoadley, A., Bass, S. B., Chertock, Y., Brajuha, J., D'Avanzo, P., Kelly, P. J., & Hall, M. J. (2022). The role of medical mistrust in concerns about tumor genomic profiling among Black and African American cancer patients. *International Journal of Environmental Research and Public Health, 19*(5), 2598.

Hoffman, K. M., Trawalter, S., Axt, J. R., & Oliver, M. N. (2016). Racial bias in pain assessment and treatment recommendations, and false beliefs about biological differ-ences between Blacks and Whites. *Proceedings of the National Academy of Sciences of the United States of America, 113*(16), 4296-4301. https://doi.org/10.1073/pnas.1516047113

Hood, A. M., Crosby, L. E., Hanson, E., Shook, L. M., Lebensburger, J. D., Madan-Swain, A., . . . Trost, Z. (2022). The influence of perceived racial bias and health-related stigma on quality of life among children with sickle cell disease. *Ethnicity & Health, 27*(4), 833–846.

Hook, J. N., Davis, D., Owen, J., & DeBlaere, C. (2017). *Cultural humility: Engaging diverse identities in therapy.* American Psychological Association. https://doi.org/10.1037/0000037-000

Hook, J. N., Davis, D. E., Owen, J., Worthington, E. L., Jr., & Utsey, S. O. (2013). Cultural humility: Measuring openness to culturally diverse clients. *Journal of Counseling Psychology, 60*(3), 353–366. https://doi.org/10.1037/a0032595

Hooper, L., Puhl, R., Eisenberg, M. E., Crow, S., & Neumark-Sztainer, D. (2021). Weight teasing experienced during adolescence and young adulthood: Cross-sectional and longitudinal associations with disordered eating behaviors in an ethnically/racially and socioeconomically diverse sample. *International Journal of Eating Disorders, 54*, 1449–1462.

Hopkins, T. E. (2021, May/June). *The truth about Black women and stress.* Retrieved June 3, 2023, from Essence.com: https://www.essence.com/lifestyle/health-wellness/the-longterm-effects-of-chronic-stress-on-black-women/

Howard, L. M., Haislip, B. N., & Heron, K. E. (2019). Associations among social connections, body dissatisfaction, and disordered eating in African American and European American college women. *PSI CHI, The International Honor Society in Psychology, 24*(1), 33–42.

Hudson, J. I., Hiripi, E., Pope, H. G., & Kessler, R. C. (2007). The prevalence and correlates of eating disorders in the national comorbidity survey replication. *Biological Psychiatry, 61*(3), 348–358. https://doi.org/10.1016/j.biopsych.2006.03.040

Huggard, D. (2020). Integrated behavioral health in a clinical primary care setting. Insight Article. Medical Group Management Association. https://www.mgma.com

Hui, B. Y., Roberts, A., Thompson, K. J., McKillop, I. H., Sundaresan, N., Poliakin, L., Barbat, S. D., Kuwada, T. S., Gersin, K. S., & Nimeri, A. (2020). Outcomes of bariatric surgery in African Americans: An analysis of the Metabolic and Bariatric Surgery Accreditation and Quality Improvement Program (MBSAQIP) Data Registry. *Obesity surgery, 30*(11), 4275–4285. https://doi.org/10.1007/s11695-020-04820-w

Hutson, D. J. (2013). Your body is your business card: Bodily capital and health authority in the fitness industry. *Social Science & Medicine, 90*, 63–71.

Institute for Cultural Diplomacy. (2024). The African diaspora: Introduction to the African diaspora across the world. https://www.experience-africa.de/index.php?en_the-african-diaspora

Jackson, J. S., Torres, M., Caldwell, C. H., Neighbors, H. W., Nesse, R. M., Taylor, R. J., Trierweiler, S. J., Williams, D. R. (2004). The national survey of American life: A study of racial, ethnic and cultural influences on mental disorders and mental health.

International Journal of Methods in Psychiatric Research, 13(4), 196–207. doi:10.1002/mpr.177

Jackson-Lowman, H. (2014). An analysis of the impact of Eurocentric concepts of beauty on the lives of African American women. In *African American women: Living at the crossroads of race, gender, class, and culture* (pp. 155–172). San Diego, CA: Cognella Academic Publishing.

Jean Baker Miller Training Institute. (2024). *The development of relational-cultural theory.* Retrieved March 2024, from Jean Baker Miller Training Institute: https://rb.gy/48ggod

Jeffrey, S. & Heruc, G. (2020). Balancing nutrition management and the role of dietitians in eating disorder treatment. *Journal of Eating Disorders, 8*(64), 1–3. https://doi:10.1186/s40337-020-00344-x

Jeffries, A. (2020, October 29). *Is plastic surgery the new Black for Black women?* Essence.com. Retrieved from Essence.com: https://www.essence.com/celebrity/is-plastic-surgery-the-new-black-for-bla/

Jetty, A., Petterson, S., Westfall, J. M., & Jabbarpour, Y. (2021). Assessing primary care contributions to behavioral health: A cross-sectional study using medical expenditure panel survey. *Journal of Primary Care & Community Health, Jan-Dec*(12), 1–6. https://doi:10.1177/21501327211023871

Jewkes, R., & Morrell, R. (2012). Sexuality and the limits of agency among South African teenage women: Theorizing femininities and their connections to HIV risk practices. *Social Science & Medicine, 74*(11), 1729–1737.

Jewkes, R., Morrell, R., Hearn, J., Lundqvist, E., Blackbeard, D., Lindegger, G., Quayle, M., Sikweyiya, Y., & Gottzén, L. (2015). Hegemonic masculinity: Combining theory and practice in gender interventions. *Cult Health Sex, 17*(2), 112–127. https://doi.org/10.1080/13691058.2015.1085094

Jimenez, D. E., Park, M., Rosen, D., Joo, J., Martinez Garza, D., Weinstein, E. R., . . . Okereke, O. (2022). Centering culture in mental health: Differences in diagnosis, treatment, and access to care among older people of color. *The American Journal of Geriatric Psychiatry, 30*(11), 1234–1251. https://doi.org/10.1016/j.jagp.2022.07.001

Johns Hopkins University. (2024). *The Legacy of Henrietta Lacks.* http://www.hopkinsmedicine.org./henrietta-lacks

Johnson, V. R., Acholono, N. O., Dolan, A. C., Krishnan, A., Hsu-Chi Wang, E., & Stanford, F. C. (2021). Racial disparities in obesity treatment among children and adolescents. *Psychological Issues, 10*(3), 342–350. https://doi.org/10.1007/s13679-021-00442-0

Jones, C., & Shorter-Gooden, K. (2003). *Shifting: the double lives of Black women in America: Women speak out about men, work, motherhood, God, and the emotional cost of being Black and female* (1st ed.). HarperCollins.

Jones, L. V., & Guy-Sheftall, B. (2017). Black feminist therapy as a wellness tool. In S. Y.

Evans, K. Bell, & N. K. Burton (Eds.), *Black women's mental health: Balancing strength and vulnerability* (pp. 201–213). State University of New York Press.

Jonsson, E. (2021). A gap in the research: Race-specific issues and difficult questions. In C. Small & M. Fuller (Eds.), *Treating Black Women With Eating Disorders: A Clinicians Guide,* 13–32, Routledge.

Just, D. R., & Payne, C. R. (2009). Obesity: Can behavioral economics help? *Annals of Behavioral Medicine 38*(1), 47–55. doi:10.1007/s12160-009-9119-2

Kamody, R. C., Thurston, I. B., & Burton, E. T. (2020). Acceptance-based skill acquisition and cognitive reappraisal in a culturally responsive treatment for binge eating in adolescence. *Eating Disorders: The Journal of Treatment & Prevention, 28*, 184–201. https://doi.org/10.1080/10640266.2020.1731055

Kanakam, N. (2022). Therapists' experiences of working with ethnic minority females with eating disorders: A qualitative study. *Culture, Medicine and Psychiatry, 46*(2), 414–434.

Keith, V. M., Lincoln, K. D., Taylor, R. J., & Jackson, J. S. (2010). Discriminatory experiences and depressive symptoms among African American women: Do skin tone and mastery matter? *Sex Roles: A Journal of Research, 62*(1–2), 48–59.

Kenny, T. E., Trottier, K., & Lewis, S. P. (2022). Lived experience perspectives on a definition of eating disorder recovery in a sample of predominantly White women: A mixed method study. *Journal of Eating Disorders, 10*(1), 149. https://doi.org/10.1186/s40337-022-00670-2

Khalil, J., Boutros, S., Kheir, N., Kassem, M., Salameh, P., Sacre, H., Akel, M., Obeid, S., & Hallit, S. (2022). Eating disorders and their relationship with menopausal phases among a sample of middle-aged Lebanese women. *BioMed Central Women's Health, 22*(1), 153. doi: 10.1186/s12905-022-01738-6

Kinavey, H., & Cool, C. (2019). The broken lens how anti-fat bias in psychotherapy is harming our clients and what to do about it. *Women & Therapy, 42*(1–2), 116–130.

Kınık, M. F., Gönüllü, F. V., Vatansever, Z., & Karakaya, I. (2017). Diabulimia, a type I diabetes mellitus-specific eating disorder. *Turkish Archives of Pediatrics, 52*, 46–49. https://doi.org/10.5152/turkpediatriars.2017.2366

Kinkel-Ram, S. S., Kunstman, J., Hunger, J. M., & Smith, A. (2023). Examining the relation between discrimination and suicide among Black Americans: The role of social pain minimization and decreased bodily trust. *Stigma and Health, 8*(4), 428–436.

Kirwan Institute for the Study of Race and Ethnicity. (2015). *Understanding implicit bias.* Ohio State University.

Kroon Van Diest, A. M., Tartakovsky, M., Stachon, C., Pettit, J., & Perez, M. (2014, June). The relationship between acculturative stress and eating disorder symptoms: is it unique from general life stress? *Journal of Behavioral Medicine, 37*(3), 445–457.

LaMorte, W. W. (2016). Institutional Review Boards and the Belmont Principles: The

Syphilis Study at Tuskegee. https://sphweb.bumc.bu.edu/otlt/mph-modules/ep/ep713_researchethics/EP713_ResearchEthics3.html

Lashley, M.-B., Marshall, V., & McLaurin-Jones, T. (2017). Looking through the window: Black women's perspectives on mental health and self-care. In S. Y. Evans, K. Bell, & N. K. Burton (Eds.), *Black women's mental health: Balancing strength and vulnerability* (pp. 215–230). SUNY Press.

Lavender, J. M., Brown, T. A, & Murray, S. B. (2017). Men, muscles, and eating disorders: An overview of traditional and muscularity-oriented disordered eating. *Current Psychiatry Reports,19*(6), 32. https://doi.org/10.1007/s11920-017-0787-5

Le Grange, D., & Lock, J. (2007). *Treating bulimia in adolescents: A family-based approach.* The Guilford Press.

Lewellen, C., Bohonos, J. W., Henderson, E. W., & Colón, G. (2021). Re-complicating intersectionality considering differences in language and personality type when considering strategies for African American women's career development. Implementation Strategies for Improving Diversity in Organizations. https://doi.org/10.4018/978-1-7998-4745-8.ch006

Lewis, J. A., Mendenhall, R., Harwood, S. A., & Huntt, M. B. (2013). Coping with gendered racial microaggressions among Black women college students. *Journal of African American Studies, 17*(1), 51–73.

Liburd, L. C. (2003). Food, identity, and African—American women with type 2 diabetes: An anthropological perspective. *Diabetes Spectrum, 16*(3), 160–165.

Lindloff, M. R., Meadows, A., & Calogero, R. M. (2024). Living while fat: Development and validation of the Fat Microaggressions Scale. *Journal of Personality and Social Psychology. 127*(2), 335–362. https://dx.doi.org/10.1037/pspi0000450

Linehan, M. M. (2015). *DBT skills training manual* (2nd ed.). New York: Guilford Press.

Liu, N. F., Brown, A. S., Folias, A. E., Younge, M. F., Guzman, S. J., Close, K. L., & Wood, R. (2017, January). Stigma in people with type 1 or type 2 diabetes. *Clinical diabetes: a publication of the American Diabetes Association, 35*(1), 27–34.

Love, C. D., Booysen, L. E., & Essed, P. (2018). An exploration of the intersection of race, gender and generation gender. *Gender, Work & Organ, 25*, pp. 475–494.

Luther, G. M., Folger, A. C., & Kelly, N. R. (2021). Body dissatisfaction and ethnic identity are associated with loss of control eating among young adult African American men. *Eating Behaviors, 43*. np. doi: 10.1016/j.eatbeh.2021.101578

Machado, C. M. (2017, June 26). Roxane Gay: Hunger is a state of being. *Guernica Magazine.* https://www.guernicamag.com/roxane-gay-hunger-is-a-state-of-being/.

Manzato, E., & Roncarati, E. (2022). Eating disorders in midlife and in the elderly. In E. Manzato, M. Cuzzolaro, & L. M. Donini (Eds.), *Hidden and lesser-known disordered eating behaviors in medical and psychiatric conditions* (pp. 23–31). Springer Nature Switzerland AG. https://doi.org/10.1007/978-3-030-81174-7_4

Marques, L., Alegria, M., Becker, A. E., Chen, C. N., Fang, A., & Chosak, A. (2011).

Comparative prevalence, correlates of impairment, and service utilization for eating disorders across US ethnic groups: Implications for reducing ethnic disparities in health care access for eating disorders. *International Journal of Eating Disorders*, *44*(5), 412–420. https://doi.org/10.1002/eat.20787 [PubMed: 20665700]

Mason, W. N., Warraich, L. K., & Haskins, N. (2024). Can you relate to me? A new approach for intersectional resilience of LGB African-American clients. *Journal of LGBTQ Issues in Counseling, 18*(2), 81–106. https://doi.org/10.1080/26924951.2023.2262327

Matacin, M. L., & Simone, M. (2019). Advocating for fat activism in a therapeutic context. *Women & Therapy, 42*(1–2), 200–215.

Mchugh, M. C., & Chrisler, J. C. (2019). Making space for every body: Ending sizeism in psychotherapy and training. *Women & Therapy, 42*(1–2), 7–21.

McLaren, L., & Kuh, D. (2004). Body dissatisfaction in midlife women. *Journal of Women & Aging, 16*(1/2), 35–54.

McMillan, D. (2021). Only a dog wants a bone! The other end of the eating spectrum. In C. Small, & M. Fuller (Eds.), *Treating Black women with eating disorders: A clinician's guide* (pp. 133–139). New York: Routledge.

Mehler, P. S., & Andersen A. E. (2010). *Eating disorders: A guide to medical care and complications*, 2nd edition. The John Hopkins University Press.

Mehler, P. S., & Rylander, M. (2015). Bulimia Nervosa—medical complications. *Journal of Eating Disorders, 3*(12), 1–5.

Merriam-Webster. (n.d.). Acculturation. Retrieved November 2023, from: https://www.merriam-webster.com/dictionary/acculturation

Merriam-Webster.com. (n.d.). Race. Retrieved 2023, from: https://www.merriam-webster.com/dictionary/race

Merriam-Webster.com. (n.d.). Sizeism. Retrieved October 19, 2023, from: https://www.merriam-webster.com/dictionary/sizeism

Merritt, M. M, Bennett, G. G., Williams, R. B., Edwards, C. L.., & Sollers, J. J. (2006). Perceived racism and cardiovascular reactivity and recovery to personally relevant stress. Health Psychology, *25*(3), 364–369. https://doi: 10.1037/0278-6133.25.3.364

Mialon, M., Ho, M., Carriedo, A., Ruskins, G., & Crosbie, E. (2021). Food industry shaping of the principles of scientific integrity. *European Journal of Public Health*, *31*(3), 319. https://doi.org/10.1093/eurpub/ckab164.844.

Michals, D. (Ed.). (2017). *Fannie Lou Hamer*. Retrieved February 2024, from National Women's History Museum: https://www.womenshistory.org/education-resources/biographies/fannie-lou-hamer

Mikhail, M. E., & Klump, K. L. (Eds.). (2021). A virtual issue highlighting eating disorders in people of Black/African and Indigenous heritage. *International Journal of Eating Disorders, 54*, 459–467.

Mimura, Y., Shimizu, Y., Oi, H., Kurose, S., Kudo, S., Takata, T., . . . Funayama, M.

(2021). Case series: Ischemic stroke associated with dehydration and arteriosclerosis in individuals with severe anorexia nervosa. *Journal of Eating Disorders, 9*(39), 1–7. https://doi.org/10.1186/s40337-021-00393-w

Mishu, M. P., Tindall, L., Kerrigan, P., & Gegg, L. (2023). Cross-culturally adapted psychological interventions for the treatment of depression and/or anxiety among young people: A scoping review. PLoS ONE. *PLoS ONE, 18*(10): e0290653. https://doi.org/10.1371/journal.pone.0290653

Mitchell, K. S., & Mazzeo, S. E. (2004). Binge eating and psychological distress in ethnically diverse undergraduate men and women. *Eating Behaviors, 5*(2), 157–69. https://doi.org/10.1016/j.eatbeh.2003.07.004

Moller, N., & Tischner, I. (2019). Young people's perceptions of fat counsellors: How can THAT help me? *Qualitative Research in Psychology, 16*(1), 34–53.

Monk, E. P. (2021). Colorism and physical health: Evidence from a national survey. *Journal of Health and Social Behavior, 62*(1), 37–52. https://doi.org/10.1177/0022146520979645

Moradi, B. (2010). Addressing gender and cultural diversity in body image: Objectification theory as a framework for integrating theories and grounding research. *Sex Roles, 63*, 138–148.

Moradi, B. (2017). (Re)focusing intersectionality: From social identities back to systems of oppression and privilege. In K. A. DeBond, A. R. Fischer, K. J. Bieschke, & R. M. Perez (Eds.), *Handbook of Sexual Orientation and Gender Diversity in Counseling and Psychotherapy* (pp. 105–127). American Psychological Association.

Morgan, J. F., Reid, F., & Lacey, J. H. (1999). The scoff questionnaire: Assessment of a new screening tool for eating disorders. BMJ, *319*(7223), 1467–1468.

Moussa-Tooks, A. B., Sheffield, J. M., Freeman, D., & Brinen, A. P. (2024). Disentangling the consequences of systemic racism and clinical paranoia to promote effectiveness of a cognitive-behavioral intervention for persecutory delusions in minoritized individuals: A case-example. *Clinical Case Studies, 23*(2), 106–126. https://doi.org/10.1177/15346501231190920

Murray, P. (1963, November 14). The Negro woman in the quest for equality. *Pauli Murray Papers, 1827–1985*. Schlesinger Library, Radcliffe College.

Murray S. B., Brown T. A., Blashill A. J., Compte E. J., Lavender J. M., Mitchison D., Mond J. M., Keel P. K., & Nagata J. M. (2019). The development and validation of the muscularity-oriented eating test: A novel measure of muscularity-oriented disordered eating. *International Journal of Eating Disorders, 52*, 1389–1398. https://doi.org/10.1002/eat.23144

Muscatell, K. A., Alvarez, G. M., Bonar, A. S., Cardenas, M. N., Galvan, M. J., Merritt, C. C., & Starks, M. D. (2022). Brain–body pathways linking racism and health. *American Psychologist, 77*(9), 1049–1060.

Nagata, J. M., Ganson, K. T., & Murray, S. B. (2020). Eating disorders in adolescent boys and young men: An update. *Current Opinion in Pediatrics, 32*(4), 476–481. https://doi.org/10.1097/mop.0000000000000911

Nagata, J. M., Ganson, K. T., Sajjad, O. M., Benabou, S. E., & Bibbins-Domingo, K. (2021). Prevalence of perceived racism and discrimination among US children aged 10 and 11 years: The adolescent brain cognitive development (ABCD) Study. *Journal of the American Medical Association Pediatrics, 175*(8), 861–863. https://doi.org/10.1001/jamapediatrics.2021.1022

Nash, J. C. (2008). Re-thinking intersectionality. *Feminist Review, 89*, 1–15.

National Alliance for Eating Disorders. (n.d.). *Members of Treatment Team.* Retrieved April 3, 2024, from: https://www.allianceforeatingdisorders.com/members-of-treatment-team/

National Center for Health Statistics (US). (2017). Health, United States, 2016: With Chartbook on Long-term Trends in Health. Hyattsville, MD: National Center for Health Statistics (US). https://pubmed.ncbi.nlm.nih.gov/28910066/

National Center for Health Statistics (NCHS). (2019, April). *Health, United States spotlight racial and ethnic disparities in heart disease.* Retrieved March 2024, from CDC National Center for Health Statistics: https://www.cdc.gov/nchs/hus.htm

National Eating Disorders Collaboration, Australian Government Department of Health and Aged Care. (2018). *The Care Team.* (B. Foundation, Producer) Retrieved April 3, 2024, from: https://nedc.com.au/eating-disorders/treatment-and-recovery/the-care

National Eating Disorders Association [NEDA]. (2005). Eating disorders in women of color: Explanations and implications. www.nationaleatingdisorders.org

National Eating Disorders Association (NEDA). (2023, September 29). Paula Edwards Gayfield Weight Stigma Video horizontal [Video]. YouTube. Retrieved from https://www.youtube.com/watch?v=sLf3RNpjHyw

National Eating Disorders Association (NEDA). (n.d.). https://www.nationaleatingdisorders.org. Retrieved from: https://www.nationaleatingdisorders.org/marginalized-voices-0

National Institutes of Health (NIH) (2022). Significant research advances enabled by HeLa cells. https://osp.od.nih.gov/hela-cells/significant-research-advances-enabled-by-hela-cells/

National Kidney Foundation (2018). African Americans and kidney disease. www.kidney.org/news/newsroom/factsheets/African-Americans-and-CKD

National Museum of African American History & Culture. (n.d.). *Let's talk about race: racial identity development.* Retrieved November 2023, from: https://nmaahc.si.edu/learn/talking-about-race/topics/race-and-racial-identity

National Public Radio. (NPR). (2016). They 'failed': 6 more Michigan employees charged in Flint water crisis. https://www.npr.org/sections/thetwo-way/2016/07/29/487934982/they-failed-6-more-michigan-employees-charged-in-flint-water-crisis#:~:text=At%20a%20press%20conference%20today,covered%20up%20significant%20health%20risks.%22

National Public Radio. (NPR). (2016, April 20). Lead-laced water in Flint: A step-by-step look at the makings of a crisis. Retrieved from https://www.npr.org/sections/thetwo-way/2016/04/20/465545378/lead-laced-water-in-flint-a-step-by-step-look-at-the-makings-of-a-crisis

National Public Radio. (NPR). (2021). The once and future 'Karen.' https://www.npr.org/2021/10/05/1043491781/the-once-and-future-karen

NBC News. (2023, June 29). Supreme Court strikes down college affirmative action programs. Retrieved from https://www.nbcnews.com/politics/supreme-court/supreme-court-strikes-affirmative-action-programs-harvard-unc-rcna66770

NBC News. (2023, August 1). Henrietta Lacks family settles with biotech company over cancer cells. https://www.youtube.com/watch?v=AENPGhVWBvE

Neville, H. A., Awad, G. H., Brooks, J.E., Flores, M. P., & Bluemel, J. (2013). Color-blind racial ideology: Theory, training, and measurement implications in psychology. *American Psychologist, 68*(6), 455–466. https://doi: 10.1037/a0033282. PMID: 24016116

New York Times. (2021, August 12). White women, Karen. *New York Times.* https://www.nytimes.com/2021/08/12/t-magazine/white-women-karen.html

Nguyen, K. H., Glantz, S. A., Palmer, C. N., & Schmidt, L. A. (2019). Tobacco industry involvement in children's sugary drinks market. *BMJ, 364,* l736. https://doi.org/10.1136/bmj.l736

Nitsch, A., Dlugosz, H., Gibson, D., & Mehler, P. S. (2021). Medical complications of bulimia nervosa. *Cleveland Clinic Journal of Medicine, 88*(6), 333–343.

Nix, Elizabeth. (2023). Tuskegee experiment: The infamous syphilis study. https://www.history.com/news/the-infamous-40-year-tuskegee-study

Njoroge, W., Forkpa, M., & Bath, E. (2021). Impact of racial discrimination on the mental health of minoritized youth. *Child and Adolescent Disorders, 23*(12). https://doi.org/10.1007/s11920-021-01297-x

The North American Menopause Society. (2023). *Body dissatisfaction can lead to eating disorders at any age.* Retrieved April 2024, from: https://rb.gy/1qh52u

Novak, J. R., Peak, T., Gast, J., & Arnell, M. (2019). Associations between masculine norms and health-care utilization in highly religious, heterosexual men. *American Journal of Men's Health, 13*(3), 1–11. https://doi.org/10.1177/1557988319856739

Nguyen, K. H., Glantz, S. A., Palmer, C. N., & Schmidt, L. A. (2019). Tobacco industry involvement in children's sugary drinks market. *The British Medical Journal*, 364-371. doi:10.1136/bmj.l736

Obesity Evidence Hub. (2022). Impact of unhealthy food marketing on children. https://www.obesityevidencehub.org.au/collections/prevention/the-impact-of-food-marketing-on-children

Office of Disease Prevention and Health Promotion. (n.d.). Food insecurity. Retrieved May 1, 2024, from: https://health.gov/healthypeople/priority-areas/social-determinants-health/literature-summaries/food-insecurity#cit17

Office of Minority Health, U.S. Department of Health and Human Services. (2013). National standards for culturally and linguistically appropriate services in health and health care: A blueprint for advancing and sustaining CLAS policy and practice. Retrieved from https://thinkculturalhealth.hhs.gov/assets/pdfs/enhancedclasstandardsblueprint.pdf

Office of Minority Health, U.S. Department of Health and Human Services. (2012). Think cultural health. CLAS legislation map. Retrieved from https://thinkculturalhealth.hhs.gov/assets/pdfs/resource-library/combating-implicit-bias-stereotypes.pdf

Office of Minority Health, U.S. Department of Health and Human Services. (2021). Retrieved from https://thinkculturalhealth.hhs.gov

Office of Minority Health, U.S. Department of Health and Human Services. (2023). Diabetes and African Americans. Retrieved from https://minorityhealth.hhs.gov/diabetes-and-african-americans

Office of Minority Health Resource Center. (2019). Profile: Black/African Americans. Retrieved from:www.minorityhealth.hhs.gov/omh/browse.aspx?lvl=3&lvlid=61

Office on Women's Health, U.S. Department of Health and Human Services (HHS). (2015a). *Diabetes.* Retrieved February 2024, from: https://www.womenshealth.gov

Office on Women's Health, U.S. Department of Health and Human Services. (2015b). *Thyroid disease.* Retrieved February 2024, from: https://owh-wh-d9-dev.s3.amazonaws.com/s3fs-public/documents/fact-sheet-thyroid-disease.pdf

Office on Women's Health, U.S. Department of Health and Human Services. (2022a). *Anorexia Nervosa.* Retrieved February 2024, from: https://www.womenshealth.gov/mental-health/mental-health-conditions/eating-disorders/anorexia-nervosa

Office on Women's Health, U.S. Department of Health and Human Services. (2022b). *Binge Eating Disorder.* Retrieved February 2024, from: https://www.womenshealth.gov/mental-health/mental-health-conditions/eating-disorders/binge-eating-disorder

Office on Women's Health, U.S. Department of Health and Human Services. (2022c). *Bulimia Nervosa.* Retrieved February 2024, from: https://www.womenshealth.gov/mental-health/mental-health-conditions/eating-disorders/bulimia-nervosa

Oh, H., Lincoln, K., & Waldman, K. (2021). Perceived colorism and lifetime psychiatric disorders among Black American adults: Findings from the National Survey of American Life. *Social Psychiatry and Psychiatric Epidemiology, 56*, 1509–1512.

Oh, H., Stickley, A., Lincoln, K. D., & Koyanagi, A. (2022). Allergies, infections, and psychiatric disorders among Black Americans: Findings from the National Survey of American Life. *Ethnicity & Health, 27*(1), 74–82.

Opara, I., & Santos, N. (2019). A conceptual framework exploring social media, eating disorders, and body dissatisfaction among Latina adolescents. *Hispanic Journal of Behavioral Sciences, 41*(3), 363–377. Retrieved from https://doi.org/10.1177/0739986319860844

Osa, M. L., Siegel, J., Meadows, A., Elbe, C., & Calogero, R. M. (2022). Stigmatizing effects of weight status on lay perceptions of eating disorder-related distress. *Eating Disorders, 30*(1), 99–109.

Oswald, F. (2024). Anti-fatness in the Ozempic era: State of the landscape and considerations for future research. *Fat Studies: An Interdisciplinary Journal of Body Weight and Society, 13*(2), 128–134. https://doi.org/10.1080/21604851.2024.2307674

Ottey, S. (2021). Treating polycystic ovarian syndrome in Black women with eating disorders. In C. Small, & M. Fuller (Eds.), *Treating Black women with eating disorders* (pp. 103–108). Routledge Press.

Oyer, L., O'Halloran, M. S., & Christoe-Frazier, L. (2016). Understanding the working alliance with clients diagnosed with anorexia nervosa. *Eating Disorders, 24*(2), 121–137.

Parker, J. E., Levinson, J. A., Hunger, J. M., Enders, C. K., Laraia, B. A., Epel, E. S., & Tomiyama, A. (2023). Longitudinal stability of disordered-eating symptoms from Age 12 to 40 in Black and White women. *Clinical Psychological Science, 11*(5), 879–893.

Paulsen, L. H., Sørensen Bakke, L., Jarbøl, D. E., Balasubramaniam, K., & Hansen, D. G. (2020). Associations between lifestyle, erectile dysfunction and healthcare seeking: A population-based study. *Scandinavian Journal of Primary Health Care, 38*(2), 176–183. https://doi.org/10.1080/02813432.2020.1753347

Payton, Gregory J. (2014). Men of color and eating disorders. In Miville, M. L. & Ferguson, A. D. (Eds). *Handbook of Race-ethnicity and Gender in Psychology* (pp. 361–378). New York, NY: Springer Science + Business Media. https://doi.org/10.1007/978-1-4614-8860-6_17

PCOS Challenge, Inc. (n.d.). *What is PCOS?* Retrieved January 2024, from PCOS Challenge Support Network: https://www.pcoschallenge.org/what-is-pcos/

Pearce-Dunbar, V., & James Bateman, C. (2021). Evolution of the fluffy ideal in Jamaica. In C. Small, & M. Fuller (Eds.), *Treating Black women with eating disorders* (pp. 195–204). Routledge Press.

Penner, L. A., & Dovidio, J. F. (2016). Racial color blindness and Black-White health care disparities. In H. A. Neville, M. E. Gallardo, & D. W. Sue (Eds.), *The Myth of Racial Color Blindness: Manifestations, Dynamics, and Impact* (pp. 275–293). American Psychological Association.

Perez, M., Voelz, Z. R., Pettit, J. W., & Joiner Jr., T. E. (2002). The role of acculturative stress and body dissatisfaction in predicting bulimic symptomatology across ethnic groups. *International Journal of Eating Disorders, 31*(4), 442–454.

Phoenix, A. (2006). Intersectionality. *European Journal of Women Studies, 13*(3), 187–192.

Physiopedia. (2021, August 10). *Eating Disorders.* (L. Hampton, Editor) Retrieved January 12, 2024, from Physiopedia: https://www.physio-pedia.com/index.php?title=Eating_Disorders&oldid=280393

Pike, K. M., Dohm, F., Striegel-Moore, R. H., Wilfley, D. E., & Fairburn, C. G. (2001). A comparison of Black and White women with binge eating disorder. *American Journal of Psychiatry, 158,* 1455–1460.

REFERENCES

Piran, N. (2016). Embodied possibilities and disruptions: The emergence of the experience of embodiment construct from qualitative studies with girls and women. *Body Image, 18,* 43–60.

Piran, N. (2017). *Journeys of embodiment at the intersection of body and culture: The developmental theory of embodiment.* Academic Press.

Policy Center for Maternal Mental Health. (2023, December). *Black maternal mental health [Report].* Retrieved January 2024, from: https://www.2020mom.org/blog/issue-brief-black-maternal-mental-health

Powell, L. M., Slater, S., Mirtcheva, D., Boo, Y., & Chaloupka, F. J. (2007). Food store availability and neighborhood characteristics in the United States. *Preventive Medicine, 44,* 189–195.

Powell, W., Richmond, J., Mohottige, D., Yen, I., Joslyn, A., & Corbie-Smith, G. (2019). Medical mistrust, racism, and delays in preventive health screening among African-American men. *Behavioral Medicine, 45*(2), 102–117. https://doi.org/10.1080/08964289.2019.1585327

Prochaska, J. O., & DiClemente, C. C. (1982). Transtheoretical therapy: Toward a more integrative model of change. *Psychotherapy: Theory, Research & Practice, 19*(3), 276–288. https://doi.org/10.1037/h0088437

Racette, S. B., Barry, V. G., Bales, C. W., McCrory, M. A., Obert, K.A., Gilhooly, C. H., Roberts, S. B., Martin, C. K., Champagne, C., & Das, S. K. (2022). Nutritional quality of calorie restricted diets in the CALERIE™ 1 trial. *Experimental Gerontology,* 165, np. doi: 10.1016/j.exger.2022.111840

Rahman, A. A. A., Al-Sadat, N., & Low, W. Y. (2011). Help seeking behavior among men with erectile dysfunction in primary care setting. *American Journal of Men's Health, 8*(1). https://doi.org/10.1016/s1875-6867(11)60033-x

Ralph-Nearman, C., Achee, M., Lapidus, R., Stewart, J. L., & Filik, R. (2019). A systematic and methodological review of attentional biases in eating disorders: Food, body, and perfectionism. *Brain and Behavior, 9.*

Ramey Berry, Daina, & Parker, Nakia D. (2018). Women and Slavery in the Nineteenth Century, in ed. Ellen Hartigan-O'Connor, Ellen and Materson, Lisa G. *The Oxford handbook of American women's and gender history,* Oxford University Press.

Raney, J. H., Al-Shoaibi, A. A., Shao, I. Y., Ganson, K. T., Testa, A., Jackson, D. B., He, J., Glidden, D. V., & Nagata, J. M. (2023). Racial discrimination is associated with binge-eating disorder in early adolescents: A cross-sectional analysis. *Journal of Eating Disorders, 11*(1), 139–148. https://doi: 10.1186/s40337-023-00866-0.

Rasmusson, G., Lydecker, J. A., Coffino, J. A., White, M. A., & Grilo, C. M. (2019). Household food insecurity is associated with binge-eating disorder and obesity. *International Journal of Eating Disorders, 52,* 28–35.

Reddy Medical Group. (2024). Breaking the silence: Unraveling the mystery of men's reluctance to seek medical care.

Reela, J. J., SooHooa, S., Franklin Summerhaysa, J., & Gillb, D. L. (2008). Age before beauty: An exploration of body image in African American and Caucasian adult women. *Journal of Gender Studies, 17*(4), 321–330.

Rein, L., & Whitlock, C. (2023). 5,000 pilots suspected of hiding major health issues. Most are still flying. *Washington Post.* https://www.washingtonpost.com/politics/2023/08/27/faa-pilots-health-conditions-va-benefits/

Reyes-Rodriguez, M. L. (2022). *Eating disorders resource catalogue.* (K. Cortese, Ed.) Retrieved November 2023, from: https://www.edcatalogue.com/wp-content/uploads/2022/02/2022GurzeCatalogue.pdf

Reyes-Rodriguez, M. L., & Franko, D. L. (2020). Cultural adaptations of evidence-based treatments for eating disorders. In C. C. Totolaini, A. B. Goldschmidt, & D. Le Grange, *Adapting evidence-based eating disorder treatments for novel populations and settings: A practical guide* (pp. 3–30). Routledge.

Reyes-Rodriguez, M., Ramirez, J., Patrice, K., Rose, K., & Bulik, C. M. (2013). Exploring barriers and facilitators in the eating disorders treatment in Latinas in the United States. *Journal of Latina/o Psychology, 1*(2), 112–131.

Richards, J., Bang, N., Ratliff, E. L., Paszkowiiak, M. A., Khorgami, Z., Khalsa, S. S., & Simmons, W. K. (2023). Successful treatment of binge eating disorder with the GLP-1 agonist semaglutide: A retrospective cohort study. *Obesity Pillars, 7*(100080), 1–4. https://doi.org/10.1016/j.obpill.2023.100080

Rienecke, R. D., & Le Grange, D. (2022). The five tenets of family-based treatment for adolescent eating disorders. *Journal of Eating Disorders, 10*(60), 1–10. https://doi.org/10.1186/s40337-022-00585-y

Rittenhouse, M. (2012). *Binge eating disorder.* Retrieved January 15, 2024, from: https://www.eatingdisorderhope.com/information/binge-eating-disorder

Rittenhouse, M. (2021a). *Effective eating disorder therapy techniques.* Retrieved January 2024, from Eating Disorder Hope: https://rb.gy/frp0cy

Rittenhouse, M. (2021b). *The effects of eating disorders on the endocrine system.* Retrieved January 21, 2024, from: https://www.eatingdisorderhope.com/long-term-effects-health/endocrine-system

Roberto, C. A., Baik, J., Harris, J. L., & Brownell, K. D. (2010). Influence of licensed characters on children's taste and snack preferences. *Pediatrics, 126*(1), 88–93.

Robinson, T. N., Borzekowski, D. L., Matheson, D. M., & Kraemer, H. C. (2007). Effects of fast-food branding on young children's taste preferences. *Archives of Pediatrics and Adolescent Medicine, 161*(8), 792–797.

Romo, L. F., Mireles-Rios, R., & Hurtado, A. (2015). Cultural, media, and peer influences on body beauty perceptions of Mexican American adolescent girls. *Journal of Adolescent Research, 31*, 474–501. https://doi:10 .1177/0743558415594424

Rosen, E. (2015). *Males, anorexia, and physical side effects.* Retrieved January 21, 2024, from: https://www.eatingdisorderhope.com/risk-groups/men/anorexia-physical-side-effects

Runfola, C. D., Von Holle, A., Peat, C. M., Gagne, D. A., Brownley, K. A., Hofmeier, S. M., & Bulik, C. M. (2013). Characteristics of women with body size satisfaction at midlife: Results of the Gender and Body Image (GABI) Study. *Journal of Women & Aging, 25*, 287–304.

Russell, H., Aouad, P., Le, A., Marks, P., Maloney, D., National Eating Disorder Reserch Consortium, . . . Maguire, S. (2023). Psychotherapies for eating disorders: findings from a rapid review. *Journal of Eating Disorders, 11*(1), 175. https://doi.org/10.1186/s40337-023-00886-w

Sabik, N. J., Cole, E. R., & Ward, L. M. (2010). Are all minority women equally buffered from negative body image? Intra-ethnic moderators of the buffering hypothesis. *Psychology of Women, 34*(2), 139–151. https://doi.org/10.1111/j.1471-6402.2010.01557.x

Sachs, A. (2023). Pilots hide mental health issues so they don't lose their wings. The Washington Post. https://www.washingtonpost.com/travel/2023/12/15/pilots-mental-health-faa-certification/

Sacks, V., & Murphey, D. (2018). The prevalence of adverse childhood experiences, nationally, by state, and by race, or ethnicity. *Child Welfare.*

Salami, T. K., Carter, S. E., Cordova, B., Flowers, K. C., & Walker, R. L. (2019). The influence of race-related stress on eating pathology: The mediating role of depression and moderating role of cultural worldview among Black American women. *Journal of Black Psychology, 45*(6–7), 571–598.

Sangha, S., Oliffe, J. L., Kelly, M. T., & McCuaig, F. (2019). Eating disorders in males: How primary care providers can improve recognition, diagnosis, and treatment. *American Journal of Men's Health, 13*(3). doi:10.1177/1557988319857424

Schafer, J., & Rutledge, T. (2003). Life without ED: How one woman declared independence from her eating disorder and how you can too. McGraw Hill.

Schlichthorst, M., Sanci, L. A., Pirkis, J., Spittal, M. J., & Hocking, J. S. (2016). Why do men go to the doctor? Socio-demographic and lifestyle factors associated with health-care utilisation among a cohort of Australian men. *BioMed Central Public Health, 16*(3), 1028. https://doi.org/10.1186/s12889-016-3706-5

Sedlak, A. J., Mettenburg, J., Basena, M., Petta, I., McPherson, K., Greene, A., & Li, S. (2010). Fourth National Incidence Study of Child Abuse and Neglect (NIS–4) Report to Congress. U.S. Department of Health and Human Services (DHHS) Administration for Children and Families (ACF) Office of Planning, Research, and Evaluation (OPRE) and the Children's Bureau.

Sellers, S. L., Govia, I. O., & Jackson, J. S. (2009). Health and Black older adults: Insights from a life-course perspective. In R. L. Braithwaite, S. E. Taylor, & H. M. Treadwell (Eds.), *Health issues in the Black community* (3rd ed., pp. 95–116). Jossey-Bass.

Shabsigh, R., Perelman, M. A., Laumann, E. O., & Lockhart, D. C. (2004). Drivers and barriers to seeking treatment for erectile dysfunction: A comparison of six countries. *BJU International,* https://doi.org/10.1111/j.1464-410X.2004.05104.x

Shafran, R., Cooper, Z., & Fairburn, C. G. (2002). Clinical perfectionism: A cognitive–behavioural analysis. *Behaviour Research and Therapy, 40*(7), 773–791. https://doi.org/10.1016/S0005-7967(01)00059-6

Shaw, H., Ramirez, L., Trost, A., Randall, P., & Stice, E. (2004). Body image and eating disturbances across ethnic groups: More similarities than differences. *Psychology of Addictive Behaviors, 18*(1), 12–18.

Sheppard, V. B., Harper, F. W., Davis, K., Hirpa, F., & Makambi, K. (2014). The importance of contextual factors and age in association with anxiety and depression in Black breast cancer patients. *Psycho-Oncology, 23*(2), 143–150.

Simone, M., Telke, S., Anderson, L. M., Eisenberg, M., & Neumark-Sztainer, D. (2022, February). Ethnic/racial and gender differences in disordered eating behavior prevalence trajectories among women and men from adolescence into young adulthood. *Social Science Medicine, 294*, 114720. https://doi.org/10.1016/j.socscimed.2022.114720

Skinner, A. C., Ravanbakht, S. N., Skelton, J. A., Perrin, E. M., & Armstrong, S. C. (2018). Prevalence of obesity and severe obesity in US children, 1999–2016. *Pediatrics, 141*(3), 2017-3459. https://doi.org/10.1542/peds.2017-3459

Small, C. (2019). Embracing relapse: For college students, consider it a gift. *Perspectives: A Professional Journal of The Renfrew Center Foundation (Summer),* 12–13.

Small, C. (2021a). Eating because we're hungry, or because something's eating us? In C. Small & M. Fuller (Eds.), *Treating Black women with eating disorders: A clinicians guide* (pp. 13–32). Routledge.

Small, C. (2021b). Introduction. In C. Small, & M. Fuller (Eds.), *Treating Black women with eating disorders: A clinician's guide* (pp. 1–10). Routledge.

Small, C., & Fuller, M. (2021). *Treating Black Women with Eating Disorders.* Routledge Press.

Smith, A. R., Zuromski, K. L., & Dodd, D. R. (2018, August). Eating disorders and suicidality: What we know, what we don't know, and suggestions for future research. *Current Opinion in Psychology, 22*, 63–67.

Smith, M. M., Sherry, S. B., Saklofskea, D. H., & Mushqaush, A. R. (2017). Clarifying the perfectionism-procrastination relationship using a 7-day, 14-occasion daily diary study. *Personality and Individual Differences, 112*, 117–123.

Sonneville, K. R., & Lipson, S. K. (2018). Disparities in eating disorder diagnosis and treatment according to weight status, race/ethnicity, socioeconomic background, and sex among college students. *International Journal of Eating Disorders, 51*, 518–526.

Sonneville, K. R., & Rodgers, R. F. (2019). Shared concerns and opportunity for joint action in creating a food environment that supports health. *Nutrients, 11*(1), 41. ttps://doi.org/10.3390/nu11010041

Stackpole, R., Greene, D., Bills, E., & Egan, S. J. (2023). The association between eating disorders and perfectionism in adults: A systematic review and meta-analysis. *Eating Behaviors, 50*. https://doi.org/10.1016/j.eatbeh.2023.101769

Stephens, D., & Thomas, T. L. (2012). The influence of skin color on heterosexual Black college women's dating beliefs. *Journal of Feminist Family Therapy, 24*(4), pp. 291–315. doi: 10.1080/08952833.2012.710815

Stiles-Shields, C., Bamford, B. H., Touyz, S., Le Grange, D., Hay, P., & Lacey, H. (2016). Predictors of therapeutic alliance in two treatments for adults with severe and enduring anorexia nervosa. *Journal of Eating Disorders, 4*(13), 1–7. https://doi.org/10.1186/s40337-016-0102-6

Stitham, K. (2021, April 15). Code switching in the workplace: Understanding cultures of power. Retrieved September 22, 2021, from: https://www.integrativeinquiryllc.com/post/the-problem-with-code-switching-addressing-the-dominant-culture

Strayhorn, G. (2009). Health disparities: The case for diabetes. In R. L. Braithwaite, S. E. Taylor, & H. M. Treadwell (Eds.), *Health issues in the Black community* (3rd ed., pp. 279–289). Jossey-Bass.

Strings, S. (2019). *Fearing the Black body: The racial origins of fat phobia.* NYU Press.

Substance Abuse and Mental Health Services Administration (SAMHSA). (2001). *Mental health: Culture, race, and ethnicity—a supplement to mental health: A report of the Surgeon General.* Center for Mental Health Services, U.S. Department of Health and Human Services. Rockville, MD.

Substance Abuse and Mental Health Services Administration (SAMHSA). (2003). *Developing cultural competence in disaster mental health programs: Guiding principles and recommendations.* Center for Mental Health Services, U.S. Department of Health and Human Services. Rockville: HHS Publication No. (SMA) 3828.

Substance Abuse and Mental Health Services Administration (SAMHSA). (2014). *Improving Cultural Competence.* HHS Publication No. (SMA) 14-4849, Treatment Improvement Protocol (TIP) Series No. 59. Rockville, MD: Substance Abuse and Mental Health Services Administration. Retrieved November 2023, from https://pubmed.ncbi.nlm.nih.gov/25356450/

Sue, D. W. (2001). Multidimensional facets of cultural competence. *The Counseling Psychologist, 29*(6), 790–821.

Sue, D. W., & Sue, D. (1999). *Counseling the culturally different: Theory and practice* (3rd ed.). John Wiley & Sons.

Sutton, A. L., He, J., Tanner, E., Edmonds, M. C., Henderson, A., Hurtado de Mendoza, A., & Sheppard, V. B. (2019). Understanding medical mistrust in Black women at risk of BRCA 1/2 Mutations. *Journal of Health Disparities Research and Practice, 12*(3), 35–47.

Talleyrand, R. M. (2006, October). Potential stressors contributing to eating disorder symptoms in African American women: Implications for mental health counselors. *Journal of Mental Health Counseling, 28*(4), 338–352.

Talleyrand, R. M., Gordon, A. D., Daquin, J. V., & Johnson, A. J. (2017). Expanding our understanding of eating practices, body image, and appearance in African American women: A qualitative study. *Journal of Black Psychology, 43*(5), 464–492.

Tarcin, G., Akman, H., Gunes Kaya, D., Serdengecti, N., Incetahtaci, S., Turan, H., . . . Ercan, O. (2023). Diabetes-specific eating disorder and possible associated psychopathologies in adolescents with type 1 diabetes mellitus. *Eating and Weight Disorders—Studies on Anorexia, Bulimia and Obesity, 28*(36), 1–8. https://doi.org/10.1007/s40519-023-01559-y

Taylor, J. Y., Caldwell, C. H., Baser, R. E., Faison, J. S., & Jackson, J. S. (2007). Prevalence of eating disorders among Blacks in the National Survey of American Life. *International Journal of Eating Disorders,* 40, 10–14. https://doi.org/10.1002/eat.20451

Taylor, J. Y., Caldwell, C. H., Baser, R. E., Matusko, N., Faison, N., & Jackson, J. S. (2013). Classification and correlates of eating disorders among Blacks: findings from the National Survey of American Life. *Journal of Health Care for the Poor and Underserved*, Feb; *24*(1), 289–310. https://doi.org/10.1353/hpu.2013.0027

Taylor, R., Forsythe-Brown, I., Taylor, H., & Chatters, L. (2014). Patterns of emotional social support and negative interactions among African American and Black Caribbean extended families. *Journal of African American Studies, 18,* 147–163.

Taylor, S. E., & Braithwaite Holden, K. (2009). The health status of Black women. In R. L. Braithwaite, S. E. Taylor, & H. M. Treadwell (Eds.), *Health issues in the Black community* (3rd ed., pp. 55–71). Jossey-Bass.

Taylor, S. R. (2018). *The body is not an apology: The power of radical self-love.* Berrett-Koehler Publishers.

Tekeste, M., Hull, S., Doyidio, J. F., Safon, C. B., Blackstock, O., Taggart, T., Kershaw, T., Kaplan, C., Caldwell, A., Lane, S., & Calabrese, S. (2019). Differences in medical mistrust between Black and White women: Implications for patient–provider communication about PrEP. *AIDS and Behavior, 23*(7), 1737–1748.

Tervalon, M., & Murray-Garcia, J. (1998). Cultural humility vs cultural competence: A critical distinction in defining physician training outcomes in multicultural education. *Journal of Healthcare for the Poor and Underserved, 9*(2), 117–125.

Thelen, M. H., Farmer, J., & Wonderlich, S. (1991). A revision of the bulimia test: The BULIT-R. *Psychological Assessment: A Journal of Consulting and Clinical Psychology, 3*(1), 119–124.

Thomas, S. P. (2022). Trust also means centering Black women's reproductive health narratives. In F. E. Fletcher, K. S. Ray, V. A. Brown, & P. T. Smith (Eds.), *A critical moment in bioethics: Reckoning with anti-Black racism through intergenerational dialogue* (pp. S18–S21). Special report, Hastings Center Report 52, no 2.

Thompson, Becky. (1994). *A hunger so wide and so deep: A multiracial view of women's eating problems.* University of Minnesota Press.

Thompson, H. S., Valdimarsdottir, H. B., Winkel, G., Jandorf, L., & Redd, W. (2004). The Group-Based Medical Mistrust Scale: Psychometric properties and association with breast cancer screening. *Preventive Medicine: An International Journal Devoted to Practice and Theory, 38*(2), 209–218.

REFERENCES

Thompson-Brenner, H., Boswell, J. F., Espel-Huynh, H., Brooks, G., & Lowe, M. R. (2019). Implementation of transdiagnostic treatment for emotional disorders in residential eating disorder programs: A preliminary pre-post evaluation. *Psychotherapy Research, 29*(8), 1045–1061. https://doi.org/10.1080/10503307.2018.1446563

Thompson-Brenner, H., Singh, S., Gardner, T., Brooks, G. E., Smith, M. T., Lowe, M. R., & Boswell, J. F. (2021a). The Renfrew unified treatment for eating disorders and comorbidity: Long-term effects of an evidence-based practice implementation in residential treatment. *Frontiers in Psychiatry, 12*(641601), 1–14. https://doi.org/10.3389/fpsyt.2021.641601.

Thompson-Brenner, H., Smith, M., Brooks, G. E., Berman, R., Kaloudis, A., Espel-Huynh, H., . . . Boswell, J. (2021b). *The Renfrew Unified Treatment for Eating Disorders and Comorbidity: An adaptation of the Unified Protocol, Therapist Guide.* Oxford University Press.

Thorpe, R. J. (2020). The Black Men's Health Project: A vision to improve the lives of Black men. Johns Hopkins Bloomberg School of Public Health. https://publichealth.jhu.edu/2020/the-black-mens-health-project

Tobacco Control Legal Consortium. (2016). *Evans v. Lorillard: A bittersweet victory against the tobacco industry.* Updated August 2016. https://rb.gy/d994la

Tong, M., & Artiga, S. (2021). Use of race in clinical diagnosis and decision making: Overview and implications. KFF.

Trawalter, S., Hoffman, K. M., & Waytz, A. (2012). Racial bias in perceptions of others' pain. *PLoS One, 7*(11), 48546.

Tribole, E., & Resch, E. (2020). *Intuitive eating: A revolutionary program that works* (4th ed.). New York: St. Martin's Essentials.

Truth Initiative. (2018, January 24). "Why are 72% of smokers from lower-income communities?" https://truthinitiative.org/research-resources/targeted-communities/why-are-72-smokers-lower-income-communities#:~:text=Why%3F,will%20continue%20to%20buy%20it.

Tuskegee University. (n.d.). Syphilis Study Legacy Committee. Retrieved from https://www.tuskegee.edu/about-us/centers-of-excellence/bioethics-center/syphilis-study-legacy-committee

Udo, T., Bitley, S., & Grilo, C. M. (2019). Suicide attempts in US adults with lifetime DSM-5 eating disorders. *BMC Medicine, 17*(1), 120.

Udo, T., & Grilo, Carlos M. (2018). Prevalence and correlates of *DSM*-5 eating disorders in Nationally Representative Sample of United States Adults. *Biological Psychiatry*, Sep 1; *84*(5), 345–354. https://doi.org/10.1016/j.biopsych.2018.03.014

Unified Protocol Institute. (n.d.). *About the Unified Protocol.* Retrieved February 2024, from: https://www.unifiedprotocol.com/about

U.S. Department of Education, Office of Civil Rights. (2008). https://www2.ed.gov/about/offices/list/ocr/504faq.html

U.S. Department of Health and Human Services. (2021). National Health Statistics Reports, Number 158.

U.S. Department of Transportation, Office of Inspector General. (2023). FAA conducts comprehensive evaluations of pilots with mental health challenges, but opportunities exist to further mitigate safety risks.

U.S. Preventive Services Task Force. (2022). Screening for eating disorders in adolescents and adults: US Preventive Services Task Force: Recommendation Statement. *Journal of the American Medical Association, 327*(11), 1061–1067.

Uzogara, E. E. (2019). Dark and sick, light and healthy: Black women's complexion-based health disparities. *Ethnicity & Health, 24*(2), 125–146.

Vaidya, V., Partha, G., & Karmakar, M. (2012). Gender differences in utilization of preventive care services in the United States. *Journal of Women's Health, 21*(2), 140–145. https://doi.org/10.1089/jwh.2011.2876

Villatoro, A. P., & Aneshensel, C. S. (2014). Family influences on the use of mental health services among African Americans. *Journal of Health and Social Behavior, 55*(2), 161–180.

Vitus, K. (2015). Racial embodiment and the affectivity of racism in young people's film. *Palgrave Communication, 1*(15007).

Vo, M., Lau, J., & Rubinstein, M. (2016). Eating disorders in adolescent and young adult males: Presenting characteristics. *Journal of Adolescent Health, 59*(4), 397–400. https://doi.org/10.1016/j.jadohealth.2016.04.00

Vyas, D. A., Eisenstein, L. G., & Jones, D. S. (2020). Hidden in plain sight – Reconsidering the use of race correction in clinical algorithms. *New England Journal of Medicine 383*(9), 874–882. https://www.nejm.org/doi/full/10.1056/NEJMms2004740

Walker-Barnes, C. (2017). When the bough breaks: The strong Black woman and the embodiment of stress. In *Black women's mental health: Balancing strength and vulnerability* (pp. 43–56). State University of New York Press.

Wall, L. L. (2006). The medical ethics of Dr J Marion Sims: A fresh look at the historical record. *Journal of Medical Ethics*; 32:346-350.Correspondence to L. Lewis Wall MD, DPhil, Department of Obstetrics and Gynecology, Washington University School of Medicine, Campus Box 8064, 660 South Euclid Avenue, St Louis, MO 63110, USA; WALLL@wustl.edu

Wall, L. L. (2021). The Sims position and the Sims vaginal speculum, re-examined. *International Urogynecology Journal,* August 32, 2595–2601. https://doi.org/10.1007/s00192 -021-04966-w

Washington Harmon, T. (2020, August 13). Code switching: What does it mean and why do people do it? Retrieved September 20, 2021, from: https://www.health.com/mind -body/health-diversity-inclusion/code-switching

Washington Post. (2023, September 19). Many of today's unhealthy foods were brought to you by Big Tobacco. Retrieved from https://www.washingtonpost.com/wellness/2023/09/19/addiction-foods-hyperpalatable-tobacco/

Welsh, L. K., Luhrs, A. R., Davalos, G., Diaz, R., Narvaez, A., Perez, J. E., Lerebours, R., Kuchibhatla, M., Portenier, D. D., & Guerron, A. D. (2020). Racial disparities in bariatric surgery complications and mortality using the MBSAQIP Data Registry. *Obesity Surgery, 30*(8), 3099–3110. https://doi.org/10.1007/s11695-020-04657-3

West, J. S. (2018). Lemons into lemonade: Black undergraduate women's embodiment of strength and resilience at a PWI. *Dissertations - ALL, 983.*

White House Office of the Press Secretary. (1997). Apology for the study done in Tuskegee. https://clintonwhitehouse4.archives.gov/textonly/New/Remarks/Fri/19970516-898.html

Whiteside-Mansell, L., McKelvey, L., Saccente, J., & Selig, J. P. (2019). Adverse childhood experiences of urban and rural preschool children in poverty. *International Journal of Environmental Research and Public Health, 16*(14). https://doi.org/10.3390/ijerph16142623

Wilcox, G. (2005, May). Insulin and insulin resistance. *The Clinical Biochemist Reviews, 26*(2), 19–39.

Williams, M. (2011). African American and psychotherapy: Why race is important. http://www.monnicawilliams.com/black-therapist.php

Williams, M. G., & Lewis, J. A. (2021). Developing a conceptual framework of Black women's gendered racial identity development. *Psychology of Women Quarterly, 45*(2), 212–228.

Williams, R. J., & Ricciardelli, L. A. (2014). Social media and body image concerns: Further considerations and broader perspectives. *Sex Roles, 71*, 389–392.

Wisniowski, P., & Samakar, K. (2023). Racial disparities in the outcomes of bariatric surgery. *Curr Surg Rep* 11, 270–276. https://doi.org/10.1007/s40137-023-00372-x

Women and the American Story (WAMS). (2022). Life story. Anarcha, Betsy, and Lucy: The mothers of modern gynecology. https://wams.nyhistory.org/a-nation-divided/antebellum/anarcha-betsy-lucy/#resource

Woodson, J. (2021). Food as a drug: Mental problem, spiritual solution. In C. Small & M. Fuller (Eds.), *Treating Black women with eating disorders: A clinicians guide,* 13–32. Routledge.

World Health Organization (WHO). (2020). Noncommunicable diseases: Childhood overweight and obesity. Retrieved from https://rb.gy/9nw1pb

Yang, P. Q. (2000). *Ethnic studies: Issues and approaches.* State University of New York Press.

Yasmin, A., Roychoudhury, S., Choudhury, A. P., Fuzayel Ahmed, A. B., Dutta, S., Mottola, F., . . . Kolesarova, A. (2022). Polycystic ovary syndrome: An updated overview foregrounding impacts of ethnicities and geographic variations. *Life, 12*(1974), 1–14. https://doi.org/10.3390/life12121974

Index

Note: Tables are noted with a *t*.

A

AAEDP. *see* African American Eating Disorders Professionals (AAEDP)

ABCD. *see* Adolescent Brain Cognitive Development Study (ABCD)

acceptance and commitment therapy (ACT), 103

accessibility, food and dietary intake and, 114–16

acculturation

Black hair and, 59

body image perceptions and, 59–60

eating disorder symptoms and, 54

ethnic identity and, 53

ethnicity and, 52

values and, 76–77

acculturative stress, 77, 158, 161

body dissatisfaction and, 51

disordered eating and, 41

EDs in Black women and, 7, 8

ACEs. *see* adverse childhood experiences (ACEs)

ACT. *see* acceptance and commitment therapy (ACT)

active listening, 7

acute medical stabilization, 10

addictions, 12. *see also* substance abuse

addiction specialists, 11

Adolescent Brain Cognitive Development Study (ABCD), 32

adolescents

Black, diet mentality and, 110

Black, identity crisis and, 119–20

with EDs, school instruction issues and, 13

family-based therapy and goal for, 98

predatory marketing practices and, 38

adultification, 63, 69

adverse childhood experiences (ACEs), 7, 8, 12, 43, 158

advertising strategies, consumer purchasing and, 38

affirmative action, repeal of, 41, 45

African American diet, 117

African American Eating Disorders Professionals (AAEDP), xix

African Americans, bariatric surgery rates among, 61

age disparities, bias and, 87

aging, fear of, 65

aging process

calorie restriction and impact on, 27

primary and secondary factors and, 28

alcohol use/abuse, 157, 159

alcohol use disorders, colorism and risk of, 32

"all foods fit" philosophy, 24, 110, 114

amenorrhea, 130, 131, 134, 145, 150, 173

AN. *see* anorexia nervosa (AN)

anemia, 130, 136*t*

Aneshensel, C. S., 121

anesthesia, Sims's gynecological procedures without use of, 36
Angry Black woman stereotype, 129
anorexia nervosa (AN), 15, 29
  binge-eating/purging type, 18
  Black men and lifetime prevalence rates for, 166
  Black men and medical complications of, 162
  Black men and symptom manifestation, 159
  Black population and age of onset for, 166
  CBT-E and, 92
  DSM-5 diagnostic criteria for, 18
  gender and symptomology of, 158
  how body is affected by, 132*t*–133*t*
  lifetime prevalence rate for, 18–19
  lymphatic system and, 148
  medical complications with, 130–32, 143
  older adults and, 106
  presentation of, in Black women, 23–24
  suicide risk with, 129
  temperament and, 158
anovulation, 150
anxiety, 12
  adultification and, 64
  anorexia nervosa and, 132
  binge-eating disorder and, 16, 137, 138*t*
  Black individuals and treatment of, 92
  Black women and, with parallel complications in eating disorders, 140–41
  Black women and prevalence of, 139
  bulimia nervosa and, 135, 136*t*
  colorism and risk of, 32
  culturally responsive treatments for, 106, 176

Appalachian State University, xviii
ARFID. *see* avoidant resistant food intake disorder (ARFID)
arthritis, 37
Asian men, cancer mortality rates for, 161
assessments, 11
  bias and, 79
  of Black men with eating disorders, 163–66
  body image attitudes and, 48
  brief, 11
  cultural factors and, 66–67
  disparities in, factors contributing to, 5–6
  nutrition, 12
  trauma experiences, 43
  see also screenings
Association of Black Psychologists, 57
asthma, binge-eating disorder and, 138
avoidant resistant food intake disorder (ARFID), *DSM-5* and essential feature of, 19

B
baby mamas, 69
balanced diets, planning, 28
Bardone-Cone, A. M., recovery model, 25
bariatricians, 13
bariatric procedures, 61
bariatric surgeons, 13
basic metabolic panel (BMP), 142
beauty and beauty standards
  body image assessments and, 55
  challenges related to, 47
  comparing oneself to others and, 59–60
  internet and, 63
  older women and Western world notions of, 27
  see also body image
BED. *see* binge-eating disorder (BED)

INDEX

bias(es), xx, 72, 120, 124
  age disparities and, 87
  checking, 79–80
  in current mental health systems, 88
  definition of, 79
  explicit and implicit, xv, 4, 29, 69, 71, 84, 175
  self-assessing for, 69
  see also stereotypes
BiDil, FDA approved use of, for Black patients only, xvi
binge eating, 12, 109
  Black population and age of onset for, 166
  Black women and, lifetime prevalence rates of, 166
  Black women and, research on, 4
  colorism, racism, and, 34
  meal deals and, xvii
  menopausal stages and, 44
  severity of food insecurity and, 115
  untreated, potential impact of, 146
binge-eating disorder (BED)
  Black men and, lifetime prevalence rates for, 166
  Black men and, medical complications of, 162
  Black women and, disparity in treatment for, 5
  Black women and, lifetime prevalence of, 15
  Black women and, presentation with, 20–22, 29
  CBT-E and CBT-BED for, 92, 93
  characteristics of, 16
  colorism and, 32
  DSM-5 diagnostic criteria for, 16
  food insecurity and, 115
  gender and symptomology of, 158
  how body is affected by, 138*t*

medical complications with, 136–38
new *DSM-5* recognition of, 173
obesity and, 140
polycystic ovary syndrome and, 149
suicidal behavior and, 129
systemic issues, systems of oppression, and, 35
bingeing and purging
  Black college football athlete and, 157, 159
  diet mentality and, 109
birth trauma, 150
Black babies, death rate for, 161
Black children
  digital media and mental health of, 33
  overweight and obesity in, 37
  racism and discrimination as reported by, 32
  sexual trauma and, 44
  unscrupulous tobacco industry salesmanship and, 38–39
Black clients
  being seen and heard, nuanced approaches to, 59, 81–83
  culturally informed providers and, 67
  "taking up space" and, 83
  treatment approach choices and backgrounds of, 89–90
Black families, food and, 113, 117
Black features not appreciated on their bodies, grappling with, 53, 60
Black female stereotypes, understanding, 69–72
  Jezebel, 69, 70–71
  Mammy, 69, 70
  Matriarch, 70
  Sapphire, 69, 71
  Strong Black Woman, 71–72, 121
Black femininity, slavery era and three dominant paradigms of, 69

Black feminism, intersectionality theory and, 77
"Black girl magic," 127
Black girls
adultification and, 63, 69
familial conflict and, 121–22
looking good and, 54
media portrayals of, 62
treating the authentic self and, 118
Black identity, food and, 118
Black men
cancer mortality rates for, 161
with Hollywood's leading ladies, 31
Black men with eating disorders, 156–73
age of onset, 166
assessment of, 163–66
barriers to care and, 167–73
causes of, 158
cultural mistrust and, 167–69
employment status and, 171–73
medical complications in, 162, 162t–163t
prevalence of, 159–61, 166
reluctance to seek care and, 169–70
symptom manifestation for, 158–59
"thug it out" and, 170
treatment options for, 161
vignette, 156–58
Black people
food insecurity in White people *vs.* in, 114
invisibility of, in EDs literature, 165, 166
Black researchers, impactful research and, 127
Black teens, racial biases in recognition of ED symptoms in, 4–5. *see also* adolescents
Black women
bulimia nervosa and prevalence in, 17
cosmetic surgery and, 61–62

defined, 3
diet mentality and, 110
eating disorders undiagnosed/misdiagnosed in, 3
eight truths health care professionals need to know about, 7–9
exploring important issues with, practical tips for, 84
familial conflict and, 121–22
fat, stigmatization of, 56–57
feminism and therapeutic work with, 90
looking good and, 53, 54–55
media portrayals of, 62–63
medical maltreatment of, 36–37, 124
older, eating disorders in, 27–28, 44–45
overweight or obesity statistics for, 13
prevalent health issues among, 139–41
restrictive eating practices and, 49
stigmatization of fatness and, 48–49
treating the authentic self and, 118
treatment of bodies of, historical context and, 48
underrepresentation of, in ED literature, 15
unscrupulous tobacco industry practices and, 38–39
vigilance in assessment and treatment for, 175–76
see also Black female stereotypes, understanding; older Black women; stressors among Black women, addressing
Black women, eating disorder presentation in, 20–24, 52–62
anorexia nervosa, 23–24, 29
binge-eating disorders, 20–22, 29
bulimia nervosa, 22, 29
desire to "look good," 53, 54–55
ethnic identity, 53–54

feeling compelled to self-compare to other women, 53, 59–60

"go get it done" attitude, 53, 60–62

grappling with Black features that are not appreciated, 53, 60

provider questions on ethnic identity, 52–53

size, shape, and weight, 53, 55–57

skin and hair, 53, 57–59

Blake, J. J., 69, 71

BN. *see* bulimia nervosa (BN)

body, respecting, 112

body dissatisfaction, 50, 53, 54, 65, 123, 160

body dysmorphia, 50–51, 53

body dysmorphic disorder (BDD), *DSM-5* diagnostic criteria for, 50

body image

body shame and, 122–23

clients' experiences, interview protocol for more accurate depiction of, 64–65

concerns of Black women *vs.* White women, 53

conversation about, 108

defining, for Black women, 47

distortions in, 50

inclusive, affirming conversations about, promoting, 66

influences on perceptions of, 59–60

media portrayals of Black women and, 62–63

men and, 164

menopause and concerns about, 44–45, 65

objectification and, 57

in older adults, 27, 65–66

self-objectification and, 57

social media and, 121

value of the Black female body and, 49

see also beauty and beauty standards

body liberation, 66

body neutrality, 66

body positivity, 66

body shame, 122–23

body size, 53, 55–57

body image and, 47

body shame and, 122

fat therapists, professionalism, and, 85

bone health, 129, 143

anorexia nervosa and, 130

Black men with eating disorders and, 162*t*

bradycardia, 152

Bray, B., 35

breast cancer, Black women and prevalence of, 139

breast lifts or reductions, 62

Brooks, R., 41

Brown children, digital media and mental health of, 33

Brownell, K. D., 38

Bulik, C., 105

bulimia nervosa (BN), 15, 29

Black men and, lifetime prevalence rates for, 166

Black men and, medical complications of, 162

Black women and, acculturative stress, and, 51

Black women and, presentation with, 22

CBT-BN for, 93

CBT-E and, 92

characteristics of, 16–18

diagnostic criteria for, 17

gender and symptomology of, 158–59

how body is affected by, 136*t*

lymphatic system and, 148–49

medical complications of, 133–35

bulimia nervosa (BN) (*continued*)
 older adults and, 106
 polycystic ovary syndrome and, 149
 suicidal behavior and, 129
 temperament and, 158
Bulimia Test-Revised (BULIT-T), 164
Burke, N. L., 164
Burket, R. C., 160

C
CALERIE 1 study. *see* Comprehensive
 Assessment of Long-Term Effects of
 Reducing Intake of Energy (CAL-
 ERIE) study
calorie restriction (CR)
 alternatives to, 29
 defined, 27
 exercise plus, optimum primary health
 and, 28
cancer, 37, 130, 160–61
Carberry, K., xviii
cardiologists, 13
cardiovascular disease
 Black women and, prevalence of, 139
 Black women and, with parallel complications in eating disorders, 140, 141
cardiovascular system, 128
 anorexia nervosa and, 131
 binge-eating disorder and, 137
 Black men with eating disorders and,
 163t
 Black women and, risk factors related
 to, 151
 bulimia nervosa and, 134, 136t
*Care and Feeding of Ravenously Hungry
 Girls, The* (Gray), 49
Caution Against Racial and Exploitative
 Non-Emergencies Act (CAREN
 legislation), 42
CBT. *see* cognitive behavioral therapy (CBT)

CBT-E. *see* cognitive behavioral therapy
 for eating disorders (CBT-E)
Centers for Disease Control and Prevention (CDC), diabetes estimates,
 146
central nervous system, anorexia nervosa
 and, 143
change, addressing ambivalence toward,
 82
"cheat foods," 109
Child Eating Disorder Examination
 (ChEDE), 164
childhood, overweight and obesity in,
 consequences of, 37–38
childhood sexual abuse, Black children
 and, 44
children
 with EDs, school instruction issues
 and, 13
 family-based therapy and goals for, 98
cholesterol levels, high, 152–53
Churchill, M., xvi
cigarette marketing, 39
Clark, K., 31
client experiences, depiction of, interview
 protocol for, 64–65
clinical interviews, 164
clinical perfectionism, definition of, 41
clinical trials for eating disorders, underrepresentation of minoritized populations in, 89
clinician assessment bias, resolving evaluation paradox and, 6
Clinton, Bill, 168
code-switching, 118–19
cognitive behavioral therapy (CBT), 161
 description of and two key principles
 in, 91–92
 limitations of, 92–93
 treatment efficacy with, 93–94

see also acceptance and commitment therapy (ACT); Unified Protocol (UP) for Emotional Disorders

cognitive behavioral therapy for eating disorders (CBT-E)
  description of, 92
  limitations of, 92–93
  treatment efficacy with, 93–94

collectivist cultures, cultural adaptations and, 106

colorblind approach to client care, xiv–xv, xvi

colorism, 8, 41, 158
  definition of, 57
  increased risk of eating disorders and, 32
  in-group, 58
  social stratification and, 31

comparing oneself to other women, 53, 59–60

complete blood count (CBC), 142

Comprehensive Assessment of Long-Term Effects of Reducing Intake of Energy (CALERIE) study, 27, 28

confidence, looking good and, 54

conflict resolution, 122

conformity
  manifesting with Black clients, examples of, 75
  in racial identity development: minority ethnic group, 74, 74*t*

constipation, 129
  anorexia nervosa and, 131, 133*t*
  Black men with eating disorders and, 163*t*
  bulimia nervosa and, 134

consumer purchasing, advertising strategies and, 38

content-related modifications, adaptations and, 107

continuous education and training, engaging in, 87

control, disordered eating and, 16, 17, 40, 116

coping mechanisms, maladaptive, adultification and, 64

cosmetic surgery, 61–62

countertransference, transference and, 85

COVID-19 pandemic, virtual learning technology and, xvii–xviii

COVID-19 vaccine, 37

COVID era, lockdowns, binge-like behaviors, and, 115

CR. *see* calorie restriction (CR)

Crenshaw, K., 77

Critical Race Theory, 77

CRON diet (CRONIES), 28–29

CROWN Act, 58

cultural adaptation(s)
  definition of, 107
  dialectical behavior therapy and, 95

cultural competence, 4, 6, 68
  additional training in, 7
  boosting, 72–73
  cultural humility *vs.*, 78
  definition of, 72
  practicing, tips for, 73–78

cultural humility, 69, 87, 175
  approach to care, embracing, xiv, xvii
  cultural competence *vs.*, 78
  definition of, 7
  practicing, 78–79

culturally competent care, description of, 73

culturally informed therapeutic alliances, building, 68–87, 176
  boosting cultural competency, 72–73
  checking your bias, 79–80
  cultural humility, 78–79

culturally informed therapeutic alliances, building (*continued*)
ensuring your clients feel seen and heard, 81–83
getting to know your client, 84
importance of, 68
multifaceted approach to, 87
overview, 68–69
practicing cultural competency, tips for, 73–78
transference and countertransference, 85–86
understanding Black female stereotypes, 69–72
understanding weight stigma, 80–81
working with older adults, 86–87
culturally sensitive lens, client care seen through, xiv–xvi
cultural mistrust, Black men with eating disorders and, 167–69
cultural racism, 123
cultural sensitivity, 126
cultural stereotypes, 63
culture
definition of, 72–73
meal plans reflecting, 113–14
therapeutic processes and, 89
currency, pilots and maintenance of, 173
cutting, 43

D
dating contexts, skin color, Black women college students, and, 31
DBT. *see* dialectical behavior therapy (DBT)
DE. *see* disordered eating (DE)
death certificate listings, eating disorders and, 141–42
DEB. *see* disordered eating behaviors (DEB)

decolonization of health care, calls for, xv, xviii
deep listening, 7
dental health, 129
Black men with eating disorders and, 163*t*
bulimia nervosa and, 133–34
dentists, 13
depression, 12
adultification and, 64
anorexia nervosa and, 132
binge-eating disorder and, 16, 137, 138*t*
Black women and, prevalence of, 139
Black women and, with parallel complications in eating disorders, 140–41
bulimia nervosa and, 135, 136*t*
culturally responsive treatments for, 106, 176
postpartum, 139
dermatologic system, anorexia nervosa and, 132
dermatologists, 13
diabetes, 160
Black women and, disproportionate impact of, 146
Black women and, prevalence of, 139
Black women and, with parallel complications in eating disorders, 140, 141
gestational, 150
overweight and obesity in childhood and, 37
overweight Black women and, xvii
see also Type 1 diabetes; Type 2 diabetes
diabetes mellitus, 12, 18
diabetic ketoacidosis (DKA), 147, 148
diabulimia, 18, 147
diagnosis, 11, 12, 13

Diagnostic and Statistical Manual of Mental Disorders (DSM-5-TR)
  body dysmorphic disorder characterized in, 50
  eating disorders defined in, 15, 16, 17, 18, 19
dialectical behavior therapy (DBT), 94–97, 161
  culturally adaptive approach in, steps for provider to take, 96–97
  description and emphasis of, 94–95
  ideographic sensitivity to clients, 95
  nomothetic approach and, 95
  treatment efficacy with, 95–97
DiClemente, C. C., 26
diet
  African American, 117
  balanced, planning, 28
  CRON, 28–29
dietary intake, being Black and, 117–18
dieticians, 11, 12–13, 28, 90, 126
dieting, 12, 49, 60
  body image in older adults and, 65
  bulimia nervosa and, 17
  strict, 109
diet mentality
  definition of, 109
  laxative use and, 145
  rejecting, 109–10, 112
diet pills, 49
digestive system. *see* gastrointestinal/digestive system
digital media, mental health of Black and Brown children and, 33
discrimination, 77, 151, 155
  adapted CBT and encounters with, 93
  darker-skinned Black women and, 58
  disordered eating and, 52
  medical mistrust among Black clients and, 35

older people of color and, 105
racial, stress of, 122
risk for binge-eating disorder and, 32
weight stigma and, 80
see also racism
disordered eating (DE)
  definition of, 109
  obsessive focus on food, body weight, and shape, 110
  stress and, 118
  subclinical depiction of, 20
  see also eating disorders (EDs)
disordered eating behaviors (DEB)
  Black adolescents and, 120
  eating disorders *vs.,* 20
disparities in health care, 158
  eliminating, strategies for, 155
  health coverage and, 26
  mental health care, older people of color, and, 105
  older Black women and, 154
dissonance and appreciating
  manifesting with Black clients, examples of, 75–76
  in racial identity development: minority ethnic group, 74, 74*t*
distorted thinking, 92–93
distress tolerance, dialectical behavior therapy and, 94
diuretics, 17, 133
divas, 69
diversity, equity, and inclusion, xviii
diversity in certain fields, need for increase in, 68
DKA. *see* diabetic ketoacidosis (DKA)
DSM-5, care for Black men with eating disorders and, 173
Dual Energy X-Ray Absorptiometry (DEXA or DXA) scan, 142, 143
Durham, A., 61

dysphoria, social media messages and, 121. *see also* body dysmorphia

E

eating
  intuitive, 110, 111–13
  mindful, 110, 113
  normalized, 110–11
  sustainable and balanced habits for, 110
  see also food; meal plans; nutrition
Eating Disorder Examination (EDE), 164
eating disorders (EDs)
  adultification and, 64
  are not about food, 116–17
  Black men and, affects of, 162*t*–163*t*
  Black women 65 years old and beyond and, 27–28, 44–45
  complexity and prevalence of, 3
  complications and mortality associated with, 142
  comprehensive approach to, importance of, 128
  co-occurring mental disorders and, 158
  deadly myths about, 46
  death certificate listings and, 141–42
  deaths related to, statistics on, 8
  disordered eating behaviors *vs.*, 20
  as emotional disorders, theoretical approaches to, 90–91
  as gendered mental health illnesses, 173
  laboratory and medical tests recommended for, 142
  levels of care for, factors related to, 9
  mortality risk for individuals with, 129
  presentation of, in Black women, 20–24
  provider types and concerns related to, 10–13
  research on Black persons and, 4–5
  self concepts and identity, and, 31

skin tone discrimination and, 58
stigma around, 68
total body systems impact of, 14
trauma and, 8, 43–44
types of, 16–20, 29
see also anorexia nervosa (AN); binge-eating disorder (BED); Black men with eating disorders; bulimia nervosa (BN); medical complications, eating disorders and
eating disorders, causes and maintenance of, 30–44
  biological and psychosocial factors, 40–41
  in Black women 65 years and beyond, 44–45
  distrust of the medical community, 35–37, 46
  internalized racism and oppression, 31–34, 46
  overview, 30–31
  politics, injustice, and violence, 41–43
  predatory food and tobacco industry practices, 37–40, 46
  systemic issues and systems of oppression, 35, 46
  trauma, 43–44, 46
Eating Recovery and Pathlight Centers, 10
EBT. *see* evidence-based treatment (EBT)
e-cigarettes, devastating health impacts of, 39
EDE. *see* Eating Disorder Examination (EDE)
EDs. *see* eating disorders (EDs)
Edwards-Gayfield, P., xix, xx, 54
electrocardiogram (EKG or ECG), 142
electrolyte imbalances, 129, 135, 136, 144, 153, 154, 163*t*
Ellis, M., 41
embarrassing or uncomfortable questions, question of avoiding, 86

embodiment
  disruptions in, 52
  lack of, description of, 51
  lack of, disordered eating and, 50,
    51–52
emergency room physicians, 10
emotional eating, 109, 110, 136
emotion regulation, dialectical behavior
    therapy and, 94
empathy, 87, 125, 127, 176
employment, race-based discrimination
    and, 122
employment status, Black men not seek-
    ing health care and, 171–73
empowerment
  of Black women with eating disorders,
    encouraging, xx
  fostering sense of, 83
endocrine system
  anorexia nervosa and, 131
  binge-eating disorder and, 137
  bulimia nervosa and, 134–35, 136t
  eating disorders, malnourishment, and,
    145
endocrinologists, 13
enhancements, cosmetic surgery and,
    61–62
Epstein, R., 63, 69
equitable care
  advocating for, 140
  cultivating, tips for, 125–26
equity issues, 26
erectile dysfunction, treatment-seeking
    behavior and, 170–71
Erikson, E., 27
ERP. see exposure and response prevention
    therapy (ERP)
esophageal tears, bulimia nervosa and, 134
ethnic identity, 52, 53–54
  definition of, 54

internalized racism and, 57
  stronger, as protective factor, 54
ethnicity
  definition of, 72
  two components within, 52
ethnic matching, 107
Eurocentric beauty standards
  Black hair and, 58
  Black women, sense of identity, and,
    120
evaluation paradox, resolving, 6–7
evidence-based treatment (EBT)
  cultural adaptations of, 89
  older adults and scarcity of, 105–6
exercise, 17, 23, 49, 60, 112
explicit bias, xv, 4
exposure and response prevention therapy
    (ERP), 103–4
eye color, 48

F
FA. see Food Anonymous (FA)
facial features, women of color and
    emphasis on, 48
Fairburn, C. G., 41
falls, calorie restriction, elderly persons,
    and, 28
familial conflict, 121–22
family-based therapy (FBT), 97–99, 161
  advantages and disadvantages with,
    98
  challenges associated with, 98–99
  cultural dynamics and, understanding,
    99
  description of, 97–98
  treatment efficacy with, 99
family dynamics, strained, adultification
    and, 64
fasting, 17, 29
fat-affirming therapy, 81

fatness
  "magic" solution to, allure of, 61
  pathologized speech about, 56
  stigmatization of, 48–49
fat phobia, 60, 80–81
fat positive attitude, 62
fat therapists, body size, professionalism,
  and, 85
FBT. *see* family-based therapy (FBT)
FDA. *see* Food and Drug Administration
  (FDA)
Federal Aviation Administration (FAA),
  nondisclosure of health issues and,
  171–73
female socialization, 90
feminist therapy, adopting, 90
fertility struggles, 149–50
fibroids, 130, 139
504 plans, 13
Flanagan, E. W., 28
Flint, Michigan, toxic water situation in,
  33
Floyd, G., 41
food
  Black families and, 113, 117
  diet mentality and constant thoughts
    about, 109
  emotional components of, uncovering
    or exploring, 117–18
  making peace with, 112
  obtaining in a socially acceptable way,
    115
  purpose of, EDs in Black women and,
    8
  see also eating; meal plans; nutrition
food allergies, 12–13
Food and Drug Administration (FDA), 26
Food Anonymous (FA), 21
food banks or food pantries, 115
food choices, influences on, 111

food deserts, 43, 46, 116
food industry practices, predatory, 37–38,
  40
food insecurity, 77, 114–16
  assistance for, 116
  hoarding behaviors, 115–16
  signs of, 115
food journal, keeping, 113
food plans, 12
food preparation, as expression of love,
  118
food stamps, discounted tobacco products
  and, 38
food swamps, 116
freaks, 69
*Freeing Black Girls: A Black Feminist Bible
  on Racism and Revolutionary Mothering* (Lomax), 9
Fuller, M., xiii, xvii, xviii, xix, 175
fullness, respecting, 112

G
gallbladder disease, binge-eating disorder
  and, 137
gastroenterologists, 13
gastroesophageal reflux disorder
  (GERD), 154
  binge-eating disorder and, 137
  bulimia nervosa and, 134
gastrointestinal/digestive system, 13, 128
  anorexia nervosa and, 131
  binge-eating disorder and, 137
  Black men with eating disorders and,
    163*t*
  bulimia nervosa and, 134, 136*t*
  thyroid disease and, 153–54
gastroparesis, 154
Gaudiani, J., 144
Gay, R., 48, 56, 62
gender

health care utilization and, 169
    intersectionality of race and, 47
gender discrimination, 93
gender identity, 119
gender inequalities, addressing, 90
general practice practitioners, 10, 11, 28
generational gaps, 86
genetic mechanisms, Type 2 diabetes and, 146
genuine connections, description of, 83
Georgetown Law Center for Poverty and Inequality, adultification study, 63
GERD. *see* gastroesophageal reflux disorder (GERD)
gerontologists, 11, 13, 28
gestational diabetes, 150
Girlhood Interrupted (Epstein, Blake, & Thalia), 69
GLP-1A. *see* glucagon-like peptide-1 receptor agonists (GLP-1A)
glucagon-like peptide-1 (GLP-1), blood sugar level regulation and, 61
glucagon-like peptide-1 receptor agonists (GLP-1A), 26
"go get it done" attitude, 53, 60–62
gold diggers, 69
Goode, R. W., 13, 175
Gordon, K. H., 4, 6, 24
Gordon, S. E., 24
Gray, A., 49

H
Haddad, C., 45
hair
    Black men with eating disorders and, 163*t*
    body image and, 47, 58
    bulimia nervosa and, 135, 136*t*
    health changes and, 129
    texture, 48, 122

Hamer, F. L., 124
Harlow, S. D., 45
Harris, S. M., 160, 163, 165
Harris-Perry, M. V., 120
hate crimes, placing racist 911 calls, 41
Hawaiian Punch, 39
HBCUs. *see* Historically Black Colleges/ Universities (HBCUs)
healing, multidisciplinary team approach to, 90–91
health
    honoring, 112
    motivation for, cautionary note on, 111
health care, inequality in, 123–25. *see also* disparities in health care
health care costs, as barrier to BED treatment for Black women, 35
health care providers
    body image discussions and, 59
    clients being and heard by, examples of, 82
    culturally-informed, 67, 176
    engagement with Black clients and, 47–48
    ethnic identity-related questions for, 52–53
    interview protocol for more accurate depiction of client experiences, 64–65
    scarcity of, as barrier to BED treatment for Black women, 35
    trust between Black clients and, 37
    types of, 10–13
health equity, advocating for and advancing, 130, 155
health-seeking behaviors, Black women and, 130
heart disease, 129, 130, 160
    anorexia nervosa and, 130
    binge-eating disorder and, 137

heart disease (*continued*)

    Black women and, with parallel complications in eating disorders, 140

    overweight and obesity in childhood and, 37

heart failure, 152

    anorexia nervosa and, 131, 132*t*

    bulimia nervosa and, 136*t*

hegemonic masculinity, maintenance of power dynamic and, 170

hematologic system, anorexia nervosa and, 131

high blood pressure. *see* hypertension

Hill, A., 41

Historical African Diaspora, creation of, 3

Historically Black Colleges/Universities (HBCUs), xviii, 31

HIV, 129

hoarding behaviors, food insecurity and, 115–16

Hoffman, K. M., 36

Hook, J. N., 78

Hopkins, T., 116

hormones

    Black men with eating disorders and, 163*t*

    disruptions in, eating disorders and, 150

housing, race-based discrimination and, 122

Huggard, D., 5

humanism, relational-cultural theory integrated with, 90

humility, 4, 6, 176

hunger, 110, 111, 112, 114

hypertension, 129, 149, 151, 152

    binge-eating disorder and, 136, 137

    Black women and prevalence of, 139

hypochloremia, 133

hypokalemia, 133, 153

hypomagnesemia, 153

hyponatremia, 145

hypophosphatemia, 153

I

IBS. *see* irritable bowel syndrome (IBS)

identity crisis, 119–20

immune system, 135

    anorexia nervosa and, 148

    bulimia and, 135, 148–49

implicit bias, xv, 4, 29, 69, 71, 84, 175

individualistic cultures, cultural adaptations and, 107

inequality in health care, 123–25

informed consent, 168

in-group colorism, within the Black community, 58

initial consultation, 7

injustice, eating disorders and, 41

inpatient (IP) care, 10

Institutional Review Board (IRB), 168, 169

insulin, 61

insulin manipulation, recognizing, 147–48

insurance coverage, lack of, as barrier to BED treatment, 35

integrative awareness

    manifesting with Black clients, examples of, 76

    in racial identity development: minority ethnic group, 74, 75*t*

intensive outpatient (IOP) therapy, 10

internalized racism, oppression and, 31–34

internet, beauty standards and, 63

interpersonal difficulties, eating disorders and, 41

interpersonal effectiveness, dialectical behavior therapy and, 94 interpersonal psychotherapy (IPT), 104, 161

interpersonal racism, 124

intersectionality, 77–78
Crenshaw's theory of, 77
of race and gender, 47

introspection
manifesting with Black clients, examples of, 76
in racial identity development: minority ethnic group, 74, 75t

intuitive eating, 110, 111–13

IOP therapy. *see* intensive outpatient (IOP) therapy

IPT. *see* interpersonal psychotherapy (IPT)

irritable bowel syndrome (IBS), 129
binge-eating disorder and, 137, 138t
Black men with eating disorders and, 163t

J

Jezebel stereotype, 69, 70–71

Jim Crow era, 45

Joe Cool character, cigarette marketing and, 39

Johns Hopkins Hospital, Henrietta Lack case, 36, 124

K

"Karen," institutional racism and self-entitlement of, 42–43

Keith, V. M., 47

Kenny, T. E., 5

Khalil, J., 44

kidney disease, 152
binge-eating disorder and, 138
Black women and, with parallel complications in eating disorders, 140, 141
kidney failure, 130, 131, 133t, 143, 144, 161, 163t

"Kool-Aid Man," 39

Kuh, D., 66

L

labels, listening for origins of, 56

Lacks, H., medical maltreatment of, 34, 36–37, 124

Lashley, M.-B., 71

Latinx teens, clinician recognition of ED symptoms in, 4, 5

laxative use/abuse, 17, 49, 133, 134, 143–45, 159

learning accommodations, 13

Lewis, J. A., 120

Linehan, M., 94

lip injections, 60

liposuction, 62

lips, 48

Lipson, S. K., 4

listening, active and reflective, 7

looking good, 53, 54–55

loss, older Black women, disordered eating, and, 87

lost childhood, adultification and, 64

M

macroaggressions, 158

makeup tutorials, 59

Mallory-Weiss tears, bulimia nervosa and, 134

malnutrition, 12, 104, 131, 132

Mammy stereotype, 69, 70

Mann, C., 70, 71

marginalization, disordered eating and, 52

marketing tactics, deceptive, in food and tobacco industries, 38–40, 46

maternal mortality and morbidity, Black women and prevalence of, 139

Matriarch stereotype, 70

McDade, T., 41

McLaren, L., 66
MDT process. *see* multidisciplinary team (MDT) process
meal plans
older Black persons and, 28
that reflect culture, 113–14
see also eating; food; nutrition
meals, variety in, 114
mealtimes, regular, 113
media
portrayals of Black women in, 30–31, 62–63
racism and representation in, 124
medical community, distrust of, 8, 35–37, 46, 123
medical complications, eating disorders and, 128–55
advancing health equity for Black women, 155
anorexia nervosa, 130–32, 132*t*–133*t*
binge-eating disorder, 136–38, 138*t*
Black men and impact of, 162, 162*t*–163*t*
bulimia nervosa, 133–35, 136*t*
cardiovascular system, 151–53
central nervous system, 143
diabetic ketoacidosis, 148
endocrine system, 145–48
gastrointestinal/digestive system, 153–54
hidden in plain sight, 141–42
lymphatic system, 148–49
musculoskeletal system, 143
in older Black women, 154–55
overview of, 128–29
prevalent, among Black women, 139–41
refeeding syndrome, 153
renal system (urinary system), 143–45

reproductive system, 149–51
sickle cell disease, 153
understanding, 129–30
untreated, severe consequences of, 128
medical distrust, description of, 124–25
medical nutrition therapy, 104
menopause
body image concerns and, 44–45, 65
medical complications with, 154–55
menstrual cycles
bulimia nervosa and, 134
irregular, 129
mental health
adultification and impact on, 64
Black men with eating disorders and, 163*t*
Black women's issues with, parallel complications in eating disorders, 140, 141
challenges, Black women and prevalence of, 139
mental health nurses, 11
mental health providers, 126
mental wellness professionals, 11–12
metabolic system
binge-eating disorder and, 137
Black men with eating disorders and, 163*t*
Black women and disruptions in, with parallel complications in eating disorders, 141
Micheaux, O., 31
Michigan Department of Health and Human Services, 33
microaggressions, 41, 158
midlife, role shifts, body image issues, and, 65
Mimura, Y., 143
mindful eating, 110, 113

mindfulness
  acceptance and commitment therapy and, 103
  dialectical behavior therapy and, 94
minority stressors, disruptions in embodiment and, 52
miscarriages, 150–51
"Mississippi appendectomy," 124
MOET. *see* Muscularity-Oriented Eating Test (MOET)
mood intolerance, eating disorders and, 41
Moradi, B., 78
multidisciplinary eating disorders, treatment center levels of care and, 161
multidisciplinary team (MDT) approach, 7
  members of team, 10–13
  to muscle mass and strength, 28
multi-organ failure, anorexia nervosa and, 132
Murray, P., 69
Murray, S. B., 164
Muscularity-Oriented Eating Test (MOET), 164–65
musculoskeletal system
  anorexia nervosa and, 132, 133*t*, 143
  binge-eating disorder and, 137
  Black men with eating disorders and, 163*t*
  bulimia nervosa and, 135, 136*t*
  recommended medical tests for, 143

N
Nagata, J. M., 32, 160
National Center for Health Statistics, 13
National Comorbidity Survey Replication (NCS-R), 166
National Public Radio (NPR), 33

National Research Act of 1974, 168
National Survey of American Life (NSAL), 18, 166
NCS-R. *see* National Comorbidity Survey Replication (NCS-R)
nephrologists, 13
neurological system
  anorexia nervosa and, 131
  bulimia nervosa and, 135
neurologists, 13
Njoroge, W., 33
non-Black providers, self-awareness of explicit biases and, xv
normalized eating, 110–11
Not All Black Girls Know How to Eat (Covington Armstrong), 9
NSAL. *see* National Survey of American Life (NSAL)
nurse practitioners, 28
nutrition
  for Black women, foundational beliefs about, 111
  gentle, 112
  non-diet approach to, 110
  see also eating; food; meal plans
nutrition, encouraging balanced approach to, 113–16
  accessibility, 114–16
  meal plans that reflect culture, 113–14
  variety, 114
nutritionists, 11, 12–13
nutrition therapy, 104

O
Obama, B., 33
obesity
  binge-eating disorder and, 138*t*
  Black children and, 37
  Black women and, prevalence of, 139

obesity (*continued*)
    Black women and, with parallel complications in eating disorders, 140
    Black women in the U.S. and, 13, 175
    weight loss surgery and, 61
obesity drugs, 61
Obesity Evidence Hub, 40
obesity label, avoiding, 56
objectification theory, 57
obstetrics and gynecologists, 13
occupational therapists, 13, 28
OCD, 43
Oh, H., 31
older Black women
    body image issues in, 27, 65–66
    cultural adaptations in treatment and, 105
    culturally informed therapeutic alliance with, 86–87
    evidence-based treatments for eating disorders and, scarcity of, 105–6
    maintaining factors for EDs in, 44–45
    medical complications in, 154–55
Opara, I., 50
opioid overdoses, 141
oppression
    internalized racism and, 31–34
    systemic issues and systems of, 35, 46
Orbach, S., xviii
organization-specific changes, adaptations and, 107
Orri Eating Disorders Treatment Clinic (UK), xviii
orthopedic surgeons, 13
orthorexia nervosa, features of, 19
orthostasis, 151
orthostatic symptoms, 152
OSFED. *see* other specified feeding and eating disorder (OSFED)

osteopenia, 143
osteoporosis, 143
other specified feeding and eating disorder (OSFED), 19–20, 129
Ottey, S., 149
overeating, 129
overweight Black children, health risks for, 37–38
overweight label, avoiding, 56
overworking, 129
Ozempic, 26, 61

P
packaging aesthetics
    children and impact of, 40
    deceptive food and tobacco industry practices and, 38
pain
    Black persons and undertreatment for, xvi
    erroneous beliefs about Black persons and, 36
paranoia in relationships, 129
parents, family-based therapy and goal for, 98
partial hospitalization program (PHP), 10
Paulsen, L. H., 171
pay inequity, 158
Payton, G. J., 166
PCOS. *see* polycystic ovary syndrome (PCOS)
PCP. *see* primary care physician (PCP)
pediatricians, 11
people of color, disparity in treatment of eating disorders in, 4
perfectionism
    clinical, definition of, 41
    disordered eating and, 16, 17, 23, 40
perfectionistic striving, perfectionistic concerns *vs.*, 40–41

perimenopause, disordered eating during, 44, 45, 65

Philip Morris, 39

PHP. *see* partial hospitalization program (PHP)

physical therapists, 28

physicians, 126

Pica, defined, 19

Pike, K. M., 5, 6

Piran, N., 52

plastic surgery, 61–62

polio vaccine, 36–37

polycystic ovary syndrome (PCOS), 145
    binge-eating disorder and, 137, 138*t*
    diagnostic criteria for, 149

population health, promoting, 126

positive self-talk, 21

postpartum depression, Black women and prevalence of, 139

postural tachycardia syndrome (PoTS), 152

power dynamic, hegemonic masculinity and, 170

Predominantly White Institutions (PWIs), xviii

pregnancy, 12, 150

preventative care, Black men and, 169

primary care physician (PCP), 90

Prochaska, J. O., 26

professional counselors, 11

proficiency, pilots and maintenance of, 173

provider language proficiency, 107

providers. *see* health care providers

psychiatric nurse practitioners, 12

psychiatrists, 11–12, 90

psychoeducation, 10, 107

psychological and psychiatric effects
    anorexia nervosa and, 132
    binge-eating disorder and, 137–38

bulimia nervosa and, 135

psychological flexibility, acceptance and commitment therapy and, 103

psychologists, 11

purging, 12
    medical complications of, 133
    methods of, 17–18

PWIs. *see* Predominantly White Institutions (PWIs)

R

race
    addressing with clients, 90
    definition of, 72
    eating disorders and importance of, xiv, xv
    intersectionality of gender and, 47
    as a social construct, 72, 73
    see also discrimination; racial identity; racism

race-based medicine, inequitable care and, xvi

racial biases
    explicit, awareness of, xv
    in medicine, condemnation of, xv
    in recognition of ED symptoms in Black girls, 4

racial discrimination, 93

racial disparities
    in health care, 123–25
    in pain assessment and treatment, 36

racial empowerment, adapted cognitive-behavioral intervention and, 94

racial identity, 73, 81, 119–20
    acknowledging and respecting, 90
    body shame and, 122
    development of: minority ethnic group, 74*t*–75*t*
    understanding, 74–76

racial identity development theory, 74

racial inequality, persistent, 73

racism, 25, 30, 130, 158, 161, 166
  adapted CBT and encounters with, 93–94
  cultural, 123
  EDs in Black women and, 7, 8, 41, 46, 175
  institutional, reincarnation of "Karen," 42–43
  internalized, ethnic identity and, 57
  internalized, fat phobia and, 81
  internalized, oppression and, 31–34
  interpersonal, 124
  large-scale forms of, BED research on, 35
  older people of color and, 105
  sizeism and, 55
  structural, 45, 123
  SWAN study results and, 45
  systemic, food insecurity and, 114
  vicarious, 124
  see also discrimination

racist 911 calls, CAREN legislation and, 41

Rahman, A. A. A., 171

randomized controlled trials, diverse populations and, 89

rapport with client, building, 84

RCT. *see* relational-cultural theory (RCT)

recovery, 24–26
  culturally responsive treatment and, 26, 176
  individual and personalized nature of, 24–25, 29
  narrative perspective on, need for, 25–26

refeeding, in acute cases, 12

refeeding syndrome, symptoms of, 153

referrals, disparities in, factors contributing to, 5–6

reflective listening, 7

rehabilitation therapists, 13

Rein, L., 172

rejection of self, 120–21

relapses, 21, 26, 29, 176

relatable therapeutic experience, need for, 68

relational-cultural theory (RCT), 66, 90, 104–5

renal system
  anorexia nervosa and, 131
  binge-eating disorder and, 138
  bulimia nervosa and, 135, 136t

Renfrew Center, The, 10, 101, 102, 113

replacement smokers, unscrupulous tobacco industry practices and, 38–39

reproductive system, eating disorder behaviors and impact on, 128, 149–51

Resch, E., 112

residential (RES) therapy, 10

resistance and immersion
  manifesting with Black clients, examples of, 76
  in racial identity development: minority ethnic group, 74, 75t

respiratory system, binge-eating disorder and, 138

restricting behavior, 12
  anorexia nervosa and, 23
  bulimia nervosa and, 17

restrictive eating, 109, 110

restrictive eating practices, White women *vs.* Black women and, 49

Reyes-Rodriguez, M. L., 77

rhinoplasty, 62

R. J. Reynolds, 39

Robinson, T. N., 40

Roe v. Wade, repeal of, 41, 45

Roux-en-Y gastric bypass surgery, 61
rumination disorder, features of, 19
Runfola, C. D., 66
Russell's signs, bulimia nervosa and, 22, 135

S
Sangha, S., 160
Santos, N., 50
Sapphire stereotype, 69, 71
satiety, awareness of, 112
satisfaction factor, discovering, 112
SCD. *see* sickle cell disease (SCD)
Schlicthorst, M., 171
school-based team, members of, 13
SCOFF, 11
screenings
early, for eating disorders, 142
routine, 11
see also assessments
seizures, bulimia nervosa and, 135
self, rejection of, 120–21
self-care, 22
self-compassion, 21
self-criticism, disordered eating and, 16, 17, 40
self-esteem, 54
adultification and, 64
inclusive, affirming conversations about, 66
low, self-objectification and, 57
self-injury, 12
self-objectification, manifestations of, 57
self-reflection, cultural humility and, 78, 79
self-report instruments, 164
semaglutide (Ozempic), 26
sexism, 57, 130
sex roles, 90
sexual abuse, childhood, 44

sexual assault, eating disorders and, 8
Shabsigh, R., 170
shape, 47, 53, 55–57
shared decision-making, 126
Sick Enough (Gaudiani), 144
sickle cell disease (SCD), 141, 153
Sims, J. M., 34, 36
single-motherhood, 43
Sister Citizen (Harris-Perry), 120
size. *see* body size
sizeism, racism and, 55
skin
Black men with eating disorders and, 163*t*
bulimia nervosa and, 135, 136*t*
eating disorders and changes in, 129
skin color or tone, 48
Black women college students' dating attitudes and, 31
body image and, 47
body shame and, 122
colorism, Black women, and, 57–58
slave trade, Historical African Diaspora and, 3
sleep apnea
binge-eating disorder and, 138
Black men with eating disorders and, 162*t*
Small, C., 30, 84
Small, T., 30
Smith, M. M., 40
SNAP. *see* Supplemental Nutrition Assistance Program (SNAP)
socialization, 63
social justice in health care, advocating for, 126
social media, rejection of self and, 121
social workers, 11
socioeconomic status (SES), onset and maintenance of EDs and, 8

Sonneville, K. R., 4
Sotomayor, S., 73
soul food, 117
Spelman College, xviii
Stephens, D., 31
stereotypes, xx, 4, 84, 120, 124
  Black hair and, 59
  body shame and, 122
  code-switching and, 119
  cultural, 63–64
  darker-skinned Black women and, 57
  ethnic identity and, 53, 54
  media portrayals of Black girls and, 62
  objectification and, 57
  Type 2 diabetes and, 147
  weight-based, 80
  see also bias(es); Black female stereo-
    types, understanding
sterilization of Black women, forced, 124
stigma
  body shame and, 123
  eating disorders in men and, 160
  food bank use and, 115
  lasting impact of, 77–78
  marginalized groups and, 78
  sickle cell disease and, 153
  Strong Black Woman archetype and, 71
  Type 2 diabetes and, 147
  weight-based, 85, 129
  see also weight stigma
Stiles-Shields, C., 81
stress, 12, 175
  acculturative, 7, 8, 41, 51, 77, 158, 161
  adultification and, 63, 64
  disordered eating and, 118
  high blood pressure and, 152
stressors among Black women, addressing,
    118–26
  body shame, 122–23
  code-switching, 118–19

cultivating equitable care, 125–26
  discrimination, 122
  familial conflict, 121–22
  identity crisis, 119–20
  inequality in health care, 123–25
  rejection of self, 120–21
Strings, S., 56
stroke, 130, 151, 152, 160
  Black women and prevalence of, 139
  overweight and obesity in childhood
    and, 37
Strong Black Woman stereotype, 71–72,
    121
structural racism, 45, 123
Study of Women's Health Across the
    Nation (SWAN), 45
substance abuse/dependence, 12, 158
  binge-eating disorder and, 138
  bulimia nervosa and, 135
substance use disorders, colorism and risk
    of, 32
suicide, 129
  anorexia nervosa and risk of, 132
  eating disorders and risk of, 142
  ideation, 12
superwoman archetype, 71–72, 116–17,
    127
Supplemental Nutrition Assistance Pro-
    gram (SNAP), 116
survival mode, 119
SWAN. see Study of Women's Health
    Across the Nation (SWAN)
Syphilis Study at Tuskegee University,
    167–68
systemic oppression, 25

T
tachycardia, 152
"taking up space," assessing Black client's
    ability for, 83

Talleyrand, R. M., 64
Taylor, B., 41
Taylor, J. Y., 17, 18, 166
team building, 126–27
   composition of treatment team, 127
   multidisciplinary team members, 126
   see also multidisciplinary team (MDT) approach
temperament, eating disorders and, 158
testing, objective of, 142. *see also* assessments; screenings
Thalia, G., 69
Theory of Embodiment (Piran), 52
therapeutic alliances
   between Black women and providers, 37
   equitable care and, 125
   see also culturally informed therapeutic alliances, building
therapeutic relationship, inclusivity and equity within, 48
therapists, 90
thin ideal
   media portrayals of, 62–63
   popularity of, during the 1960s, 48
Thomas, T. L., 31
Thompson, B., 34
"Thug it out," 170
thyroid disease, Black women and impacts of, 153–54
thyroid dysfunction
   anorexia nervosa and, 131
   bulimia nervosa and, 135
TikTok, 170
tobacco industry practices, predatory, 38–39
toxic water in major U.S. cities, racism and, 33–34
transdiagnostic processes, eating disorders and, 40–41

transdiagnostic treatments, emergence of, 100
transference, countertransference and, 85
Transtheoretical Model of Behavior Change, Stages of Change component of, 26
trauma, 12, 41, 158
   eating disorders and, 8, 43–44
   EDs in Black women and, 7, 175
   high blood pressure and, 152
Treating Black Women with Eating Disorders (Small & Fuller), xiii, xvi, xvii, xviii, 9
treatment centers, levels of care in, 9–10
treatment of eating disorders
   barriers to, systemic and personal, 68
   cultural factors and, 66–67
   treatment models, Black women, disparities, and, 88
treatment plans
   developing, 11
   person-centered and culturally sensitive, 126
treatment team, composition of, 9–10
Tribole, E., 112
triple jeopardy, older Black women and, 154
trust in body's cues, rebuilding, 113
tummy tucks, 62
Tuskegee Syphilis Study, xvi
Tuskegee Syphilis Study Legacy Committee, 168
Type 1 diabetes, 146, 147–48
Type 2 diabetes, 26, 61, 146
   binge-eating disorder and, 136, 137, 138*t*
   Black men with eating disorders and, 163*t*
   Black women and, disproportionate impact of, 146
   Black women and, with parallel complications in eating disorders, 140

Type 2 diabetes (*continued*)
bulimia nervosa and, 133
polycystic ovary syndrome and, 149
stigma and, 147

U
unconscious bias, 69
Unified Protocol (UP) for Emotional
Disorders
acknowledgment of cultural factors in,
100–101
description of, 100
limitations with, 100
UTM based on, 101
Unified Treatment Model for Eating Dis-
orders (UTM)
benefits and limitations with, 101–2
overview of, 101
treatment efficacy with, 102–3
University of North Carolina, Chapel
Hill, xviii
University of the West Indies, Dying to Be
Beautiful conference, xix
unspecified eating disorders, older adults
and, 106
UP. *see* Unified Protocol (UP) for Emotional Disorders
urgent care, 10
U.S. Department of Health and Human
Services, Adolescent Brain Cognitive
Development Study, 32
U.S. Department of Health and Human
Services, Office of Minority Health
on practicing cultural competency, 73
on practicing cultural humility, 79
U.S. Preventative Services Task Force, on
false-positive results, 165
U.S. Public Health Service (USPHS),
Tuskegee Study of Untreated Syph-
ilis in the Negro Male, xvi, 167–68

UTM. *see* Unified Treatment Model for
Eating Disorders (UTM)

V
Vaidya, V., 169
values
acculturation and, 76–77
fostering sense of, 83
variety in meals, 114
vertical sleeve gastrectomy, 61
vicarious racism, 124
Villatoro, A. P., 121
violence, disordered eating and, 41
virtual IOP therapy, 10
virtual learning, COVID-19 pandemic
and, xvii–xviii
vomiting, 133, 134

W
Wake Forest University, xviii
Warner, K. D., 38
water boil alerts, 34
weathering, 150
weight, 53, 55–57
conversation about, 108
excess, binge-eating disorder and, 138,
138*t*
weaponizing, 56
weight loss
CALERIE 1 study on, 27
diet mentality and, 109
"go get it done" attitude and, 53, 60–62
medications, 26
weight loss surgery, 61
weight management
counseling for Black women, foundational beliefs about, 111
dieticians and, 12
weight stigma, 85, 129
definition of, 80

reinforcing, 56
understanding, 80–81
Westcott, A., 36
White children, sexual trauma and, 44
White girls, adultification of Black girls
 vs. of, 63
White people, food insecurity for Black
 people *vs.* for, 114
White supremacy, body image messages
 and, 47
White teens
 binge-eating prevalence rate and, 4
 clinician recognition of ED symptoms
 in, 4, 5
White women
 lifetime prevalence of BED among, 15

overweight or obesity statistics for, 13
restrictive eating practices and, 49
stigmatization of fatness and, 48–49
Whitlock, C., 172
WHO. *see* World Health Organization
 (WHO)
WIC program. *see* Women, Infants, and
 Children (WIC) program
Williams, M., xv
Williams, M. G., 120
Women, Infants, and Children (WIC)
 program, 116
World Health Organization (WHO), on
 overweight and obesity-related diseases,
 37–38
Wright, D., 41

About the Authors

Charlynn Small, PhD, LCP, CEDS-C, is assistant director of health promotion, at the University of Richmond, Virginia, a frequent speaker at national and international conferences, and an advocate for awareness and treatment of eating disorders affecting Black women and underrepresented groups. She received her PhD from Howard University. Dr. Small is president of the board of directors of the International Association of Eating Disorders Professionals Foundation and cofounded their African-American Eating Disorders Professionals Committee. She is the coeditor of *Treating Black Women with Eating Disorders*, Taylor & Francis (2021) and of *Antiblackness and the Stories of Authentic Allies*, Oxford University Press (2024).

Paula Edwards-Gayfield, LCMHCS, LPC, CEDS-C, BC-TMH, is a regional assistant vice president and diversity and inclusion cochair at The Renfrew Center. She is an advocate for increasing awareness about eating disorders affecting Black, Indigenous, and People of Color (BIPOC) groups and is passionate about access to culturally sensitive, inclusive, and equitable care. She is a contributor to the book *Treating Black Women with Eating Disorders: A Clinician's Guide*. Edwards-Gayfield is a certified member and approved consultant (CEDS-C) of iaedp™ and serves on the National Eating Disorders Association (NEDA) Board, clinical advisory council, and the advisory board for Eating Disorder Recovery Support (EDRS).